Please return/renew this item by the last date shown
on this label, or on your self-service receipt.

To renew this item, visit **www.librarieswest.org.uk**
or contact your library

Your borrower number and PIN are required.

and what "sil‹   ›ndent

D1382086

CONTEMPORARY PLAYS BY BLACK BRITISH WRITERS

Selected and introduced by Natalie Ibu

Misty Arinzé Kene

Nine Night Natasha Gordon

Princess & The Hustler Chinonyerem Odimba

Burgerz Travis Alabanza

40 Days Firdos Ali

a profoundly affectionate, passionate devotion to someone (—noun) debbie tucker green

NICK HERN BOOKS

London

www.nickhernbooks.co.uk

A Nick Hern Book

Contemporary Plays by Black British Writers first published in Great Britain in 2021 as a paperback original by Nick Hern Books Limited, The Glasshouse, 49a Goldhawk Road, London W12 8QP

Burgerz was first published in 2018 by Oberon Books, an imprint of Bloomsbury Publishing Plc, and is reproduced with permission

Cover image: *Misty* by Arinzé Kene (Bush Theatre, 2018), photograph by Helen Murray/ ArenaPAL
Designed and typeset by Nick Hern Books, London
Printed in the UK by Mimeo Ltd, Huntingdon, Cambridgeshire PE29 6XX

A CIP catalogue record for this book is available from the British Library

ISBN 978 1 84842 984 0

Contents

Introduction
Natalie Ibu

In the preface for *Misty*, Arinzé Kene tells us about a series of –
maybe real, maybe not – encounters in which the question 'What is
a Black play and what do we *really* mean when we say it?' causes
seismic disruption for all who spend a moment thinking about it. In
his retelling, faces fall apart, tears are shed, minds are blown, jobs
are lost, disillusionment felt, the industry abandoned, a system
crumbles, nothing makes sense any more.

For me, the descriptor 'Black plays' is rooted in racism. It implies
that plays – by Black artists and/or about Black people – can only
speak to Blackness. It implies that white stories – by white artists
about white people – are about the universal, about the human
experience and anything that is not is limited in its scope. So, in my
practice, I have rejected it. I talk not of the race of the play but
about the specific lived experience of who wrote it, about who the
play spends time with, about its perspective, about what it's
screaming into the darkness of the auditorium, about the questions
it's asking.

But labels, per se, aren't bad. Labels, in the wrong hands, are lazy
and limiting, but labels used with care and intention can be useful.
Labels help us make sense of things: they can help us find things
that might be otherwise lost or overlooked, they help us create
community, they welcome you, warn you, get your attention. They
help orientate you, help you find what you're looking for. Labels
can be an invitation.

So, you're holding in your hands an invitation. An invitation to sit
in the worlds, and with the characters, created by six brilliant Black
British writers between 2010 and 2020. That's the only thing
defining these plays. They are diverse in all ways – setting, form,
style, location, scale, content and concerns. The writers are all
Black, yes, but they come from a variety of lived experiences and
identity intersections. But, not all identity intersections. I started
collating this collection with a commitment to making sure no one,
no Black intersection, was left out or behind, but that's impossible

to do in a book of just six plays. It's a burden that too often lies at the feet of Black artists and makers – we cannot be the (only) soldiers of representation.

By bringing these plays together under this label, we can see so clearly – and celebrate – the diversity and multiplicity of stories authored by Black playwrights in the last decade. Culture moves, shifts and changes in phases. I've learnt about the radical and flourishing diversity of stories by Black artists being produced in the 1970s and 1980s as a result of groundbreaking independent theatre companies like Talawa, Black Theatre Co-operative, Carib Theatre Company, Dark and Light Theatre and Theatre of Black Women. And then a narrowing and returning to a singular narrative – a narrative that is obsessed with deprivation, arrival, othering, and where we are just Black – as a result of a tightening of resources available to independent companies and, therefore, a growth in power of the (so often) white gatekeepers of our cultural venues. But, this anthology – including work from the National Theatre, the West End, the Edinburgh Festival and venues from across the UK, as well as an unpublished work – celebrates the return of a time of multiplicity, variety and complexity.

Ishmail Mahomed – the CEO of Market Theatre in Johannesburg – said: 'Arts and culture is the canary in a mine. It alerts us to risks and changes in our environment.' I think that we have underestimated the work of Black artists: we insist that it's a mirror and never a window. It's been thrilling to return to these works, with all we know now in 2021, and explore what they were heralding, what they were warning us about.

All these plays are rich and full of observations, but the thing that screams off the page in *Misty* by Arinzé Kene – produced at the Bush, London, in 2018, before a West End transfer to the Trafalgar Studios in the same year and a pandemic-postponed transfer to The Shed in New York – is its vivid vision of a virus infecting city life. Kene uses the language of infection as a metaphor to talk about the gentrification of place and home. At times, the virus is Black people before being flipped to become those – so often white – moving in and squeezing original communities of colour out of their homes. This collision of virology language and race politics predicts the perfect storm of the summer of 2020 when the Black Lives Matter movement reached another peak – following the tragic murders of Breonna Taylor, Ahmaud Arbery and George Floyd – in the middle of a global pandemic.

In *Nine Night* by Natasha Gordon – produced at the National Theatre in 2018, before a West End transfer to Trafalgar Studios – is a moving yet hilarious exploration of grief rituals. When Gloria, the matriarch of the family, dies, the traditional Jamaican Nine Night wake begins. Revisiting the play in 2021, it takes on a new significance as we meditate on those across the globe who not only lost loved ones to Covid-19, but who, because of quarantine and lockdowns, were robbed of their own mourning rituals and left with a grief that's yet to find its home. Rereading it, we're given permission to grieve the things we've lost over the last year – jobs, plans, relationships, health, people, dreams and momentum.

Protest and grief also feature in *Princess & The Hustler* by Chinonyerem Odimba, produced at Bristol Old Vic Theatre by Eclipse Theatre, Bristol Old Vic and Hull Truck Theatre, before going on a UK tour. This domestic drama, set in 1963 in the home of a Black family, combines the politics of colourism with the Bristol bus boycott – a seminal Black British Civil Rights action that led to the Race Relations Act of 1965. As part of Eclipse Theatre's Revolution Mix – a theatrical intervention to undo the erasure of Black British Stories across five centuries – Odimba, in 2019, brings a recent but under-celebrated story into our consciousness, forcing us to confront the history of race politics in Bristol. Just a year later, the statue of Edward Colston was toppled and pushed into Bristol Harbour during that summer's Black Lives Matter protests – an action that demanded the city acknowledge but not celebrate the city's role in the slave trade.

Whilst Kene is telling the story of the colonisation of parts of London that sees his neighbour Dreadlock Rasta being replaced by Redhead Eddie, Odimba explores the legacy of colonisation in Britain: Jamaican-born-and-bred Wendall goes into the service to fight for Britain and is discharged after an incident and with a lung condition. He is promised a job and a future in England only to be disrespected and made invisible – kept from being able to make a living and support his family in a land that wants his life but not him or his labour.

In Travis Alabanza's *Burgerz* – produced by Hackney Showrooms in 2018 before touring to the Edinburgh Festival Fringe in 2019, to be followed by a national and international tour, which was postponed due to the pandemic – Travis helps us think about the decolonisation of gender as they invite us into their mourning of safety and as they model, for us, how to wrestle for agency over trauma. There is so much grief bubbling under the surface of all of these plays – expressed in such dynamic and different ways – but Travis knew we needed help grieving what had been lost, what was being lost and what was ahead.

In *Misty* and *Princess & The Hustler*, we are encouraged to think about how we protect women and girls in the face of misogyny and colourism, whereas in Firdos Ali's *40 Days* we join Black Muslim parents as they wrestle with how to protect their Black Muslim son as well as preparing him for the hostile world they live in. On the morning following the Brexit vote, a British Black Muslim boy goes upstairs after seeing the results on TV, lays down on his bed and never gets up again. He stops speaking, moving, responding to touch and sound. Through the play, Ali explores the impact of state violence on Black and brown children, but also the consequence of bringing that news into the home on young lives. Doom-scrolling before doom-scrolling was a thing. Written in 2017, there is a chilling moment when the Boy lists the deaths of Black men and boys at the hands of police – he says: 'Black boys / Black boys die / Black boys die in the summer.' And it hasn't stopped.

Burgerz is a beautiful dedication to pain. Alabanza gave the world a language for allyship before Black squares, reading lists and liberal guilt reached an all-time high. *Burgerz* had the courage to ask for it and the generosity to teach it.

We move from allyship to relationships in debbie tucker green's *a profoundly affectionate, passionate devotion to someone (–noun)*, produced at the Royal Court Theatre in London in 2017. A timeless meditation straddling the past, the present, the future and the possibilities. tucker green's exquisitely detailed dialogue draws so deftly the physical and emotional highs, lows, mundanity and complexity of intimate relationships.

Welcome. Welcome to Bristol in 1963. Welcome to Waterloo Bridge in 2016. Welcome to a house in May 2017. Welcome to three couples and what might be, what once was and what could have been in 2017. Welcome to a West Indian household in 2018. Welcome to London in 2018. Welcome to the past, present and – crucially – the future.

MISTY

Arinzé Kene

For my sister,
Ndidiamaka Mokwe

2

Misty was originally produced at the Bush Theatre, London, on 15 March 2018. The production transferred to Trafalgar Studios, London, from 8 September 2018, presented by Trafalgar Theatre Productions, Jonathan Church Productions, Eilene Davidson and Audible in association with Island Records.

Performer & Playwright	Arinzé Kene
Director	Omar Elerian
Set Designer	Rajha Shakiry
Musical Director & Musician	Shiloh Coke
Musical Director & Musician	Adrian McLeod
Little Girl	Sedonna Henok, Mya Napolean & Rene Powell
Lighting Designer	Jackie Shemesh
Sound Designer	Elena Peña
Video Designer	Daniel Denton
Dramaturgs	Stewart Pringle & Kirsty Housley
Movement Director	Rachael Nanyonjo
Sound Associate	Richard Bell

Preface

I've been told to write a Preface. So I guess I'll just launch right in and tell you how *Misty* came about.

I went to the Young Vic Theatre a few years back to see a play. I'm being ushered into the theatre and I get talking with the usher. He's a tall young wide-eyed baby-faced black guy. His name is Raymond (his name ain't actually Raymond, I've changed it to protect his identity). Raymond is fresh out of drama school, excitable, optimistic about the industry and full of young actor jizz. You know the stuff. He's energetically talking at me about acting stuff and so my mind was drifting until he goes, 'Oh I saw this good play recently... ah man I've forgotten the name of it... it's on upstairs at the Royal Court... it's a black play that's blah blah blah...' And he carries on describing the play but my mind goes off on a tangent and I'm thinking to myself... 'A *black* play?'

Now I'd heard this term used plenty before but that evening for some reason, it really landed and I said to Raymond, 'Raymond. A black play? What do you mean by "a black play"?'

'How do you mean?'

'I mean, *how* was the play black?'

'Well... it had black people in it.'

'Hmm. Right. Okay. Okay. Right okay. Okay. Right.'

Raymond tears my ticket, shows me my seat. I watch the play. I leave the theatre. Heading to Waterloo Station now, heading home, and I see Raymond, he's just finished his shift so we walk out together. He asks me what I thought of the play and I think for a moment then, I say fuck it...

'Yeah man, pretty standard white play.' I knew what I was doing.

Raymond's all like, 'Hold up. What do you mean "white play"?'

'Raymond, it had white people in it, it's a white play.'

'No-no, I've seen it… I wouldn't call it a white play… It wasn't about like… being white or whatever, it was a dysfunctional family, it was a family play.'

'Okay, okay right, right, okay, right. But Raymond. The play you were telling me about earlier, the one that you recommended to me, that's a black play right? It's about black people right?'

'No-no, that… that play was… it was about people-trafficking, it's a people-trafficking play.'

'THEN WHY CALL IT A BLACK PLAY, RAYMOND? If it was a people-trafficking play, why call it a black play?'

'Because… be… because…'

He looked out into space. His face fell apart. Then he said, 'I don't know.'

Then he fainted and I caught him just like in the movies. Nah not really, he didn't faint but he did go kind of pale. He got upset.

We were still on The Cut so I walked Raymond back to the theatre, sat him down and got him some water. He placed his head on the table. Said he was feeling dizzy but I know when a man is trying not to cry. About a minute went by in silence, he hadn't sipped his water. He really needed to process this whole black-play/white-play shit. He raises his head, his eyes squinted, he says something along the lines of, 'I don't know why I called it a black play, bro. I don't know anything any more. Just because there's mainly black people in it, it doesn't make it a black play. Why is it that in my head, the race of the characters in the play, or the person who wrote the play, comes before the actual play itself? As though that's what's most important about it.' He was shaking his head.

'It ain't just you, Raymond. We all do it. It's our mindset.'

'Fuck that mindset! Let's reset that mindset!'

The whole of the Young Vic Theatre bar look around to us. Raymond was sacked from his front-of-house job the following day.

After that night, Raymond was never the same again. He'd text me nearly every day and stalk me into having coffees with him where he'd chew my ear off about the whole black-play/white-play thing. The baby-faced optimistic Raymond was now a distant memory. He had become disillusioned. Making all of this worse was that around that time everyone started using the D-word again. 'Diversity.' It was everywhere. In the *Guardian*. *The Stage*. *Evening Standard*. *Metro*. David Harewood commenting on it... and Raymond would harass me over coffee like, 'I looked the word up "Diversity", bro, the Oxford definition is "point of difference", bro. A point of difference. Am I a point of difference? When they say we need more diversity, do they mean they need more points of difference? If I'm the point of difference, what's the norm? Is white theatre the norm? Is white theatre a thing? Are Adrian Lester and debbie tucker green points of difference? Diversity yeah... this diversion to the norm, tell me, who gets to say what's a diversion and what's ordinary? I don't wanna be a diversion. I've been on buses that have been diverted. That shit ain't fun. Pisses everyone off. It's long. And maybe that's the reason why Suzman was pissed off, read this paper here, bro, right here, theatre's veteran, Janet Suzman says, "Theatre is a white invention." She says black heads don't go theatre, her exact words, to quote her: "they don't bloody come." If we don't bloody come then where did I meet you, bro? Am I delusional? Let me know if I'm delusion, bro.' Delusional would be a reach but he was definitely not okay any more.

A few months later Raymond and I are back at the Young Vic again. We've just seen a play and I bump into a black actress I know. We'll call her Donna. Donna tells me there's an awesome play I should go see.

'What's the name of the play, Donna?' I ask.

Donna says, 'Oh man... it's the black play on at the blah blah blah...' Now beside me, I could feel Raymond begin to turn. He wasn't gonna let it slide. Raymond was 'woke' now. So the words 'black play' to him, meant, 'let us fight'... he responded like a shark to a drop of blood.

'Whoa whoa whoa. Black play?' he said.

'Yeah. Yeah, it's a black play and...' Donna continued.

'As opposed to – ?' asked Raymond.

'I'm sorry?'

'As opposed TO – ?'

'I… I don't get what you're asking me.'

'As opposed to it being a white play? Answer me!'

'No-no, just, well, it's a black play – '

'Why's it a black play? Like. Why though.'

'Because it is! It's a black play innit! Arinzé, who is this guy? The play was written by a black woman, there's black people in it, therefore – '

Now, Raymond leans in for the kill. I tried to stop him but I was too late. He says…

'Donna, are you an actress, or a black actress? Is *Hamlet* a play, or a white play?'

Donna was done. She could not answer, her mind was blown. She had to quit acting. Cos she didn't know whether casting directors wanted to see her as an actress or a black actress. Didn't know whether to greet them with a 'hello' or an 'eh-yo'. It messed with her so much that she was neither an actress, or a black actress, she'd become a shit actress. Never in the moment, never in the scene. Only ever thinking about her blackness.

Maybe Donna's made up. I don't know. She's real somewhere. Anyway. Whatever happened, it led me to write this thing.

Onstage

ARINZÉ
MUSICIANS

Also

VIRUS / BLOOD CELL
VOICEMAIL
RAYMOND
DONNA
PRODUCER
GIRL
DIMPLES
LUCAS
ASSISTANT STAGE MANAGER
AGENT'S ASSISTANT
AGENT

Track List

01. City Creature
02. Apparently
03. Locked Out
04. Uncle
05. *Knock Knock Knock* (*freestyle*)
06. Mutiny

Interval

07. *Reversal* (*freestyle*)
08. Sleep Paralysis
09. Chase
10. Geh-Geh
11. *Jungle Shit* (*freestyle*)

ACT ONE

Scene One

Lights up. The VIRUS *goes to the mic.*

'City Creature'

VIRUS
A lot of crazy shit happens on the night bus,
One shouldn't settle disputes on the night bus,
Shouldn't settle disputes after ten at night, boss,
It's only ever gonna end up in a fight, truss.

Here is the city that we live in,
Notice that the city that we live in is alive,
Analyse our city and you'll find, that our city even has
bodily features,
Our city's organs function like any living creature,
Our city *is* a living creature,
A living breathing city creature broken in to boroughs,
Mostly living creatures are broken in to organs,
For the city creature each borough is an organ,
And if we're saying that the boroughs be the organs now,
You might liken the borough that I live in to the bowel,
So if boroughs be the organs of our city creature,
Then our motorways are the arteries of city creatures,
The high streets be arterioles of city creatures,
And each road is a capillary.

You'll notice that travelling down these blood vessels of our living
city creature,
Night buses are packed with blood cells, red and white,
Them's the passengers, you and you, it's a normal night,
Some of you alight, more of you get on and pack it tight,
But all is well,
Cos blood cell to blood cell there's nothing to fear,
Not unless something sneaks in through the back door before the
driver has a chance to shut it
And it's pushing

and it's nudging
and it's shoving up the place
and you can't see its face, cos it's got a
hoodie on its head
but *can* see its waist, cos it's got its
trousers down its legs,
so you can see its [boxer shorts].
[But of course],
you ain't judging,
cos it's nothing
that you ain't seen before.
You're just collectively 'aware' of him, and nothing's wrong with
that
cos he jumped in through the back,
and blood cells don't like scraggy surprises coming through the
back door in dark baggy disguises,
it peaks the nervousness, the whole blood temperature rises,
and for safety purposes, word to the wise, avert your eyes, and sit
in silence.
The doors close, the night bus pulls away, so now there's no getting
off,
And if you're wise enough! You'll know not all of us! Aboard this
bus! Are blood cells...
Nah,
One of us is virus.
Geh-geh.

Some toxic irreversible shits are bound to visit the night bus,
One shouldn't settle disputes on the night bus,
Shouldn't settle disputes after ten at night, boss,
You're only gonna get infected by some virus.

I jump the night bus,
And it's packed,
That's the only reason I came in through the back,
Cos when it's packed the driver won't open the front,
But I ain't gonna stand in the rain like a cunt

As soon as I'm on, I realise I'm the only virus one
Apart from the driver chauffeuring in the front,
But he's sat there in the glass cage
which implies that he's had his last days of virus rage
Anti-viral oppression probably rendered him depressed and
submissive

bereft of the spirit,
compliant, not a breath of defiance left in him
since they arrested him and disinfected him.

I'm on the lower deck,
The bus is so rammed, I have to stand, by the door,
I keep getting (*Nudge.*)
Nudged in the back by this (*Nudge.*)
Drunk prick and I swear (*Nudge.*)
He nudges me one more –
'Oi oi oi, watch it yeah. You see *me*? I'm standing here. I'm
already pissed off tonight so – ' (*Nudge.*)

I must look like a pussy,
Because this dickhead pushes me,
The whole bus goes silent,
How can I not get violent?

I look this blood cell in the eye like 'what's happening?'
I crack my knuckles, step to him and start cackling,
Other passengers back away fearfully nattering,
I get to happy slapping him, blood cell splattering,
Batter him, nothing else mattering,
Bet he won't ever, consider, doing that again.

Get off the bus,
Don't have to run,
I just *walk* away,
That's how it's done,
No need to panic,
Keep calm and carry on.

Scene Two

We hear a voicemail left by RAYMOND. ARINZÉ *listens to it.*

VOICEMAIL. Welcome to your EE voicemail.
    To listen to your messages, press one –
    (*Beep.*)
    You have, one, new message,
    left today, at,
    6:47 a.m.

As our two MUSICIANS *become* RAYMOND *and* DONNA *and caption is projected above their heads reading:*

'Raymond, Arinzé's friend, thirty-three, chef.
Donna, Raymond's wife, thirty, school teacher, loves cycling.'

RAYMOND. Arinzé, hey dude, tis Raymond here.
Sorry I didn't stick around last night to give you feedback,
I had daddy duties –
(*Sound of the baby in his arms fretting, he shushes her.*)
She's been… difficult –

DONNA. Every time I change her diaper she does another shit!

RAYMOND. She's been driving Donna crazy, so forgive me for
keeping this brief.
Bro, I hope you appreciate me telling you this as a friend,
I had issues, with your story –
(*The baby frets, as if responding to what he's said,* DONNA
shushes her.)
I mean, the whole 'guy beats someone up on a night bus' thing?
It felt like another…

DONNA. Generic angry young black man!
(*The baby begins to cry a little.*)

As ARINZÉ *listens he produces a balloon. He blows it up.*

RAYMOND. I looked around and most of the audience were…
most of them don't look like us.

DONNA. They seemed to love it!

RAYMOND. As soon we walked out Donna turned to me and said
'Arinzé sold out and wrote an *urban* play.'

DONNA. Nah that's not what I said. I said 'Arinzé sold out and
wrote a nigga play.' You wrote a nigga play so your work would
get on. Ain't nothing but a modern minstrel show.

The baby begins full-out high-pitched crying, RAYMOND *can't*
shush her.

RAYMOND. Arinzé, I gotta sort this child out, man.
Listen, bro, I'm sorry if this sounds harsh but… (*Pause.*) do not
have kids, man.
You don't want none of this.
This will turn you into an angry young black man for real.

The message ends.

VOICEMAIL. To save message, press –
(*Beep*.)
Message, deleted.
To return the call, press –
(*Beep*.)

It rings. No answer. ARINZÉ *goes to the mic behind the gauze to leave a voicemail.*

You have reached the voicemail box, for,
'*Raymond*'
Please leave a message after the beep.
Once you have left your message,
key hash for more options.
(*Beep*.)

ARINZÉ. Raymond.
Donna.
Arinzé here.
Hope you guys are good.
Just got your fucking voicemail.
I don't know if you guys are aware but…
You're not writers.
Raymond, you're a chef.
Maybe you should stick to… fucking chefing?

VOICEMAIL.
(*Beep*.)
If you would like to re-record this message please press –
(*Beep*.)
Message deleted.
Please leave a message after the beep.
Once you have left your message,
key hash for more options.
(*Beep*.)

ARINZÉ (*after a beat*). Raymond! Donna!
I got your message… so lovely to hear from the three of you.
Donna is a joker, that whole 'nigga play' thing gave me pure jokes.
I'm still laughing now. Was she joking?
I've never heard of that term before.
She *was* joking though right?

Because this ain't just some nigga play. My nigga characters have well-thought-out nigga story arcs and shit. Haha...

As ARINZÉ *walks away from the mic his voice (pre-recorded) continues to leave the rest of the message.*

(*Pre-recorded.*)... Haha! I'm playing, man.
Anyway broski... thanks for the advice, I'm gonna let it marinate and uh...
We'll talk soon.
Beaucoup blessings,
Slugs and fishes, hugs and kisses, my bro.

ARINZÉ *has come from behind the gauze and is now downstage. He takes in the balloon in his hand. He holds it in front of him. He lets the balloon go. The air gushes out of it. It flops around until it drops, deflated.*

Scene Three

The VIRUS *takes position near a large cube at the side of the stage. He uses the chair as a bike.*

'Apparently'

VIRUS
Later that night,
After the night bus fight,
I walked about...
And then... then...
I stole a bike!
And then I rode about,
I'm really good at bikes,
Wheelie,
I thought I'd ride and see the sights,
Wheelie,

A virus on the corner selling white,
Wheelie,
Lady of the night in fishnet tights,
Wheelie,

Red and blue anti-viral siren,
Wheelie,
I politely wave as I wheelie by them,
(*Middle finger up.*)
Wheelie,

I mean, it's one of them nights,
Not much to do,
So I call up Jade,
See what she's up to,
Jade's an old friend,
We don't speak much,
But every now and then,
She lets me beat it up,
I like Jade nuff,
Cos we don't discuss,
About 'How's life' and,
All of that stuff nah,
I text her 'are you able?'
She texts me 'come now'
I text 'ten minutes tops',
She lets me beat it up –

Jade's a virus from round the way
And even though she's proper safe, and proper sweet
It's only ever proper late, when we meet
You won't catch us broad day strolling down the street
Cos Jade's got a complic-ated history
And I don't want my name dragged into her misery
It's hard enough as it is out here on these streets
Let alone to be mixed up in some fuckery.

Jade was just a normal chick,
But apparently her mum and dad were crazy strict,
Apparently they wouldn't ever let her out the yard,
They'd crack the whip apparently and make her study hard,
Apparently that put Jade under nuff stress and with it,
The good girl, apparently began to rebel,
Apparently at school she started acting parasitic,
She bit a teacher apparently and got expelled.

Apparently there was a house party –
Apparently Jade drank too much and got wavery,
Jade started apparently acting unsavoury,

Apparently she was kinda fucked, like, proper fucked, like,
collapsed and shit.

Apparently when the party was over –
Apparently her friends tried to find her but they had to go cos,
Apparently, Jade was nowhere to be seen,
Apparently they searched every bedroom, toilet, mezzanine.

Apparently 'I don't know' that was the answer people gave when
they asked 'where's Jade?'
'Ptshh, I don't know',
Apparently, they tried calling her phone
Apparently, they assumed, Jade had already gone home.

Apparently while all of that was happening,
Apparently in the stairwell just under the scaffolding,
Apparently Jade was on the floor collapsed again,
Apparently when they found her they had to call an ambulance,
Cos apparently Jade was sat there in a pool of blood,
And there was something in that pool of blood apparently,
A little lump of something rolled up –
Apparently she kept saying 'get it away from me, I don't know
how it came from me.'

Apparently ambulance rode up and picked it up and didn't even do
much before they wrote it off and wrapped it up
And Jade apparently stood up and tried to walk it off like – say
nothing happened and so caught her up like 'hold up, you're
in shock'
and they wrapped her up, in a cloth, and took them both off and
rode off, apparently,
the sirens were turned off, cos there was no rush apparently,
vomit and guts on her dress,
it was all a bloody mess, apparently.

Reputations in the city creature, stay
Rumours in the city creature, don't go away,
Whispers haunt the place like ghost and people say,
'Jade had to be a ho,
What kind of girl don't know?'
She let them beat it up
She let them beat it up
There goes that virus Jade who lets them beat it up,
She's easy like that,

Derelict building fuck,
Splinters on her back,
Gave birth in a shack.'

I'm outside her house,
Dump the bike in the hedge,
I climb up to her window,
Where I sit on the ledge,
She comes to open it,
But goes 'shhh' before she lets me in,
Just so that I know that her dad is in.

I sit with her this night,
She massages my wrist,
It's aching from the bus fight,
I'm kind of liking this,
Cos no one touches me,
Not properly,
Most people cross the street,
Or watch me microscopically, but –

I hate it when she's nice,
I hate it when I come through the window and she's got me
a Lilt with a cup of ice,
I hate it when she tells me I ain't like them other breddas,
I hate it when she says the two of us should be together,
I hate it when we're hugging in the bed,
Cos I don't wanna put the wrong idea in her head,
So I go over to the window sill,
To smoke, but I can feel her staring at me still,
And she goes:
'Babe, I'm not being funny but,
Your hatred of blood cells hurts me as well,
I'm worried that if you don't mind your Ps and Qs,
Your mugshot will end up on the antiviral news.'

'Jade. Lissen. I'm gonna have to stop you there mate,
Cos you're chatting as if you're a saint, when you
blay-tantly ain't,
Plus, you're sounding like my mum,
Sticking up for the blood cells as if you wanta be one.

And I've already had her shit today,
Mum, of all people, saying that I've been acting strange
as of late,

She actually asked me "am *I* stable?" She blamed it on
the spliff –
She sat me at the table, she said she's worried stiff,
She said *I* act bizarre, she was all la-di-dah –
Steady chatting blah blah blah, said I'm being blasé blah
about it –

But "it's serious!"
"Not gonna watch you smoke your life away"
When she smokes nearly forty a day,
She raised her voice a bit,
Pounding her fist on shit –
I sit and let her grow her fit,
Chewing my ear to bits but then –
Then I try to leave the yard,
Before I fucking switch,
But here's what takes the piss,
Here this,
Mum,
She rummaged through my stuff,
And left it looking mash –
But as if that weren't enough,
When she found my stash,
She gave it all a flush,
She likes to keep it brash –
And bom, that's what set me off,
"The fact it ain't your ting to throw away,
I bought it with my JSA,
Respect? What you on about?
I never smoke it in the house,"
That's when I went upstairs to find her purse,
I reimburse myself for whatever she flushed was worth,
The whole time she's pulling me back, proper pulling shirt –
But I storm out, slam the door, stomp the earth…

And then I catch the bus to come see you,
And now I'm here it's nuffin but aggro you give me too,
So I'm gone, cos maybe I am going through some shit,
But I ain't gonna get criticise by some hypocrite.'

Me on the street again,
Bicycle seat again,
Wheelie-ing down the concrete again,
Wheelie!

> The virus on the corner selling white is still there,
> Wheelie!

> The lady of the night in fishnet tights gives me the eye as
> I wheelie by but I'm all right
> Wheelie! –

A balloon has suddenly dropped down into the audience. ARINZÉ
*sees it and stops performing. He gets audience members to pass the
balloon to him. They pass it down.*

A beat as ARINZÉ *inspects the balloon. Just as he goes to burst it
he's SNAPPED into –*

Scene Four

– a meeting with PRODUCER. ARINZÉ *quickly hides the balloon
behind him, under his shirt. He sits into the chair, which places him
in the meeting with the* PRODUCER. *His back is to the audience but
they can see his face because there's a camera pointed at him and his
face is being projected onto the cube. The camera is slowly zooming
into* ARINZÉ's *face as the meeting gets more and more intense.*

[PRODUCER *is voiced by sound bites of Morgan Freeman from
various movies.*]

PRODUCER. 'CONCENTRATE!'

ARINZÉ (*hiding balloon behind his back*). Sorry. I've been…
    getting distracted –

PRODUCER. 'Look at me boy!'

ARINZÉ (*hiding balloon*). I just, I keep getting these –

PRODUCER. 'Look at me dammit!'

ARINZÉ (*faces* PRODUCER, *he's on camera now*). Okay, I… I
    think I need a little bit more time to write this. It's taking a bit
    longer than I thought because… well…

PRODUCER. 'What have you been thinking about all this time?'

ARINZÉ. Well I… okay so, this is gonna sound weird. I have this
    friend, his name is Raymond. Him and his wife, Donna… they

basically, they say I'm selling out by writing this and, well, ever since they... ever since they said that I've been getting these... you know what, forget it, it's just... the whole virus guy, getting violent and... I'm worried that the whole thing is lacking 'Theatre' and it's too... 'Ffeat-uh' and uh...

PRODUCER. 'I like that story.'

ARINZÉ. Yeah, yeah okay. But what I'm getting at is... they called it a... and I hate using this word but... they called it a 'nigga play' and, I mean –

PRODUCER. 'It's just a bullshit word.'

ARINZÉ. It *is* bullshit but –

PRODUCER. 'To me it's just a made-up word.'

ARINZÉ. Yes but, the implications, it's extreme. To call it a 'nigga play'.
It's really got me thinking now... are they... do they have a point? Is that what this is? Is that what I'm really doing?

PRODUCER (*beat*). 'To tell you the truth... I don't give a shit.'

ARINZÉ. Uhm... it's just, this thing is gonna have my name on it, and if people think I'm out here churning out nigga plays and straight up defecating on my community, that's not a very good look for me. They'll crucify me out here. So I give a shit.

PRODUCER. Do you?

ARINZÉ. Yeah it's, you know, the whole point of me talking about this with you right now.

PRODUCER. 'You're quite sure about this are you?'

ARINZÉ. Well. I've been getting these...
(*Decides not to tell him about the balloon.*)
... I've been thinking about it a lot.

PRODUCER. 'That's cos you're a baby and you don't know shit.'

ARINZÉ. See I didn't want you to get mad –

PRODUCER. 'You think I'm stupid, son?'

ARINZÉ. Stupid? No. You're an accomplished theatre producer, well educated, I don't think you're stupid.

PRODUCER. 'Yes you do!'

ARINZÉ. I just… I mean, maybe sometimes you can be a little *insensitive* –

PRODUCER. 'You question my judgement, my competence, my intelligence!'

ARINZÉ. I… no, I trust your judgement, you produce such incredible work, and I'm grateful for this opportunity, I just, I don't want to be out here contributing to the whole 'nigga play' canon, if such a thing exists.

PRODUCER. 'You're no earthly good at all, unless you take this opportunity and do whatever you have to!'

PRODUCER *is gone. The meeting is over.*
ARINZÉ *takes the balloon out from under his shirt. A beat. Facing us, he bursts the balloon –*
He's surprised to find that the balloon was filled with orange dust, and upon bursting it he finds himself covered in dust. Some of it in his mouth. He splutters.

Scene Five

The VIRUS *is locked out of his house. He knocks on the door. Nobody comes to answer.*

'Locked Out'

VIRUS
Okay, this ain't funny no more,
Tracy I beg you tell Mum to open up the door,
My clothes by the bin though, you're taking man for joke,
If you let me in though, I'll maybe let this go,
At least come to the window, I know you're there you know,
I see the television glow, when I look through the post…
Like how can I win though, I'm on a slipping slope cos,
Everything I do's a sin though, man ain't sniffing coke,
Man ain't pimpin' ho's, man ain't dealing dope,
You see me hustling? See me stealing?
It's that new blood cell bloke of yours, it must be him, I'm gonna kill him.

You pick him over me yeah?
You, him and Tracy – one big happy fucking family yeah?
Cool, that's fine with me yeah,
But tomorrow when the day's in,
If I don't see the rest of my stuff, you just watch, that's all I'm
saying.

And by the way, there's no keeping me away from Trace!
I raised that girl, just me,
She'll leave you too, you'll see,
When she's old enough,
And she knows enough,
Nah, you know what?
Man's fighting for custody – bom.

I'm the one helping her with her homework,
I'm the reason Tracy's been achieving,
I'm the one who's been to all of her assemblies,
You couldn't even show up to parents' evening –

ARINZÉ *hears knocking at the door which leads backstage.*
ARINZÉ *ignores it.*

'Uncle'

Seriously, what are uncles for?
If not to help you out when your parents can't no more.
I'll be quiet and I swear I won't take up much space,
I won't bring anyone over, I won't get in your face,
I'll sleep on the sofa, won't disrespect your place,
I'll keep it clean and kosher, I'll even wash my plates,
I'll even use a coaster for every drink I take,
And when I use the toaster I'll brush my crumbs away,
I know you like the poker and your friends come here to play,
Plus you're a Casanova, if you need me out? Just say,
I know we haven't spoke for – who's counting anyway,
I know I stole your phone but that was back in the day like,
That was two months ago, plus, may I elaborate,
It was a Motorola, let's not exaggerate,
But that is the shittest mobile, on the planet mate,
I swear down, I've grown up, and I'd appreciate,
If you'd accommodate, seriously wait, seriously.

Seriously, what are uncles good for?
Remember the time when you were late dropping me off
to football?

I missed the game. And what did I say? I forgave you Uncle,
Covered for you nuff times, you were my favourite Uncle,
But now it's *my* rough times I see you're changing Uncle,
I'm at your door, you're clocking me like I'm a stranger Uncle,
Want me to beg? Get on my knees? You wanna see me crumble?
Is that it? Fuck this. You used to be more humble,
Yeah I'll admit that I'm a virus but you're proper fungal,
I got some shit on you Uncle, Imma give you a lungful,
I know you used to pick me up from school completely drunk,
You'd be swaying into other lanes and you'd mumble,
You'd overswerve and hit the curb, it happened more than once,
We'd get out, you'd faff about and then you'd take a stumble,
Think you're a saint or some shit? Think you're
a Buddhist monk?
I happen to know different, Imma give you a lungful,
I know you have genital herpes, Auntie told my mum,
I know that Auntie was banging that man at church Uncle,
I know you lost your job for laundering yet carried on –
Dressing up every day as if you were still going work, Uncle,
But there's a dodgy flat I used to go to buy my skunk,
I saw you hanging outside it, looking disgruntled,
I watch you go inside and after like hours gone,
I watch you stagger out, tie off, your shirt crumpled,
You walk the streets, sleeves rolled up, your eyes have sunk,
And every now and then you shudder, smile and grumble,
You slide down the wall and fall asleep in a slump,
That is until you are approached by a police constable,
They throw you in the meat wagon and I know what you done,
Cos shortly afterwards they raid the place and everyone,
Comes up with charges and somehow you get none,
Which means not only did you open your mouth, you sung,
If I were them I'd hold you down and I'd cut out your tongue,
I don't associate with snitches, don't know why I come,
You can keep your fucking sofa cos it smells like bum,
Think I actually need your help, think I need anyone?
I'm gone.

The knocking at the door persisted. Now the door bursts open.
Smoke and light pours out of the door, before a giant shadow is
cast across the stage, and walking out of the door is –

Scene Six

– a cute little GIRL, *about ten years old.*
She's holding a sheet of paper and a helium balloon.
She goes to a microphone. Adjusts it to her height. Puts on her
reading glasses.
Puts the sheet on a music stand and reads as if she's speaking from
a pulpit.

GIRL. From: sistakene@aol.com
    To: arinzé-kene@gmail.com
    Date: Thursday, February 10th, 9:48pm.
    Subject: Do not be the naked beggar!

Hey little bro,

Long time no speak.

All is good over here. I'm sat under the opepe tree as I write
this. I've just put the kids to bed, they're growing up so quick.
Small chickens are playing behind me.

I tried Skypeing you a few times to see if you could make it out
here for my fortieth! You didn't call me back so… I went behind
your back and phoned Dimples. She said you're okay but you're
stressing, busy writing. Mama and I are glad that you have a
writing job, but why didn't you tell us? Were you embarrassed?
She said you're writing a searing contemporary urban gig theatre
piece? Is that the kind of play I imagine it is?

Bro, I know that too much cross-examination can be
destabalising to a piece of art, so I'll just say this:

The GIRL *gives a nod to the band and they begin playing*
motivational music to underscore the little GIRL's *speech.*

You better not be writing some red-hot buffoonery to pander to
the voyeuristic needs of the bourgeoisie.
Because unlike the past brutalities inflicted upon us, this modern
war is in the mind, working from a psychological perspective.
This psychosocial engineering programme is disseminated to
you through news, education, radio, television, film – deployed
in all sectors right from the government to…
the *theatre*.

The GIRL *indicates to the band and they begin to crescendo as*
she drives her point home.

It engenders in our people feelings of self-doubt, self-hatred, and when that's what you're feeling, you could totally make up stories like, well, the one you seem to be writing right now. Or even worse, you could be writing some gun-crime – (*BEEP!*)

ARINZÉ *produces an orange water pistol.*

The type of story you're telling creates a national climate that is insensitive to our plight. Thus fostering a consensual national setting wherein which our people are more easily mistreated and oppressed!
And this leads to our people being harassed and even killed by the authorities for reaching for our keys! For reaching for ID! Or for walking down a street to go buy a bag of Skittles!

The music and her speech has hit the climax, she indicates for the band to decrescendo. They do.

I know you probably have producers breathing down your neck telling you what to write but you must still retain
your integrity!
As Dad used to say:
'A dressed beggar can get fed, but a naked beggar cannot!'

…but what do I know? I'm not an artist. Why not get advice from Dimples?

ARINZÉ *scoffs at this.*

I mean, she's doing so well. Her paintings are classy as ever. And the collective that she's a part of, wow, I follow them on Instagram, they look so cool.

ARINZÉ. Nah, they ain't cool man.

GIRL (*to* ARINZÉ). I know you don't think they are but they're ahead of the curve, little bro.

ARINZÉ. It's all a façade. They're tasteless private-school kids, who come to East London, put on a pair of dirty jeans, say 'yeah deffo' and call themselves artists.

GIRL. You shouldn't be jealous of their success.

ARINZÉ. I'm not jealous, I just don't wanna be a part of some phoney collective.

GIRL. You should seek their advice.

ARINZÉ. They're glorified cultural tourists.

GIRL. But I know you hate asking for help. Maybe if you weren't
so proud, you wouldn't be writing a nigga play –

ARINZÉ *has had enough. He shoots her balloon with his water
pistol. The balloon bursts.*
It frightens the little GIRL *and she begins to cry.* ARINZÉ *feels
guilty.*

The ASSISTANT STAGE MANAGER *appears. She shakes her
head at* ARINZÉ *as she ushers the little* GIRL *offstage.*

ARINZÉ (*to* ASM)…. I mean, you wouldn't get it, you wouldn't
understand… I'm got getting advice from Dimples… anyone
can sell a painting…

He begins to freestyle.

'Knock Knock Knock' (freestyle)

she sold a couple paintings and her ego inflated and…
…cos her work blew up, she got these new friends, and they're
so successful,
they're so grown up cos they're pop-up shop owners,
their art work is critically exhibited, they're cool magazine
contributors, designers and editors,
tastemakers with three thousand disciples and Twitter followers,
and their Instagram pics are so like 'nuhnhuhnhunhunhun you
can't sit with us.'

Anyway, she's part of that collective, and they're like… so
respected, cos they're like… so selective, and like,
part of me wants the play to do well just so the collective could
be like
'Dimples, wow, your boyfriend's so respected, his play is so
impressive, we want him in the collective.'
At which point, I'll be like 'Wow. Thank you, collective,
I mean, I'm flattered but, I'm not interested.'
Cos that would show Dimples that I don't need a seal of
approval from them or acceptance,
and Dimples would see that I'm a true artist and she's just been
pretentious
I mean, I was writing the other day, in the kitchen as I do,
And they made me feel like a dickhead for begging them to
keep it down in the living room.

I was like knock knock knock. Hi everyone, sorry to interrupt.
I'm Dimples' boyfriend.

DIMPLES. Yeah, everyone, this is my boyfriend.

ARINZÉ. Hi.

DIMPLES. What's up?

ARINZÉ. I know you lot are having a collective meeting and
you're drinking – sounds like fun,
but I'm in the next room, trying to get work done, and I can't
hear myself thinking,
so whichever one of you who keeps making that duck sound
I would really appreciate if you stop making the duck sound cos
it's so fuckin annoying
Enjoy the rest of your evening.
I'll just get back to my writing.
Thanks for your cooperation. Goodnight then.

ARINZÉ goes to write. Moments later. ARINZÉ returns.

Knock knock knock – Hi everyone, I asked you to stop but you
just carried on with the duck sounds, even more duck sounds
than before, it's immature, and hard to ignore, why you laughing
for?

DIMPLES. We'll keep it down, go back to your virus.

ARINZÉ. Dimples may I have a word, with you in private.

First of all, I think it's deep how you don't stand up for me in
front of company, I'm a commissioned writer now and I deserve
to be treated more respectfully

DIMPLES. You are the one who was rude just now

ARINZÉ. How was I rude just now

DIMPLES. You burst in and said we were making duck sounds

ARINZÉ. You were making duck sounds

DIMPLES. No, that's just his laugh

ARINZÉ. Whose laugh?

DIMPLES. Redhead Eddie, Redhead Eddie laughs like that

ARINZÉ. Which one's Redhead Eddie?

DIMPLES. He's the redhead one, he lives downstairs now

ARINZÉ. Dreadlock Rasta lives downstairs

DIMPLES. Dreadlock Rasta moved out, Redhead Eddie's moved in

ARINZÉ. Nah, you sure? Dreadlock Rasta loves it here, he
    wouldn't leave these ends

DIMPLES. If you don't believe me you can ask him

ARINZÉ. Dreadlock Rasta wouldn't just up and go,
    Dreadlock Rasta part of the cultural infrastructure – wouldn't
    just up and go,
    this is his home,
    Dreadlock Rasta you know, you sure?
    Dreadlock Rasta moved out?
    Nah I'm pissed off now.

DIMPLES. What are you on about?

ARINZÉ. I'm on about the fact that Tony's laundrette is
    a swanky coffee shop now
    I'm on about Betty hairdresser's turning into a Bikram
    yoga premises,
    Plus isn't it weird that we're the only ones left in this building
    who was originally here?
    People like Dreadlock Rasta and Handyman Andy slowly begin
    to disappear
    I ain't got nothing 'gainst Redhead Eddie, but I'm not a fan of
    how the Rasta man keeps getting replaced but the trust-fund
    man,
    it ain't fair... it ain't morally right.

DIMPLES. Wow, like, as if you have the right to discuss what's
    morally right?
    What you write ain't morally right.

ARINZÉ. Says who?

DIMPLES. Says me. Says the whole inner city, that you're
    exploiting,
    Calling us viruses,
    Yeah that's very nice. Yeah that's morally right.

ARINZÉ (*beat*). I'm gonna go for a walk.

DIMPLES. Cool.

ARINZÉ. When I come back. I think we should talk.

DIMPLES. Cool.

Scene Seven

The VIRUS *is alone on the streets.*

'Mutiny'

VIRUS
The streets are mine again,
But it ain't like before,
Something's different –
The breeze don't feel nice any more,
Cos there's blood cells everywhere…
And their smell lingers in the air,
I ain't used to seeing so many of them round here…

That's a next ting,
When I'm by myself?
That's the only time I ever feel that I'm myself,
My self is weird man,
Need someone here –
Need Tracy in my ear man,
Yeah.

Everything about Trace, the way I love that girl,
She's the purest most adorest thing in this world,
She got a glittery soul, her heart's completely gold –
She deserves the things I was deprived of, tenfold,
Not even big things, the simple little things,
Things that's, normal, just normal like…
Things like, things like: listening,
Things like,
'Come here, sweetheart. Are you all right?
You're so kind. You're very bright.
Have I told you? You're the perfect height.
Thought I'd surprise you, look, that thing you like.
What do you want to be? What do you want to see?
You'll be that. You'll see that.'

Nah with me yeah? I had to beg for shit,
Either that or prove I absolutely needed it.

Just fucking… nuff basic things I felt to do,
Sounds silly but, I nuff wanted to go to the zoo,
And no one took me,
The time my year went at school,
Mum was tired after back-to-back night shifts and lost the
permission slip and when they tried to phone her,
They couldn't get through.

The VIRUS *recieves a phone call.*

Hello?
Tracy is that you?
Come this weekend, we're going to the zoo me and you
Why you sniffling?
Who's that in the background?
Why we whispering?
The antivirals? She let them in?
Yeah? They talking to her now?
What they talking 'bout?
They said I did what on the bus?
What proof they got?
How'd they know it was me?
CCTV – ?
You sure that's what they said?
He suffered what to the head?
It was a normal fight –
Who's that laughing in the back?
Oh… then why's she crying like that?
Yeah the zoo, you wanna go?
Deffo, don't tell Mum though, she can't come with us,
Yeah there'll be nuff candy floss,
Yo Trace, listen,
You're very bright. You're the perfect height,
And listen – Hello?

When a virus shakes up a blood cell, the organ doesn't cope well,
the city creature goes pale, the body's feveral,
Antivirals administered by hypodermic needle go on patrol, in
search of us virus people,
As they police through the blood vessels, we scatter like roaches,
we scuttle into the shadows like beetles,

They don't want us roaming in the city creature, they don't want us
multiplying, they don't want an upheaval,
A mutiny, cos they know I'm polyhedral and there's not much they
can do to me but lock me up and ask that I be peaceful,
They ask that you stay away from us, don't play with us and never
lay with us, they make you heedful,
They wanna eat my soul, they want us barefooted and broke, they
portray us as dark hearts and evils,
And it's deceitful cos they created us and now they hating us, turn
away from us, label us medieval,
We get angry and we shout and switch, they say we're primitive,
and that we're limited, uncongenial,
Yeah that's why it's deceitful, cos they created us and now they
hate us, turn around and put the onus on us,
now you wanna blame it on me? It's all my fault, the way that
I be? You're taking *no* responsibility?
Ah makes me wanna multiply and infect you so's you die, the
whole city creature,
makes me wanna rally all my viruses and start a massive riot, start
fires and pull off car tyres
and loot shops and the whole lot, and when the cops try to kettle us
we give them the heat like kettle pots,
give them that hot volcanic rock, raise our tops, pull out our metal
glocks, blow them out their socks,
gun shots like blop blop blop, the street cleaners are gonna need
bigger mops to soak what's coming up!

There's a persistent knocking at the door again.
ARINZÉ *acknowledges it but ignores it.*
The ASM *appears and rudely chucks him a wetsuit. She's still
disappointed in him for making the* GIRL *cry so she doesn't help
him put it on.*
ARINZÉ *talks to us directly.*

ARINZÉ (*as he puts on the suit*). Dimples and I had that talk… she
left me.
She basically left me because, to quote her,
I was writing was some 'urban safari jungle shit'.
Raymond, Donna, and some other friends, no longer wanted to
be associated with me.
They didn't exactly ostracise me but my opinion in the
Whatsapp no longer had gravitas?

ARINZÉ *gets a random audience member to help zip up the back of his wetsuit.*

And my sister?

ARINZÉ *now unlocks the backstage door. The little* GIRL *pushes in a shopping trolley full of water balloons.*
ARINZÉ *gets against the wall and braces himself and she begins to throw them at him.*
He tries to dodge. Some will miss him, some will hit him. But maybe he doesn't duck at all. Maybe he takes his punishment.

She kept sending emails – (*Dodges water balloon.*)

The two MUSICIANS *join in throwing water balloons at* ARINZÉ.

'Why would you tell this (*Dodges.*) depressing-as-fuck story, Arinzé?'

'Why would you (*Dodges.*) make this shit up, Arinzé?'
'What about your responsibility as a writer?'

'Don't you care about the impact it'll have on people?'
'When you reach official Uncle Tom status, is there like, a special handshake?'

'What about (*Dodges.*) people who actually live this shit life, Arinzé? Have you asked them how they feel about you telling this story?'
And I was like
(*They're all out of water balloons.*)
I was like, 'Well, it's funny you should ask that.'

ARINZÉ *dries his hands. He gets the Dictaphone. He presses play.*
We begin to hear ARINZÉ *interviewing a young man named* LUCAS.
On the recording there's background noise implying they're in some kind of communal space like a prison or a psychiatric ward:

… Okay so it's recording, just, test it for me, say something…

LUCAS. Wha'gwan, this is Lucas, mic check one two –

ARINZÉ. We're good just speak up a bit.

LUCAS. Cool, and I just talk?

ARINZÉ. Yeah just tell me like, everything that happened.

LUCAS. From where, from the beginning?

ARINZÉ. Yeah from the start.

LUCAS. Cool, well it started on the night bus then cos... I just
jumped on the bus, through the back door, when it opened. And
I'm there now, just standing there and there's a drunk guy,
swaying, and like I said. I wasn't even trying to start anything
but he couldn't stand straight, and it ain't my fault he can't
stand straight, so I said to him... I just told him to watch it. He
kinda fell on me again, so like, I switched, and we got in a fight.
It was mad quick. The bus driver stopped the bus so I get off the
bus. And... yeah...

ARINZÉ. When did you see Jade?

LUCAS. I saw Jade that night because, when I got off the bus,
I was bopping past a corner shop and someone left their bike
there outside it so I just jumped on the bike –

ARINZÉ. You stole it?

LUCAS. I *took* it. It was in my way when I was walking past it so I
took it. Minor. Stealings different innit. I didn't go out of my way,
it was literally on the pavement *in* my way. Anyway. I ride to
Jade's now... Jade was still living round my sides them times so,
when I got to Jade's, I see that her bedroom light was on, so I just
put the bike in the hedge bit, I hid it in... the bush across the road,
where there's a little park.
Jade was...
...It's mad cos all the 'blood cells and viruses' stuff, it's just the
way I see the world, I tried to like, tell Jade about it... she said I
was tweaking out haha said I was buggin out cos of some bad
weed so we argued about that for a bit... I just see things
differently, the whole blood cells verses virus thing is like, I
don't think it's down to anything I was smoking... anyway
things escalated and I left Jade's...

ARINZÉ. Where'd you go?

LUCAS. Went home. Rode home. Clocked that Mum had locked me
out. It wasn't the first time but like... I knew it was serious
because all my stuff was in bin bags outside. Proper raw. Ike,
I didn't even do nothing to deserve it this time...

While the recording plays, ARINZÉ *leaves the stage.*
He returns with an air blower and a huge balloon.
He begins to inflate the balloon with the blower. It gets bigger
and bigger until it explodes with a massive BANG!

Lights out is simultaneous with the loud bang.

End of Act One.

Interval.

ACT TWO

Scene One

When the audience re-enter the theatre there is a balloon centerstage, six foot in diameter. Our MUSICIANS *go behind the gauze and become* RAYMOND *and* DONNA.

VOICEMAIL.
 (*Beep*.)
 You have, one, new message,
 left today, at,
 2:04, a.m.
 From, Raymond,
 And, Donna,
 And, the baby.

RAYMOND. ... and okay, it's a true story, but like, so what.
 It doesn't matter that it's a true story. It doesn't make it okay to tell a story, cos it's true. What I'm saying is that you're falling into the trap that some of our black writers fall into.
 It seems that some black writers 'conveniently' wanna write narratives that majority white audiences are interested in seeing about black people.

DONNA. 'Conveniently.'

RAYMOND. And that narrative my brother, is –

DONNA. Black trauma.

RAYMOND. I would've just said 'trauma'.

DONNA. Black trauma ought to be a genre of its own cos under the umbrella of black trauma comes your typical stories of racism, slavery, crime and violence you know...

RAYMOND. ... drugs, gangs, poverty.

DONNA. *Django*? *Django Un*-fuckin-*chained*. Give me strength. Why do you think *Django* and *12 Years a Slave* are always gonna be box-office hits?

Meanwhile something like *Love Jones* or *Brown Sugar*,
where the black folk are just going through normal
mundane things,
like being unlucky in love, those stories don't do well,
know why?
Cos the black folk in those stories ain't suffering.
We never get a cycling-through-the-city montage in films.
I want a cycling-through-the-city montage of a girl who looks
like me.
Cos I love a cycle. I really like cycling.

RAYMOND. And I ain't saying you've written *Django* but, you've
written just another hood story.
(*Their daughter frets.*)
Do you really want for our daughter to see yet another one?

DONNA. Is that the only story about us that there is to tell her?

RAYMOND. I don't believe that your story being true excuses it.

DONNA. But, you know, put your little nigga play on sweetie,
haha,
You do what you gotta do and we'll do what we gotta do.

RAYMOND. Donna, don't say that –

DONNA. No, don't censor me, I mean it.
If we can shut down some Barbican-arts-centre-human-zoo-
slavery bullshit,
then we can set fire to a little bush –
(*The baby is crying now.*)

RAYMOND. She's joking man.

DONNA. Joking as ever but I'm serious as fuck though.

The voicemail ends.

VOICEMAIL. To save –
(*Beep.*)

Message, deleted.
To return the –
(*Beep.*)

It rings once then goes to voicemail.
A light slowly comes up on the balloon and we realise that
ARINZÉ *is inside it. He's on his phone, leaving a message.*

You have reached the voicemail box, for,
'*Raymond*'
Please leave a message after the beep.
Once you have left your message,
key hash for more options.
(*Beep*.)

ARINZÉ. Hey, Raymond, Donna. Arinzé here. Erm.
    Sorry if it sounds a bit echoey, I'm just...
    Listen, I don't think you can dismiss Lucas's story on account
    of...
    it being depressing as fuck.
    I grew up with him and,
    he'd never been to see any of my work and when I asked why...
    Well... you know what he said would make him come to
    the theatre?
    He wanted to see himself there. That's what he said. He wanted
    to see himself.
    So me putting him on stage so he could see himself, is that so
    bad? Am I fucked up, for doing that? Doesn't his story deserve
    to be told too?
    I mean, he's been through so much in his life and... given
    what's happened with him since I started writing the play...
    It's felt like my duty or that I owe it him to...

ARINZÉ *repositions himself in the balloon. He continues
talking while he does. Eventually he's upside down, half in and
half out of the balloon, his back facing the audience while
balancing on his shoulders. His hands are gesturing as he's
speaking. It's absurd.*

Know what, if anything, going back to the recording made me
wanna tell the story even more because,
I realised that I heard it wrong. The whole blood cells and
viruses thing, I had it wrong.
Lucas was saying that *he* was the blood cell and *they* were the
viruses.
Which makes more sense now because... scientifically...
If viruses invade the body, and raid the body, then Lucas and I
have witnessed viruses invade our area.
It started with them building the overground train...

ARINZÉ *starts freestyling. The* MUSICIANS *join in when they
pick up his rhythm.*

'Reversal' (freestyle)

– and because of this overground train the viruses came, from
far and wide.
Viruses raise the rent price so high that small businesses, local
businesses
that have been here a long time, can no longer survive
so they close down, so the viruses turn it into a Starbucks now,
which causes the property value to rise even more,
buildings are privatised even more,
which attracts even more virus vultures
pushes out even more business owners,
and we lose even more of our culture,
and even more people who used to live here can't afford to,
people like me, Lu, and Dreadlock Rasta too, that's what
viruses do.
So I had it the wrong way round. We're the blood cells. We've
been the blood cells all along
A virus can't replicate itself all alone, it must infect a cell
They inject themselves into a cell and convert that cell into
a mindless virus-producing cell –
It's what Redhead Eddie did to my girl –
And it was happening in the story as well.

ARINZÉ *pulls himself out of the balloon. He's still wearing his*
wetsuit.

Scene Two

ARINZÉ *doesn't seem to be able to move.*
As he performs this song, the ASM *gets him out of the wetsuit and*
dresses him.

'Sleep Paralysis'

BLOOD CELL
The sun rises,
My brain's awake,
My body ain't,
Sleep paralysis,
I'm always having this,

I can breathe,
But fear that any moment someone's coming to suffocate me,
Which makes me anxious,
Which makes my heart race,
All they need to do is hold a pillow on my face,
Or pull a plastic bag over my head,
Or pinch my nose,
Can't even fucking wiggle my toes.

I hear people walking,
With their hard shoes,
On their ways to work,
In my area, no one used to wear hard shoes to work,
But my area's been changing,
They've been replacing, us blood cells with more viruses,
Viruses who wear suits to work,
And hard shoes to work,
And us blood cells, who they say don't choose to work –
Who they say refuse to work,
Have to leave our places as the rent inflates beyond our wages.

I hear drilling,
Builders shouting,
Employed by new viruses –
Fitting extensions on their houses,
I hear women,
Here come yummy mummies and French au pairs,
Pushing wide-as-fuck prams everywhere,
Now there's ramps, where there used to be stairs,
Soon there's gonna be a separate lane for prams,
Cos they're the single leading cause of pavement traffic jams,
It's pramageddon,
This is my nightmare, I need to wake up!

They've even built coffee shops where they used to sell beers –
Where arty viruses meet up and chew off each other's ears,
And further down the road, they've built a theatre,
But us blood cells don't watch bearded men in leotards,
Thank you very much but fuck Shakespeare,
This is where I grew up,
The other day I was on the bus, and I missed my stop,
I did not recognise it,
Cos these viruses have come here and gentrified it,
And to be fair it does looks nice, but I don't like it.

Scene Three

'Chase'

BLOOD CELL
'Now, I know you hate it when I visit while you're working, Jade,
I know you've got all these viruses to be serving, Jade –
And, I would've texted you, but my battery's done –
Which is probably for the best cos, if I switch it on...
Huh, don't even wanna say with all these viruses watching –
Come we step outside a sec, gotta tell you something,
I did not come all this way to be ignored,
Don't make me have to switch, why you acting silly for?
Telling customers you've never seen me before,
Like last night we weren't mashing on your bedroom floor,
You gonna blank me yeah? Pretend like I'm not here?
You think I won't start flipping tables and dashing chairs?'

She goes and gets a next waiter to cover,
She pushes me through the kitchen and out the back door –
Screaming in my face, says I'll get her in trouble –
She's up for a promotion and why am I trying to get her
sacked for.

She knows that there's a warrant out for my arrest,
Knows I'm already front page of the *Daily Gazette*,
Apparently it's quickly circulating via text,
Apparently her dad texted her, 'have you seen it yet?'
Apparently her dad got five brothers,
Apparently he's got a couple nasty cousins,
Apparently they wanna catch me before the police,
Apparently man ain't safe any more on these streets,
Apparently a normal person would be scared –
Apparently the fact I'm smiling and don't care is kind of weird, to
her,
Jade says my time is up, and she should be working,
She thinks I'll let her storm off without getting a word in.

I grab her arm and say –
'I won't let go unless you promise to meet me later with food
money and clothes.'
She pulls away from me and
She storms off without saying yes or no but I know she's
gonna show.

When I go –
I walk with my head low, and stay away from main roads, cos
they're the arterioles.
And when I'm passing people on the pavement
I cover my face a bit, pretending I'm speaking on the phone.
When I hear sirens
I'm diving, hiding, in phone boxes, behind a bin, behind a skip.
That's where I see
Kids bunking off of school so I tax each of them, for enough to buy
fish and chips.
I eat it facing the wall
Down a cul-de-sac, looking over my back, I've never been hungry
like this.

I feel like an animal
Scoffing it down so quick, the salt and vinegar's stinging
off my lips.
I have a bit of change
So I get a drink, from the corner shop, a can of Lilt, I finish it, in
two sips.
I arrive at the gates
of Tracy's school, for three-thirty, just in time, to hear the pips.
I decide to wait
Across the street, disguised by this random hat, that I found, laying
on the ground.
The kids pour out of the school
And my eyes are peeled for Tracy, because she don't hang around.

I spot my little sister
Power-walking through the crowd, but she looks upset, got her
head down.
A couple kids
Trying to bully her, but I can't make out what they're saying, over
all the sound.
I'm tempted to fuck them up
But I don't wanna blow my cover, so I just watch it carry on.
And turns out she didn't need me anyway
She smacks the bully in his face and sends him crying to
his mum
I walk over to her
And I whisper in her ear, telling her when to meet me and where.
But then some kids
Start shouting 'it's him, it's him', then the antiviral appear.

I run like a dog
Run like an animal, run like a beast, through alleyways
and streets.
Run till I can't feel my feet
But I still hear police dogs, barking, they're closing in on me.
The dogs can smell me easily
Cos I'm sweating, from the running, and I ain't had a shower.
So I tek off all my clothes
I dump them in the bushes, and then I jump in the canal.

When I was young
I never got my certificate for swimming ten metres cos I can't
fucking swim.
I dove in this canal on a whim
Hoping that after a few bad strokes my *instincts* would kick in.
They *don't* kick in
I breathe in water, I'm guzzling nuff water, I'm drowning
in the water.

I'm really trying
To be breast-stroking in the water, but all's I'm doing is choking in
the water.
I come to terms
With the fact that I'm gonna die so I stop panicking and let myself
go.
That's when I feel
Something under my toes and come to realise, yep this canal's
quite shallow.

I wade through the water
I get out, I tiptoe to a park, and hide behind trees.
I'm butt naked
It's really windy, and now my nose is blocked, cos it's zero
degrees.
So when I spot a hipster
Walking through the park, I rob his clothes, he's about my same
build and height
I put it on but
Something's wrong cos, somehow, it ends up proper tight.
I cannot walk in these jeans
I can't even bend my knees, I can see every muscle in my thigh.
But my area's been gentrified
So dressing like an arty virus, is not a bad disguise.
I stop, to see the clock

Through the window, of a shop, and remember that I got to meet
Jade.
But with no means to tell her
I'll be late, cos I lost my phone, when I dashed my clothes, in the
escapade.

I run
With a wedgie chafing in my bum, down arterioles, and I'm
wearing *hard* shoes.
People still look at me
But now it's differently, not suspiciously, like what I'm used to.
I get to
The corner of the road, where I told Jade to go, but I don't see Jade
there.
But I know
She was here recently, the smell of her Blue Freeze hair gel, lingers
in the air.
Do I go left
Go right, straight ahead, or do I just wait here instead?
The longer I contemplate
is the further that she's possibly walking away, but I know Jade's
head.
I wait five minutes
Then Jade approaches, slurping a can of Coke, and 'I know who
the Lilt's for.'
I locate an open car
I put Jade in the back, get in after, and I shut the door.

It's been a tough long day
It's been such a rough day, my stress levels have been
gone crazy.
It feels good
To just sit down a sec, to catch my breath and decompress with
Jade but.
I get vex when she
Hands me only ten pounds, and explains 'that's all the money
I can spare.'
I get vex when she goes
'I can't steal my dad's clothes, he would notice, there's nothing he
don't wear.'

I get vex at
'why would I lie, if there was leftovers at the restaurant

I would've brung it.'
I get vex cos
Up to now she's been all over me and now she's acting like she
ain't on it.
Nonetheless
I try warn her regardless about the viruses taking over the city
creature.
She says I'm crazy
Says I need to see someone, she says bye, and she's gone.

It's like I'm the only one who can see what's going on.
Call it virus invasion,
Call it gentrification,
Call whatever you want,
It's nothing but modern-day colonisation.

We gotta wake the fuck up outta this nightmare,
I've had enough of being powerless, enough sleep paralysis,
Can't you see what's going on, we're being ousted,
By these shiny-shoe-wearing viruses,

They up the rent and kick out the blood cell tenants,
They shutting down the youth clubs and youth centres,
To build a bar & grill with a garden terrace,
There's enough to impel us to desperate *measures*,

Let us wake up out of our night *terrors*,
Let us stand united 'gainst the *oppressors*,
Let us activate and organise *vengeance*,
Let us bring back our small *businesses*,

Let us kick them out of our *premises*,
Then let us gather all of these *aggressors*,
And make *them reside,* in death-trap *housing*,
See how *they* like all the heat, and *howling*,

There's gonna be black smoke *rising again*,
Cos my people are done *internalising again,*
Cos we don't wanna hear *apologising* again,
It's time to start *Penalizing!*

To high heaven we've been *compromising,*
But they're down with Lucifer *harmonising,*
That's why no justice is *materialising,*
It's time we start *chastising!*

A member of the audience's phone begins to ring.
This makes ARINZÉ *break character and stop performing.*

ARINZÉ (*to audience*). You gonna switch it off?
Is that you?

> *Eventually,* ARINZÉ *realises the ringing is his personal phone*
> *that he left somewhere on stage. He's very apologetic...*

Ah shit, my bad...
I was texting at the interval and...

> *He turns the ringer off but it's vibrating in his hand.*
> ARINZÉ *looks at the caller ID.*
> *He goes behind the gauze to take the call –*

Scene Four

ASSISTANT. Hi Arinzé, it's Rebecca from the agency, can I patch
you through to your agent, is this a good time?

ARINZÉ. Well... not really, no –

ASSISTANT. Great, please hold.

> ARINZÉ*'s put on hold for a beat. Then –*

AGENT. 'Listen, you have just a little bit more attitude than I like.'

ARINZÉ. What? I don't have an attitude.

AGENT. 'Yes you do have an attitude. If you didn't have an
attitude you would not raise your voice to me now would you?'

ARINZÉ. I'm not raising my voice, I'm engaging my diaphragm,
projecting my voice because I'm at the theatre. Listen, I'm not
gonna change the play –

AGENT. 'You don't seem to understand what I'm saying.'

ARINZÉ. Yeah I do, listen, if the producers think it's too political
just because of the gentrification thing with the virus turning out
to be blood cell then –

AGENT. 'This would not be the place to begin a career.'

ARINZÉ. – Firstly, it's not even that political. And even if it was, so what?
If the audience ain't ready to be challenged, maybe they shouldn't go to the theatre.

AGENT. 'People like going to theatres.'

ARINZÉ. I... I don't wanna discuss this with you, I'm gonna go.

AGENT. 'I'm the good guy – Do you understand? – I'm the good guy.'

ARINZÉ. If you were the good guy you'd be fighting my corner, you'd have my back on this one. I'm gonna worship Lucas's story, I think it's... the right thing to do.

PRODUCER. 'That's cos you're a baby and you don't know shit.'

ARINZÉ. Who is... is that... you're with him right now aren't you?

AGENT. 'Oh he's a handsome man – Got a good old head on his shoulders.'

PRODUCER. 'Your left nipple is a quarter inch higher than your right nipple.'

AGENT. 'You think so?'

PRODUCER. 'That's exactly the way I like it.'

AGENT. 'I'm really glad you're into this.'

Blast of porn noise.

ARINZÉ. Wow! Can you just, fucking, not do that in front of me.

AGENT. 'I made a mistake, I'm sorry, it will never happen again.'

ARINZÉ (*turns to* PRODUCER). Listen... I...

PRODUCER. 'What do you want from me? What the hell do you want?'

ARINZÉ. I just wanna get to the end with no one telling me how and what I should write. Is that too much to ask?

PRODUCER. 'You smoke crack don't ya?'

ARINZÉ. I... what?

PRODUCER. 'YA SMOKE CRACK DON'T YA?'

ARINZÉ. Crack cocaine?

PRODUCER. 'DON'T YOU SMOKE CRACK?'

AGENT. I… No. I don't smoke crack.

PRODUCER. 'It kills your brain cells.'

ARINZÉ. I just. I write. I just wanna write my shit
unencumbered… and not even… I don't even *wanna* write the
enlightening play that ticks all the boxes and bridges the racial
and sexual and LGBT abyss, that some people expect of me. I
just wanna write a play, man. A regular play. It's really not that
deep. Everybody's just… the pressure, from both sides… can't
this just fucking exist? Without it being a… an exotic… urban
thing to someone, or a nigga play or without you thinking it
ought to be unpolitical – what the fuck can you possibly know
about what *I* wanna say? Can't it just be a play? Can a play
from a person like me just be a fucking play already? Can we
just hurry up and stop being weird about people like me writing
plays and shit?

PRODUCER. 'You disappoint me brother, you disappoint me.'

ARINZÉ. It's just a story, about Lucas, about people like me, who
don't want wanna get displaced by flat-white-sipping yoga
addicts.

PRODUCER. 'I don't want you to blame the white man.'

ARINZÉ. No, I said 'flat white' not… I'm not blaming white
people.

PRODUCER. 'Three of us will put our heads together and… I'm
sure we'll be able to help you decide what's best for you to
do – '

ARINZÉ. See that's exactly what I'm not trying to have us do,
didn't you listen to *anything* I just said?

AGENT. 'It's gonna be a little different around here.'

ARINZÉ. I just wanna –

PRODUCER. 'This is not a damn democracy! – There's only one
boss in this place and that's me!'

The call ends.

Scene Five

ARINZÉ *bounces his stress ball against the wall of the cube. This goes on for a while.*
All of a sudden, every time the ball hits the wall of the cube, there's a thundering bass.
ARINZÉ *throws the ball at the cube again but now, the ball has turned into a water balloon – we only know that when it bursts against the cube.*

There's sounds coming from within the cube.
ARINZÉ *goes to the cube and puts his ear to the wall, listening.*
ARINZÉ *begins to open the cube, he pulls the wall down until the interior of the cube is visible.*

This whole scene is like a nightmare.
Inside the cube is ARINZÉ*'s study: desk, laptop, chair, lamp, etc., but everything is covered in orange and the room is filled with balloons. It's as if his room is the interior of a balloon. Sitting at the desk typing away is the little* GIRL. *She swivels around in the chair and faces* ARINZÉ. *When she talks, her voice is deep and demonic.*

GIRL (*demonic voice, barely audible*). Oh, hey little bro!
    I didn't notice you there.
    I was just busy rewriting your play.
    (*Maniacal laugh.*)

She hands ARINZÉ *a ghost balloon. Then she leaves through the cube.*
ARINZÉ *goes in after her but she's disappeared.*
Out of frustration ARINZÉ *starts bursting the balloons.*
He bursts as many as he can.
As he bursts the balloons a song begins to play (not by the MUSICIANS).
Some of the balloons have an orange powder in them. ARINZÉ *becomes covered in orange powder. He removes his shirt which is covered in the powder, so now the powder gets right on to his body. All over him. Bursting them becomes a dance. It represents the torment he's living with.*
It will go on for as long as necessary.

By the end of this, all the balloons are burst, ARINZÉ *is topless, exhausted and covered in orange powder. However, even though there are none left, he's still bursting balloons. They're inside him now. They're inside his head. It's endless.*

*Then there's a moment of surrender. A moment of acceptance.
He gives in to them being there. He embraces them. He lets
himself be influenced by them.*

Scene Six

The BLOOD CELL *paces around topless... He gets rid of the mic-
stand and paces with the mic on the wire. It's tense. It's like that
moment an hour into a hip-hop concert where the artist is drenched
in sweat, the stage is theirs. The audience is theirs. The length of
the pauses between geh-geh's don't matter. There's conviction there.
We've not seen the* BLOOD CELL *or* ARINZÉ *this bold before.
When he begins performing, he gives everything, unashamed of
who he really is, of his roots and of what people may think.*

'Geh-Geh'

BLOOD CELL
Geh-geh.
Geh-geh.
Geh-geh.
Geh-geh.

Geh-geh.
Geh-geh.
Geh-geh.
Geh-geh.

I'm at an arty virus cafe.
Geh-geh.
I told Tracy to meet me here.
Geh-geh.
I thought it was the old adventure playground.
Geh-geh.
Reached here to find out they've knocked it down.
Geh-geh.

And built this arty virus cafe.
Geh-geh.
I sit at a table, in the corner.
Geh-geh.

Dressed as this hipster, I've blended in.
Geh-geh.
Skinny virus waiter approaches me.
Geh-geh.

Is this, your only food menu?
Geh-geh.
So you don't even do a full English.
Geh-geh.
Yet you call yourself a cafe.
Geh-geh.
Ooh, 'Café' my bad.
Geh-geh.

Right. What is a croque madam?
Geh-geh.
So it's just egg, bread, cheese, ham.
Geh-geh.
And somehow costs eleven pound.
Geh-geh.
…wow.
Geh-geh.

I'll just, I'll geh-get a coffee.
Geh-geh.
You have a separate menu, for coffee.
Geh-geh.
Which one's, the normal coffee?
Geh-geh.
Just get me the one, everybody geh-gets.
Geh-geh.

Right, so, is this meant to be my coffee?
Geh-geh.
Why is it in such a tiny mug?
Geh-geh.
Why does the milk come separately?
Geh-geh.
I just like my milk inside my coffee, I'm crazy like that.
Geh-geh.

Know what, take it back, bring me a tea.
Geh-geh.
You can't have a separate menu for tea, bro.
Geh-geh.

You just, you can't.
Geh-geh.
No I do not wanna see the tea menu. No.
Geh-geh.

Get me a tea, just get it.
Geh-geh.
Just get it. A normal tea.
Geh-geh.
I know you have it. I know you do.
Geh-geh.
Get it if you wanna skateboard ever ageh.
Geh-geh.

Just want a tea and two slices of toast.
Geh-geh.
I'd like the milk inside my tea if that's okay.
Geh-geh.
White toast, buttered if that's okay.
Geh-geh.
Oh, and buttered, with butter, by the way.
Geh-geh.

I've been geh, like, geh-geh, and.
Geh-geh.
Think I'm infected geh, by geh geh, cos.
Geh-geh.
Ever since Jade geh, in the car, I've.
Geh-geh
I can't hold in, the geh, people are watching me,
Geh-geh!

Newspaper says police are still after me.
Geh-geh.
News is the man I beat died, of his injuries.
Geh-geh.
Now this hipster waiter has clearly noticed me.
Geh-geh.
He goes in the back, I geh-geh the fuck up and I leave.
Geh-geh!

I go to Tracy's school, pull her out of class.
Geh-geh.
We take the Tube, all the way to Regent's Park.
Geh-geh.

Get to London Zoo, Tracy joins the queue.
Geh-geh.
With a random school group, they let her through.
Geh-geh!

While the security guy was looking away,
Geh-geh.
I sneak through, the disabled-access gate,
Geh-geh.
But then he sees me at the last second,
Geh-geh.
He grabs his radio, I grab his neck and,
Geh-geh.

I tell him, to keep it stepping,
Geh-geh.
I take his radio and me and Tracy go,
Geh-geh.
Into the crowd, of people,
Geh-geh.
To find us now is like a haystack needle.
Geh-geh.

Tracy look! The kangaroo,
Geh-geh.
I told you we would go to the zoo, me and you,
Geh-geh.
You're the perfect height, you're very bright,
Geh-geh.
You can become any thing you like,
Geh-geh.

Taser! Taser! Taser!
Geh-geh.
Police tackle me down to the ground,
Geh-geh.
My shoulder pops out, I hear the sound,
Geh-geh.

Bones crack, knees on back, ow!
Geh-geh.

Struggling to breathe,
Geh-geh.
They're folding me like a long sleeve,

Geh-geh.
My ears pop,
Geh-geh.
Everything <u>stops</u>.

Everything does stop.
House lights come up.
ARINZÉ *pulls the plug out of the microphone.*
The band stopped playing immediately.

Scene Seven

The little GIRL *from earlier enters with the Dictaphone.*
She presses play on the Dictaphone.
We begin to hear ARINZÉ *and* LUCAS*'s interview continued.*
ARINZÉ *and the band continue packing away as this plays.*

LUCAS.... and I'm just there kinda on my side now and my ears
pop. I remember that, my ears pop.
And sounds just went a bit different. Everything went different
after that.
Then I get this... everything goes, cloudy, but it's nice.
And that's when I died.

ARINZÉ *(on Dictaphone)*. Wow. That's... mad.

LUCAS. Tell me about it.

ARINZÉ *(on Dictaphone)*. What was the last thing you saw?

LUCAS. Before I died?

ARINZÉ *(on Dictaphone)*. Yeah, can you remember?

LUCAS. I was looking up. Last thing I saw... Yeah man. Yeah. I
saw the balloon.
Orange balloon floating away. Tracy was holding it before
everything kicked off.
Can't even remember how / she got it now.

ARINZÉ *(on Dictaphone)*. / Fam you died! Fuck the balloon, you
died!

LUCAS. Haha. I know man! When you die it's weird. It's like the sound of a choir.
A choir of little girls. Sounds kinda sick. It's something to look forward to when you die.

ARINZÉ (*on Dictaphone*). So how are you even talking to me right now?

LUCAS. I don't know haha. You wrote this. You tell me.

ARINZÉ (*on Dictaphone*). I wrote this?

LUCAS. Yes.

ARINZÉ (*on Dictaphone*). So, I just made all this depressing shit up.

LUCAS. Haha. Yes.

ARINZÉ (*on Dictaphone*). WHY?

LUCAS. Haha I don't know. Ask yourself.

ARINZÉ (*on Dictaphone*). Arinzé, why man?

ARINZÉ *stops what he's doing. A beat.*

(*Live.*) I don't know.

LUCAS. You in the theatre now?

ARINZÉ (*resumes packing*). Yeah.

(*On Dictaphone.*) They looking at you?

(*Live.*) Yeah.

(*On Dictaphone.*) This is awkward, man. You're a weird guy out here in these playwright streets. Seriously, why write this though urban safari jungle shit? You ain't thought about the responsibility and all that?

LUCAS. Arinzé don't care about no responsibility.

ARINZÉ (*on Dictaphone*). How you gonna end this jungle shit? –

ARINZÉ *stops playback from the Dictaphone. He puts it away. It's the end of the gig so they're packing away, winding up wires, turning off equipment, putting the drum sticks into the bag, the mics are zipped into their bags.*
STAGE MANAGEMENT *begin to clear the stage. During this…*

ARINZÉ *or one of the two* MUSICIANS *pound their fists on
the desk or the floor.*
*The others pick up on it and start chanting the words
'Jungle Shit'.*
ARINZÉ *freestyling one last time, the* MUSICIANS
back him with the 'Jungle Shit' chant after every line. ARINZÉ
*vibes to it, dances to it. He's free. Free from it all. He enjoys it
more and more, becoming more tranced as it goes on.*

'Jungle Shit' (freestyle)

Jungle Shit,

Urban safari jungle shit?

Jungle Shit,

'Jungle shit', let's begin,

Jungle Shit,

Juh-juh-juh-juh-juh-juh,

Jungle Shit,

Apparently wrote jungle shit,

Jungle Shit,

Is that a sin?

Jungle Shit,

Is it for-bid-den?

Jungle Shit,

Firstly, define jungle shit,

Jungle Shit,

Our depiction on your TV screen?

Jungle Shit,

Radio, news, magazines?

Jungle Shit,

Is that what you mean?

Jungle Shit,

Lock your window and your door?

Jungle,

We're coming through the ceiling and the floor?

Jungle Shit,

Shithole country shit?

Jungle Shit,

An African? An animal?

Jungle,

An afric-animal? A cannibal?

Jungle,

Afric-animal cannibal satanical?

Jungle,

Primitive? Neanderthal?

Jungle Shit,

Jungle where we ought to be?

Jungle Shit,

Cracking nuts at the base of a tree?

Jungle Shit,

Banana eating?

Jungle Shit,

Chest beating?

Jungle Shit,

That what they mean by jungle shit?

Jungle Shit,

Does 'urban youth' come under it?

Jungle Shit,

I'm forbidden to write 'bout it?

Jungle Shit,

You hella protective over it,

Jungle Shit,

It's like it's some sacred shit,

Sacred Shit,

You mad that I lied?

Jungle Shit,

Does it even matter?

Jungle Shit,

That I told white lies,

Jungle,

White lies about black matters,

Jungle,

Don't you know black lies matter,

Jungle Shit,

If this shit was jungle shit,

Jungle Shit,

It won't be just any jungle shit,

Jungle Shit,

It be rainforest jungle shit,

Jungle Shit,

It be Jumanji jungle shit,

Jungle Shit,

Wakanda jungle shit,

Jungle Shit,

But this ain't jungle shit,

Jungle Shit,

This might be some Featre shit,

Featre Shit,

With a capital 'F',

Featre Shit,

Cos where I'm from we say 'fanks man',

Featre Shit,

If they don't like my theatre shit,

Featre Shit,

They can suck my big black theatre dick.

Crash to BLACK.

End of Play.

NINE NIGHT

Natasha Gordon

To Ella and Reuben

Nine Night was first performed in the Dorfman auditorium of the National Theatre, London, on 30 April 2018 (previews from 21 April). The cast was as follows:

ROBERT	Oliver Alvin-Wilson
LORRAINE	Franc Ashman
UNCLE VINCE	Ricky Fearon
TRUDY	Michelle Greenidge
SOPHIE	Hattie Ladbury
ANITA	Rebekah Murrell
AUNT MAGGIE	Cecilia Noble

Director	Roy Alexander Weise
Designer	Rajha Shakiry
Lighting Designer	Paule Constable
Sound Designer	George Dennis
Movement Director	Shelley Maxwell
Fight Director	Bret Yount
Company Voice Work	Rebecca Cuthbertson
Dialect Coach	Hazel Holder
Staff Director	Jade Lewis
Assistant to the Movement Director	Sarita Piotrowski

The play transferred to Trafalgar Studios, London, on 1 December 2018, with the following changes to the cast:

LORRAINE	Natasha Gordon
UNCLE VINCE	Karl Collins

Acknowledgements

This play was born from the support network of an incredible
group of women.
Sisters, your belief in me has birthed a playwright.
Amelia Adrian, Michele Austin, Rakie Ayola,
Sharon Duncan-Brewster and Ashley Miller.
Thanks forever.

Many thanks to:
Rufus Norris
Ben Power

To the cast and creative team at the NT

To Katie Haines

To Ruby Gordon

To my family

For your support and encouragement, special thanks to:
Emily McLaughlin
Indhu Rubasingham
and especially to Dominic Cooke for making this happen.
I am eternally grateful.

Lastly, to Tom Anderson for absolutely everything.

N.G.

Characters

ANITA, *Lorraine's daughter, twenties*
LORRAINE, *Gloria's daughter, mid-forties*
MAGGIE, *Gloria's cousin, seventies*
VINCE, *Maggie's husband, seventies*
ROBERT, *Gloria's son, early forties*
SOPHIE, *Robert's wife, mid-forties*
TRUDY, *Lorraine and Robert's half-sister, early fifties*

Note on Text

Where there is a / in the text, the next character starts speaking.

Scene One

Lights up on: a roomy seventies-style kitchen. The furniture is old-fashioned. Deco is typical of an elder West Indian. There is elaborate wallpaper that has been up since the 1970s, lots of house plants, pictures and relics of Jesus and the Virgin Mary on the walls, shelves full of ornaments and crocheted placemats. Around the room there are several headshots of a boy and girl taken together at school, throughout the years.

There are three doors in this room: one upstage-right slightly off-centre, one upstage-left and one downstage-left. The upstage-left door leads to the front room, the upstage-right door leads to the hallway, front door and rest of the house. The downstage-left door is the back door, leading to the garden. There is a sink and some cupboards downstage-right. There is also a table and chairs and a sofa.

We open on ANITA *at the kitchen sink making a pink powdered drink that looks a bit like milkshake. We watch her put three heaped teaspoons of powder into a mug.*

ANITA. Shit!

She pours water from the kettle into the mug. She lifts the mixture up with the spoon and allows it to fall back into the mug. She stirs it, then sniffs it.

Rank.

She is about to head up the stairs, through the door upstage-right, when she realises she has forgotten something. She goes back to the sink and starts rummaging through the drawers.

She checks the cupboards.

She walks to the bottom of the stairs and shouts.

Can't find the straws.

Beat.

Mum?

Beat.

Shall I just bring a teaspoon?

From upstairs we hear –

LORRAINE (*offstage*). Have you looked in the drawers?

ANITA. Yes.

LORRAINE (*offstage*). Have you checked in the cupboards?

ANITA. Yes.

LORRAINE (*offstage*). They were there yesterday.

ANITA. I know. I put them there.

LORRAINE (*offstage*). So, just bring a spoon, Anita. A tablespoon. Teaspoons are fiddly.

The doorbell rings.

ANITA. Bloody hell.

Beat.

It rings again.

LORRAINE (*offstage*). Anita, the door?

ANITA. Yes, I know. I'm going – Answering doors, looking for straws – Anything else?

ANITA *turns to go –* MAGGIE *and* VINCE *enter from upstage-right.*

ANITA *jumps.*

Jesus Christ!

VINCE. De door left open.

ANITA. Was it?

MAGGIE. Yuh mad? Any and anybody could jus' walk in.

ANITA. Tell me about it.

MAGGIE. Be careful, not carefree.

ANITA. The lock keeps sticking. Uncle Robert's been promising to fix it. Does Mum know you're coming?

MAGGIE. Me ring ha dis morning. Where yu grandmadda?

ANITA. She's upstairs.

VINCE. It turn bad-bad?

ANITA.... Yes.

MAGGIE. But, is just the udda day me a sit down and a chat wid ha, good-good. It's like she just give up after me leave.

ANITA. No, I don't think so. / It's just taken its toll.

MAGGIE. Lord have mercy. (*To* VINCE.) Me tell yuh. She shoulda drink de bush tea whe me tell ha fi drink. You know how many people life dat ting save in Jamaica?

Beat.

ANITA. Shall I take your coats?

VINCE. Tank yuh, dawta.

VINCE *takes off his coat and hands it to* ANITA.

MAGGIE. Dees doctor inna dis country, don't know dem head from dem foot! All now, dem a look right, dem a look left fi find cure for dis cancer business. If she, Gloria, was in Jamaica, dem woulda stop dis nonsense long time!

ANITA. Your coat, Auntie Maggie?

MAGGIE. No, tank you. It might be summer dem call dis, but I feeling de cold. Where yuh madda?

ANITA. Upstairs, with Grandma.

MAGGIE. Tell her fi come down.

VINCE *and* MAGGIE *sit down.*

ANITA *walks to the bottom of the stairs and calls out.*

ANITA. Uncle Vince and Auntie Maggie are here.

Beat.

She'll be down in a minute.

MAGGIE *eyes* ANITA.

MAGGIE. Yuh know, back home in Jamaica, me have dis cousin. Rosemary. She big suh, like yuh grandmadda. Last year, she phone me. Bawling – di doctor seh she have diabetes and him ready fi chop off she foot. Now me tell ha, 'Rosemary, save yuh eye water, nuh badda cry', and I tell ha fi mek dat same bush tea whe me advise yuh grandmadda to tek. Rosemary boil up di leaf dem; chamomile, cerasee, duppy-gun and donkey-weed. As God is my witness, mek Him strike me down if one word I speak is a lie! You tell me where dat diabetes is now? Ehh?

Beat.

It gawn!

ANITA. Yeah. Or maybe they misdiagnosed it. Speaking of tea, would you like a drink?

VINCE. Yu have anyting harder dan tea?

ANITA. I'll have a look. Auntie Maggie?

MAGGIE. Which kinda tea yuh 'ave?

ANITA. Dunno. Builder's? Peppermint?

MAGGIE. Dat's all?

ANITA. It's not my kitchen, so –

MAGGIE. Just give me some wata – Not from de tap, if yuh please.

ANITA. I'll see what I can find.

ANITA *exits upstage-right, taking* VINCE's *coat.*

VINCE *and* MAGGIE *sit in silence.* MAGGIE *sniffs the air.*

MAGGIE (*whisper*). You smell it, Vin?

VINCE. Smell wha?

Beat.

MAGGIE. She travelling, alright.

ANITA *returns without the coats carrying an open bottle of brandy and a small can of Coke.*

ANITA. You're in luck, Uncle Vince. I found some brandy.

VINCE. God bless yu.

ANITA. Can of Coke to go with it?

VINCE. Nah sah, dat's a woman's drink. I tek it as it comes.

ANITA *pours brandy for* VINCE *then heads to the fridge to get water for* MAGGIE.

MAGGIE. Nah badda start pon dat drink business and turn fool pon me yuh hear? Me nah carry yuh home tonight.

VINCE. Calm yuh nerves, woman.

ANITA. How did you get here?

VINCE. Yvette drop we off.

ANITA. Did she?

MAGGIE. In she new brand car.

ANITA. Nice.

MAGGIE. It is. Very, very nice indeed.

ANITA. She didn't fancy popping in?

MAGGIE. Yuh know how she always busy. We lucky that she even in the country this week to give us a lift.

ANITA. The job's working out, is it?

MAGGIE. She living de life, my dear. Last week she travel business class to New York. Next week she travelling premium class to – to… Whe she a go, Vince? India?

VINCE. Indonesia.

MAGGIE. Indonesia. She spreading she talent across de whole world.

ANITA *gives them their drinks.* VINCE *take a sip of brandy.*

ANITA. Yeah. I don't know how she does it, balancing all those drinks and dinners midair. She always did love make-up, I suppose.

Beat.

MAGGIE *watches* ANITA.

MAGGIE. Yu turn Rasta now?

ANITA. Sorry?

MAGGIE. Yu new hair style.

ANITA. It's an experiment actually.

MAGGIE. Experiment?

ANITA. Nathan and I are challenging the subtleties of
    discrimination – how long can we go without combing our hair
    before we feel –

MAGGIE. Headlice?

ANITA. Pressure to conform.

VINCE. Dat sound interesting.

ANITA. People are still trying to define us by our roots, Uncle V,
    literally. People wanna check out their politics before they're
    checking my hair.

MAGGIE. How is Nathan? Him still not working?

ANITA. He's finishing his PhD.

MAGGIE. / Still?

VINCE. How de baby?

ANITA. Rosa? She's fine, thank you.

MAGGIE. How old she is now?

ANITA. Nine months.

VINCE. She gettin' big.

ANITA. Yeah, she's growing fast.

MAGGIE. She a good baby?

ANITA. She's a great baby.

MAGGIE. She sleep good?

ANITA. Yep.

MAGGIE. Right through the night?

ANITA. Yep.

MAGGIE. She like she food?

VINCE. Jesus Christ! Is why yu a interrogate de chile?

MAGGIE. Is not an interrogation fi ask a simple question –

ANITA. She's mostly on breast milk / and –

MAGGIE. Breast milk?

ANITA. Yep.

MAGGIE. At nine months?

ANITA. The antibodies in –

MAGGIE. Poor ting must be longing fi a piece of chicken.

MAGGIE takes a glug of water and chokes.

ANITA. Are you alright? Sorry, I didn't get a chance to say, it's sparkling. I hate that, when things get up your nose. I better take Grandma's drink up.

ANITA exits, upstage-right.

MAGGIE (*speaking quietly*). I wonder if dem ring Trudy yet?

Beat.

I bet dem nuh ring ha.

Beat.

Remind me, fi ring ha dis evening.

Beat.

A nuh yuh me a talk to?

VINCE. Lard, Maggie. Lef people business alone nuh, man.

MAGGIE points to a picture of Gloria up on the wall.

MAGGIE. Pssst…

VINCE. Wha?

MAGGIE. Me bet a dat one dem a go use. Fi di coffin.

She gets up and throws her glass of water away. She waters a dry-looking plant.

She picks up an ornament of a glass fish.

Me did 'ave one like dis, remember?

VINCE. Put dat down, Maggie.

MAGGIE jumps as LORRAINE enters with the powdery drink that ANITA made. LORRAINE clocks MAGGIE with the fish. VINCE stands up. MAGGIE puts the fish back.

LORRAINE. Hello, Auntie Maggie, Uncle Vince.

They greet each other with hugs and kisses.

Nice of you to visit, you didn't / say –

MAGGIE. Me couldn't believe when me ring dis morning and yuh tell me seh Gloria gawn down suh.

VINCE. We can see ha?

LORRAINE. It's a bit awkward. She's only just got back off to sleep.

MAGGIE. After me travel all dis way on me bad hip?

LORRAINE. I wasn't expecting you. / If you had said –

VINCE. We understand.

LORRAINE. She's had a rough night – maybe / tomorrow –

MAGGIE. Last night me dream seh, me see ha, flying high pon a white dove. She land right in front of me, stretch out she neck like ostrich and seh 'Maggie, me beg yuh read me Psalm 23.' So, me tell Vincent, even if me haffi cripple wid pain dis marning, dis day can't pass and me nah see Gloria, me good-good cousin.

Beat.

LORRAINE. You'll need to be really quiet.

MAGGIE goes to her bag and rummages for her Bible.

VINCE. How long?

LORRAINE. Weeks… Days.

VINCE. Jesus-Christ-Almighty-Farda-God-in-Heaven.

MAGGIE. Stop bawl down de Lard name. 'Im busy enough. Come, mek we go and see.

MAGGIE and VINCE head up the stairs.

LORRAINE goes to the sink and throws away the powdery drink. She takes her phone out of her pocket and dials.

LORRAINE. Robert. It's me. Again. Call me back.

Scene Two

ROBERT *and* ANITA *are at opposite sides of the table.* SOPHIE *is standing.* LORRAINE *is chopping vegetables. There's a vase of big sunflowers on the table.*

ROBERT. Is she ever gonna wake up?

ANITA. What's the time?

SOPHIE. Half past two.

ANITA. You need to put a permit in your car, Mum.

ROBERT. Can anyone smell that?

SOPHIE. Smells delicious.

ROBERT. Not the food – Kinda dank smell.

Beat.

She hasn't budged. I've been here since ten.

ANITA. Eleven.

ROBERT. What?

ANITA. You got here at eleven.

ROBERT *looks at* ANITA.

ROBERT. What's that thing in her arm?

Beat.

Lorraine?

ANITA. It's a subcutaneous needle.

ROBERT. A what?

ANITA. It automatically administers the morphine.

ROBERT. So, that's why she's knocked out – Lorraine?

ANITA. It doesn't knock her out, it keeps her comfortable.

ROBERT. It's not right. She can't move, can't / talk.

ANITA. She smiled this morning when we were changing her.

SOPHIE. Showing off those fantastic teeth, no doubt.

ROBERT. Why are you changing her?

ANITA. As oppose to?

ROBERT. The nurses.

ANITA. What / nurses?

SOPHIE. Is it me, or is it unbearably hot?

ROBERT. They're qualified professionals, carrying out proper procedures.

SOPHIE. Anybody mind if I open the window?

SOPHIE *gets up.*

ROBERT. There's a proper way to do things. What if you drop her?

SOPHIE *opens the window.*

ANITA. You want us to leave her to lie in her piss while we wait for qualified professionals to carry out / proper procedures.

ROBERT. When I left on Monday she was compos mentis.

SOPHIE. Can I help with anything, Lorraine?

ROBERT. She was lively, sitting up, cracking joke.

ANITA. No, she wasn't.

ROBERT. Yes, she was.

SOPHIE. Why don't I chop the rest of the veg.

ROBERT. You weren't even here.

ANITA. Yes, / I was.

ROBERT. Not / at the same time as me you weren't.

SOPHIE. I must have told you, I was the fastest chopper in Home Economics. I could dice a seven-inch carrot in under twenty seconds. Still can. So, happy to / help if –

LORRAINE. Fuck!

SOPHIE. Oh God, did you slice through?

LORRAINE. Fuck!

ANITA. Is it deep?

SOPHIE. I'll mop up vomit, but I cannot stand the sight of blood.

LORRAINE. It's not my finger. It's the chilli.

ANITA. Chilli?

SOPHIE. Ah. In the eye. I did that once. Hurts much more than it should. Here, let me –

LORRAINE. I'm fine. Can everyone just…

> LORRAINE *goes to the sink.*

> *Silence.*

SOPHIE. Any news, Anita?

ANITA. Not really.

SOPHIE. Oh. Well, I suppose Rosa takes up all your time these days. We'd babysit, you know, / if you wanted to go out – give the establishment what for. Or just have a night out.

ROBERT. Would we?

ANITA. Thanks.

SOPHIE. I talk about you and Nathan all the time. To my students. I hold you up as an example. Your responsibilities haven't held you back – a new wave of radicals –

ANITA. We're not radicals.

SOPHIE. No, I wasn't / implying –

ANITA. Self-empowerment is not radicalism. That's exactly the kind of rhetoric the media use. Throw around buzzwords as a means to distract while their government drags us deeper into oppression.

SOPHIE. I was referring to your chutzpah, really.

ROBERT. I bet they love you at baby groups.

ANITA. I don't do / baby groups.

SOPHIE. How's the eye, Lorraine?

> *Beat.*

ROBERT. Mum doesn't eat chilli.

LORRAINE. It's not chilli, it's a soup. I saw a recipe on a forum – foods that fight cancer. Thought it might be worth a try.

Beat.

SOPHIE. Any news on Trudy?

ROBERT. What?

SOPHIE. Just wondering if there's been an update.

Beat.

I think it would be a shame if she didn't come over. Do you think she realises – ?

ROBERT. Of course she realises.

SOPHIE. Yes, but has she taken in, how / quickly –

ROBERT. She's not interested.

SOPHIE. Have you actually explained to her – ?

ROBERT. What difference would it make?

SOPHIE. It's an opportunity for her to say goodbye to her mother.

ROBERT. It's an opportunity for her to get her foot on British soil, suffocate some poor bastard with her pum-pum / and start seeking a British passport and whatever else she can get her hands on.

ANITA. Pum-pum, are you for real?

SOPHIE. She's your sister.

ROBERT. Half-sister.

SOPHIE. I don't mind phoning her –

LORRAINE. No, thank you, actually, Sophie –

SOPHIE. Just imagine if she did make the trip from Jamaica, the difference it could make to Gloria.

ROBERT. How's she going to notice when she's practically in a coma.

SOPHIE. She can still hear us, smell us even. For all you know she could be lying there / waiting –

ROBERT. She's not.

SOPHIE. You don't know that –

ROBERT. I know my mum. She's not lying there waiting for Trudy. She stopped waiting for that woman years ago.

LORRAINE *looks out the window.*

ANITA. She's not in a coma. She knows exactly what's going on.

LORRAINE. Is that rain? It's bloody raining. Anita, get the basket.

ANITA *goes to get the basket.*

ROBERT *kisses his teeth and gets up to go.*

Hold up – where are you going?

ROBERT. What d'you mean, where am I going? – to see if she's woken up.

ANITA. Where is it, Mum?

LORRAINE. You'll have to wait ten minutes.

ROBERT. Wait / for what?

ANITA. Mum?

SOPHIE. Under the sink, Anita.

LORRAINE. It's time for her to have her Complan. Anita, get one ready.

ROBERT. Her what?

LORRAINE. It's better she drinks it before she has visitors.

ROBERT. Visitors? Are you taking the –

SOPHIE. I'll make the Complan –

LORRAINE. No thank you, actually, Sophie – She hasn't seen you for a couple of a days. She'll get distracted and she won't swallow properly.

ANITA. You can get the washing.

ANITA *hands* SOPHIE *the basket.*

ROBERT. What are you carrying on with, Lorraine?

LORRAINE. You said yourself – there's a proper way to do things.

ROBERT. I've been waiting since ten o'clock.

ANITA. Eleven.

ROBERT. Who's talking to you?

SOPHIE exits downstage-left with the basket.

LORRAINE. It'd be a shame wouldn't it; to fight the cancer, but die from choking.

ANITA. Mum, she can't fight the –

LORRAINE. No. But, I'm not just going to write her off, am I?

ROBERT sits back down. They sit in silence as LORRAINE chops and ANITA prepares a Complan.

What was that?

ANITA. What was what?

Slight beat.

Mum?

LORRAINE. Is it ready?

ANITA. Yes.

ANITA takes a spoon out of the drawer.

LORRAINE takes the glass and the spoon from ANITA. She throws the spoon in the sink.

LORRAINE. The straws are next to the fridge.

LORRAINE exits upstage-right. ANITA gets a straw and follows.

SOPHIE re-enters.

She puts the washing down.

Silence.

SOPHIE. Funny weather. The sun's back out.

Beat.

Beautiful flowers. Fresh. Where did you get them?

Beat.

Sunflowers were our first success. Do you remember? In the garden of the old flat. You used to look good in pair of wellies. Funny to think now, but we got quite into that garden, before we gave up and covered everything in evergreens.

ROBERT *gets up.*

ROBERT. Why bring up Trudy?

SOPHIE. Look – I know you don't see eye to eye, but I thought if I offered to call, it might help.

ROBERT. Help? Can't you see Miss Seacole's driving this ship. There ain't no room for Florence.

SOPHIE. We're not at war, Robert.

ROBERT. Don't come running to me when she flings your arse overboard.

SOPHIE. Probably not your best analogy – given I'm the only one here that can actually swim.

ROBERT. What?

SOPHIE. Look, Robert –

ROBERT. You know, for a music teacher, you've got a shit sense of timing.

SOPHIE. You're absolutely right. There is something in the air – it's insufferable.

LORRAINE *appears at the doorway with the Complan.*

LORRAINE. You can go up.

ROBERT. She didn't even drink it? After all that?

ROBERT *exits upstage-right.*

LORRAINE *empties the Complan down the sink.*

SOPHIE. I bet she's saving her appetite for the soup.

LORRAINE *picks up her jacket and makes for the upstage-right door.*

LORRAINE. I'll be back in a bit.

SOPHIE. Shall I turn the soup off?

LORRAINE. No... Yes.

SOPHIE. Permit?

LORRAINE exits, without the permit.

SOPHIE watches her go.

SOPHIE alone.

She rubs her stomach.

She lifts up her top, puts her hands on her belly and closes her eyes.

She sits for a few moments in silence.

We hear footsteps coming down the stairs very fast. SOPHIE *opens her eyes and quickly drops her top.*

ANITA (*offstage*). Mum!

ANITA enters.

Where's Mum?

SOPHIE. I –

ANITA. Where is she, Sophie?!

SOPHIE. I don't know. She / said –

ANITA. Grandma, her breathing. She's –

SOPHIE. Oh, God.

ROBERT (*offstage*). No, no / no, no, no, no, no, no, no, no, no, no, no, no, no, no, no...

ANITA. Find her, / Sophie.

SOPHIE. Oh, God – she can't have got far –

ANITA. Just get her. Get her quickly.

ANITA exits upstage-right – heading back upstairs.

SOPHIE exits upstage-right – heading for the front door.

Scene Three

In the kitchen. There are lots of bouquets of flowers. The table is full of bottles of wine, rum, beer and finger snacks. LORRAINE is holding onto the back of a chair. ANITA stands by the upstage-left door, holding a tray. 'Dollar Wine' by Colin Lucas is blaring from the front room.

We are into the third night of the Nine.

LORRAINE and ANITA are still as the music plays for a few beats.

ANITA moves from the door.

ANITA. How many more nights?

Her next door's already complained. Can't Uncle Robert hold this shindig at his house? They've got a big enough gaff. You're done in. Nathan's taken Rosa home early, cos Auntie Maggie keeps trying to sneak chicken bones in her mouth. I don't know who half of them are in there. They don't know me, yet seem to think my name's 'Waitress'. And what's-her-name with the bright purple weave – Miss Stacey – looks more like she's going to Carnival than coming for a wake. Why don't you just stay at home tomorrow night? Let them congregate in a pub if they wanna drink and make noise.

Beat.

Mum?

LORRAINE. Three things you don't mess with when it comes to Jamaicans, Anita. Their money, their food and their traditions. You, of all people, should understand that. Nine nights of mourning. They're paying their respects.

ANITA. They're nyaming out our food and drink. Right, that music's going down.

ANITA exits upstage-left.

LORRAINE pours herself a drink.

The music becomes quieter.

MAGGIE enters from upstage-right.

MAGGIE. Vincent is in 'ere?

LORRAINE. No.

MAGGIE. Yuh see 'im?

LORRAINE. No.

MAGGIE. Suh, wheh dat man gawn?

LORRAINE....I don't know.

MAGGIE. Me tell him already dat we not stopping long. Me wan fi get home fi watch *EastEnder*. Big tings are gawn in de Queen Vic tonight!

MAGGIE *exits upstage-right.*

ANITA *enters from upstage-left.*

ANITA. Spoons. We need serving spoons.

ANITA *goes to the cutlery drawer.*

Feisty Miss Stacey just cussed off Sophie for dipping her hands into the peanut bowl – 'Yuh hand clean?' And she's one to talk. Her hands have been all over Uncle Vince. Twice she's pulled down her top to show him a scar on her shoulder, 'Left over from me operation.'

She'll need another one if Maggie catches her.

SOPHIE *enters from upstage-left.*

You alright?

SOPHIE. No harm done.

ANITA *exits upstage-left with spoons.*

Right. Time I was heading off.

Slight beat.

Lorraine?

LORRAINE. Yeah. Sorry about the peanuts. She's –

SOPHIE. No, no, my fault. I forgot myself – I probably shouldn't be eating them any way – well – not that I shouldn't be – it's just – it's – goodness, I had an early start this morning, I think it's finally catching up with me... It's been lovely tonight. Really, it has. Not sure I can make it tomorrow, end-of-term reports to write –

LORRAINE. You don't have to –

SOPHIE. No, I'd like to attend each night. For Gloria. I hope you liked the cake. I didn't know what else to bring. It was lively tonight... With the music. I didn't think they'd be dancing. Is that usual?

Beat.

Lorraine?

LORRAINE. Those pills you gave me?

SOPHIE. Brilliant, aren't they?

LORRAINE. They're for depression. I'm not depressed.

SOPHIE. No. But –

LORRAINE. Are you alright? I / mean –

SOPHIE. They help me to sleep. The one thing I've never been any good at. Still, it's improved since I started yoga – it's – I – I – Sorry –

LORRAINE. It's alright.

SOPHIE. I thought the pills might help you to – but – you're – God, sorry, Lorraine. You're the one that should be –

LORRAINE. You're allowed to be upset.

SOPHIE. I miss her. She was one of the kindest people I ever – I'm really sorry.

LORRAINE. You don't need to apologise.

SOPHIE. I don't know how you're managing it, but you're doing brilliantly. All of this company must be of comfort. It – it was nothing like this when my dad passed away. I think a neighbour brought food round for the first few days, but it felt like people were avoiding us mostly. Some people couldn't even look me in the eye. Funny, how some people don't know what to say, whereas others say too much.

LORRAINE. Yeah.

SOPHIE. Oh, God. Sorry – am I – ?

LORRAINE. No.

SOPHIE. Dad passed away in the middle of the night and my mother decided it'd be better if I got a full night's sleep rather than wake me. My sister was there. I think about that less now. You nursed Gloria till the very end. That's all that really matters.

Beat.

LORRAINE. I've been dipping into this book, about the different layers of grief. Apparently, your loved ones only appear to you in a dream once your subconscious has processed the loss.

SOPHIE. Funny. Robert dreamt about her last night.

LORRAINE. Did he?

SOPHIE. Oh, I think it was very brief… It was months before I dreamt about Dad. I sat up for three nights after he died; in the kitchen, waiting, cross-legged, staring at a candle.

LORRAINE. In the kitchen?

SOPHIE. Well, you wouldn't want a ghost to appear in your bedroom – that would be spooky.

LORRAINE. So did he? Appear?

SOPHIE. No, but he did send a sign. On the day of his funeral. We were driving to the crematorium and a white feather flew in from the window and landed on my shoulder. He was mad for birds.

Slight beat.

LORRAINE. I hope I get a sign.

SOPHIE. You're bound to.

LORRAINE. Not a feather though – too subtle. More like a frying pan / in the back of my head.

SOPHIE. In the back of your head.

/ Ha!

LORRAINE. Ha!

Beat.

Why shouldn't you be eating peanuts?

SOPHIE. Sorry?

LORRAINE. You / said –

SOPHIE. Oh, they're fattening, aren't they?

LORRAINE. Peanuts?

MAGGIE *re-enters from upstage-right.*

MAGGIE. Yuh find him?

SOPHIE. Who?

MAGGIE. Vincent.

LORRAINE. Have you checked outside, Auntie Maggie?

MAGGIE. No.

LORRAINE. Well, he's probably out there.

MAGGIE. I don't know.

SOPHIE. I'll check on my way out?

MAGGIE. Yuh leaving already?

SOPHIE. Early start tomorrow.

MAGGIE. Me too. Lorraine, please – beg yuh go look fi him. Di hip giving me problem. Tell 'im me ready.

SOPHIE. I'll go –

MAGGIE. Lorraine will do it.

LORRAINE *exits upstage-right.*

What a beautiful evening. Word really travel pon mout. Me never even notice de time fly so quick. Yvette was going to pick we up dis evening, but she haffi work. Suh, we haffi brace de cold, cold, freezing cold.

SOPHIE.... Would you like a lift?

MAGGIE. I like to use my Freedom Pass. It's de only decent ting me get from dis teefing Government, an' me intend to get full use outta it before me dead. Look pon Gloria. She get good use outta it before God call she. De whole of North London she travel with it. The 41 bus. The 444. The 43. The 236 –

SOPHIE. Yes, she certainly was one for getting around.

MAGGIE (*lets out a dirty laugh*). You can say dat again.

SOPHIE. Sorry?

MAGGIE. Wheh you live again?

SOPHIE. Hackney.

MAGGIE. Yuh still live round dem side? Wheh dem a stab up people like it a competition? Yuh good.

SOPHIE. You really wouldn't recognise it now.

MAGGIE. Well, yuh can live de risky life. Yuh nuh 'ave any pickney fi tink bout. Is where Yvette used to live. But, she move, with the help of Jesus. She have a very nice flat in Muswell Hill now… Wid seh fiancé.

SOPHIE. Goodness. Yvette's getting married?

MAGGIE. Well, I'm not suppose to tell anybody really. (*Whispers.*) Between me and yuh.

SOPHIE. Congratulations! That's great news.

MAGGIE. It's wonderful news. Shame Gloria won't be here to see it. Gloria love a wedding. And yuh know what happen after marriage? / Finally, I will be a grandmadda. And dat pickney will have tall, Indian-like hair. Like my side of de family. Gloria always admire my Yvette hair. Lorraine could shave off she head and mek a back scrub – Yuh enjoy dis evening?

SOPHIE. Divorce?

I'm not sure 'enjoy' is the right word.

MAGGIE. How yuh mean? Is not fi yuh. Is fi Gloria.

ROBERT *enters from upstage-right, carting a bottle of rum.*

ROBERT. Evening all.

MAGGIE. Ah! De prodigal son return! Where yuh been hiding?

ROBERT. Good to see you, Auntie M.

She gives ROBERT *a warm hug.*

MAGGIE. Me sorry for yuh loss, darling. But, such is life. The Lard giveth, suh him haffi tek wheh.

ROBERT. Yep.

MAGGIE. Yuh put on weight. Wifey must be looking after yuh good.

ROBERT. And you're looking well.

MAGGIE. Oh, yuh know, with the help of Jesus.

LORRAINE *re-enters from upstage-right.*

LORRAINE. He is outside, Auntie Maggie.

MAGGIE. Wheh him a do out deh?

LORRAINE (*to* ROBERT). Decided to put in an appearance? (*To* MAGGIE.) Chatting to George.

MAGGIE. Mad George?

ROBERT *gets a message through on his phone. He replies.*

LORRAINE (*to* MAGGIE). George Carter.

MAGGIE. Him mad, yes. I bet dem a chat pure fart.

LORRAINE. They were talking about you actually.

MAGGIE. Me?

LORRAINE. Yeah. Some dance you went to in the sixties. Uncle Vince says he arrived at that party with Mum / but –

MAGGIE. Sophie, come on –

LORRAINE. He left the party with you.

MAGGIE. Time fi tek we 'ome –

LORRAINE. He's calling it an ambush.

MAGGIE. Blasted man, yuh wait...

MAGGIE *storms out.*

SOPHIE. I think he might be in trouble.

MAGGIE (*offstage*). Sophie!

LORRAINE. He's too drunk to notice – you might be though.

SOPHIE. Wish me luck.

ROBERT *puts the rum on the table.*

See you later, darling.

ROBERT. Yeah.

Beat.

SOPHIE. Night, Lorraine.

LORRAINE. Night. And thanks.

SOPHIE. Any time.

SOPHIE *exits.*

LORRAINE *watches* ROBERT *pour himself a drink.*

ROBERT. Thanks for what?

LORRAINE. She made a lovely cake.

Beat.

ROBERT. Is it busy in there?

LORRAINE. Not as busy as it was. People have been asking for you.

ROBERT. Like who?

LORRAINE. Show yer face and you'll find out.

Slight beat.

ROBERT. There's no rush. Chris sends his condolences, by the way.

LORRAINE. When does he get back from Hong Kong?

ROBERT. Not for a bit.

LORRAINE. So he's not coming to the funeral?

ROBERT. He can't.

LORRAINE. How many dinners has he eaten in this kitchen?

ROBERT. It's a stressful time, alright? He can't just drop everything.

LORRAINE. Peas in a pod.

ROBERT. Sorry?

LORRAINE. You and Chris.

ROBERT. You make patties, Lorraine. We make bread.

LORRAINE. What's that supposed to mean?

ROBERT. Don't worry about it.

ROBERT *picks at the snacks.*

LORRAINE. How are you sleeping?

ROBERT. Not great.

LORRAINE. Sophie said you dreamt about Mum.

ROBERT. Did she?

LORRAINE. What was she doing?

ROBERT. What?

LORRAINE. In the dream.

ROBERT. I don't know.

LORRAINE. How can you not know?

ROBERT. I can't remember.

LORRAINE. You must remember. You told Sophie.

ROBERT. I didn't tell Sophie anything. She heard me talking in my sleep.

LORRAINE. What did you say?

ROBERT. Lorraine – It's been the longest day. I just told you, I can't remember –

LORRAINE. Was she well? Did she –

ROBERT. We need to talk, Lorraine.

LORRAINE. Talk? Talk about what? –

ANITA *bursts in from upstage-left.*

ANITA. That's it. I'm gone. If I stay in that room a minute longer, it'll be more than Grandma that needs burying.

ANITA *starts to gather her things together.*

ROBERT. So what? You're not going to say anything?

LORRAINE. Say anything about what?

ROBERT. It's not the time to be cracking jokes.

ANITA. Who's joking? I'm going home to my baby, before I commit murder.

ROBERT. Everything for you is joke, innit? You should've skipped uni and gone to clown school –

LORRAINE. Robert – Don't rise, Anita.

ROBERT. I'm serious. Do you know how much money them mans make at Covent Garden juggling balls on a unicycle? You could actually pay your way instead of relying on your mum to bring you, your daughter and your man out of penury.

LORRAINE. Oh, / God –

ANITA. Remember that time when I was two and I pissed in your shoe –

LORRAINE. No, Anita. No.

ANITA. It wasn't because I didn't know any better. It was because of your shit taste in shoes –

ROBERT. See, this is what happens when you raise them without a father, / they lack breeding. You shouldn't even let her loose in there. She doesn't know how to speak to big people.

ANITA. Here we go same old, old, lame – at least I turn up.

I'm twenty-three!

ROBERT. I couldn't care if you were three hundred and five!

ANITA. Three hundred and five?

LORRAINE. Both / of you, stop it, now.

ANITA. That doesn't even make any sense! What's my name – Methuselah, from the Bible?

ROBERT. Maybe if you studied the Bible more closely, you'd have come home with a degree, instead of a baby.

ANITA. I came home with both – two things you can't buy on Amex.

ROBERT. I buy whatever I like. I'm not interested in children, or dressing up like Harry Potter for the day prancing around in a gown, like a prick!

LORRAINE. You two really believe she's gone. That's why it's alright for you to come in here, raise your voice and sharpen your teeth. But this is still her house and she's still in it. Next time you come, hang your bad-mindedness by the door. Or don't bother coming at all... And, Anita, this isn't the place to protest. Turn up tomorrow looking like Krusty the Clown, and you'll leave looking like Ghandi.

LORRAINE *exits upstage-left.*

Scene Four

The middle of the same night. LORRAINE *sits in the kitchen, cross-legged on the floor, staring at a candle.*

Scene Five

Night Four.

LORRAINE, ROBERT *and* VINCE *in the kitchen.* LORRAINE *puts together bowls of finger snacks and drinks. She places them on a tray.* ROBERT *and* VINCE *are at the table, mid-conversation.*

VINCE. Stop it. Me belly a go bust!

ROBERT. Lorraine was there.

VINCE. Gloria was vex!

ROBERT. She was so adamant.

VINCE. She ring me cussing that marning.

ROBERT. I said, 'Mum, it's a bank – Are you sure the cashier short-changed you?'

VINCE. 'Dat woman teef me twenty pound!'

ROBERT. The commotion with the bank manager the next day –

VINCE. 'I'm sorry, Mrs Green, but we checked Cassandra's / till' –

ROBERT. Cassandra! That's it!

VINCE. 'It was perfectly balanced.'

ROBERT. Do the rest, Uncle V. I can't –

VINCE. 'Well, yuh can tell Cassandra; me twenty pound, whe she teef, me hope she tek it, buy food, it run she belly and she shit fi de whole week!'

    ROBERT *and* VINCE *crack up.*

ROBERT. The look on his face.

    LORRAINE *picks up the tray and exits upstage-left.*

    VINCE *refills their glasses. He raises his in the air.*

VINCE. Gloria.

    ROBERT *raises his glass.*

ROBERT. Mum.

    They tip some rum onto the floor – a libation to Gloria – chink glasses and drink.

VINCE. Travel in peace.

    Beat.

ROBERT. You were good to her, Uncle V. Good to us. You gave her strength, you know? Like Popeye drinking spinach. Remember the days you'd pick me up from school. In your Rover V8?

VINCE. Dat car did hold de road good. Best vehicle me ever 'ave.

ROBERT. The look on those kids' faces, like, 'Raa – where'd they get the money for that?'… And that Christmas, when you drove round to pick us up in it. The day Alvin walked out. I tried to lock myself in my room. Didn't want to see anybody. Mum near brock down the door.

VINCE. She used to seh, 'Shake off yuh dust; rise up – Isaiah 52.' As long as I know Gloria, nuttin ever keep she down fi long, and I see ha wrestle some real hardship.

ROBERT. It was you who talked me round though. In the absence of a father, we had you, and God. The other mums would shout,

'Wait till your father gets home.' Whereas Mum would say, 'When yuh get to Heaven, yuh see, God will deal wid yuh.' I was never sure if that was an incentive to behave or not.

VINCE. You farda wasn't a monster, Robert.

ROBERT. His name's Alvin, Uncle V.

Slight beat.

When I was a kid, I'd watch a black man walking down the street with his kids. I'd look at the kids and think, 'Are you gonna be one of the lucky ones? Or is he gonna fuck you up too?'... Yvette was one of the lucky ones, Uncle V.

VINCE. What about, Anita?

ROBERT. What about her?

VINCE. That farda she 'ave? Wid dem steely blue eye, as 'im look pon you, yuh blood freeze over. Anita wasn't lucky.

ROBERT. What? With all those summer holidays she gets to spend with him in the South of France. Most youth I know, Uncle V, ain't got money to top up their bus fare. All Anita's got to worry about is topping up her tan.

VINCE. She 'ave a small baby.

ROBERT. Whose fault is that?

Beat.

Yuh and I are quite similar, though.

VINCE. Yuh tink suh?

ROBERT. Yeah. We've both done well. Despite the odds.

VINCE. Well, yuh haffi elevate yuh self.

ROBERT. You took that to another level – the RAF.

VINCE. Fe a short while –

ROBERT. Your own garage –

VINCE. Fe over thirty years.

ROBERT. Did you give her money, Uncle V?

VINCE. Wha?

ROBERT. Mum. To keep the house.

VINCE....

ROBERT. It's alright. She didn't tell me. I worked it out.

VINCE. Look, Robert –

ROBERT. Maggie doesn't know, does she?

VINCE....No. And dat's de way it will stay.

ROBERT. How much?

VINCE. Robert –

ROBERT. Don't worry. I'm not going to say anything. How much?

VINCE. Dat's between / me and –

ROBERT. I'm gonna pay you back.

VINCE. Pay me back?

ROBERT. It's the least / I can –

VINCE. No, Robert, dat's not / what –

ROBERT. It's what she would want, Uncle V.

VINCE. Is trouble yuh a look, Robert?

ROBERT. She's sending me omens.

VINCE. How yuh mean?

ROBERT. Look, you know how Chris – business-partner Chris – has been back and forth to Hong Kong? Now get this, and I'm not a man big into dreams and dem tings, but the other night I dreamt she was calling me. I could hear her voice, but couldn't find her. I ran downstairs into the kitchen and Alvin was standing there staring at me. Mum came up behind him, carrying this big-arse machete. Just as I shouted, 'Mum, don't!', she split his head in two / and bare ten-, twenty- and all fifty-pound notes splattered across the room – I woke up drenched.

VINCE. Wha?

    Serious ting.

ROBERT. Serious – it's a sign.

VINCE. She split 'im head inna two?

ROBERT. Like a melon –

VINCE. Jeeezzzz...

ROBERT. The business is gonna be big, Uncle V. I'm stepping it up.

VINCE. Fi real.

ROBERT. Come in on it.

VINCE. Wha?

Beat.

ROBERT. I've seen mans make thirty grand in less than an hour.

Beat.

The more you put in the bigger the margin.

Beat.

This time next year, you can build two houses in Jamaica.

VINCE *laughs.*

What's funny?

VINCE. I wish yuh all de luck / inna –

ROBERT. No, hold up a minute –

VINCE. Robert, yuh madda only jus gwan –

ROBERT. And I can't look after her any more but I can still look after you, Auntie Maggie –

VINCE. Me and Maggie live good. We alright –

ROBERT. Who's talking about being 'alright', I'm talking / about –

VINCE. Robert, yuh 'ear / whe me –

ROBERT. The Vince that grew me wasn't driving a Rover V8, cos he wanted to be 'alright'. We need to get clued up, Uncle V. It's not even about you, it's about Yvette, Yvette's children. Look how the Asian man's got it sorted. With what we spend in their shops, food and hair alone – we're feeding their families for generations to come. Well, what about us? I haven't been grafting since I was sixteen to just end up 'alright'. When you used to pick me up, Uncle V, the way those kids used to stare at us as we drove off. Those eyes still follow me wherever I go, whichever building I step into; only now they sit on the faces of grown men. They look at me same way, scratch their heads and wonder. The more they scratch the deeper I get under their skin. Let them feel us, Uncle V. Come in on it.

Beat.

VINCE. Yuh really wan lift up dis family, Robert?

ROBERT. Absolutely –

VINCE. Den yuh look after yuh sister dem. Lorraine, Trudy –

ROBERT. Trudy?

VINCE. See it deh –

ROBERT. This has nothing to do / with –

VINCE. A yuh sister –

ROBERT. I know who she is!

VINCE. Is because of yuh farda dat Trudy never reach England / and –

ROBERT. How was he gonna mind next man's baby, when he couldn't look after his own –

VINCE. It cut up Trudy inside, bad / bad, bad.

ROBERT. Mum always provided for Trudy. How many barrels did me and Lorraine watch travelling to Jamaica? Filled to the brim with things we couldn't touch –

VINCE. Yuh nuh how many times you madda beg yuh farda? –

ROBERT. Alvin!!

VINCE. She beg 'im fi send fi Trudy –

ROBERT. Uncle V, no disrespect, but, I'm trying to show you an opportunity. I don't want to discuss Alvin or Trudy right now –

VINCE. Yuh remember me friend from back 'ome?

ROBERT. What?

VINCE. Frank Thomas –

ROBERT. Who?

VINCE. We used to call him Tiger, because him love de solitary
life –

ROBERT. Uncle –

VINCE. When me first meet 'im, 'im 'ave whole heap a property –
Five house inna one street in Brixton. One night, 'im tek me to
di pub, buy me a drink. / He must be ask about ten man dat
night what dem want. If a man seh 'beer', Tiger buy 'im two, If
a man seh 'rum', Tiger buy double. Tiger line up alla de drinks
dem, pon de table one by one like a domino run. You tell me
what 'im do next?

ROBERT. Uncle Vince –

I don't / know.

VINCE. Wham! 'Im box off all a di glass fi show, seh, 'im a big
money man. You tell me wheh Tiger end up now? –

ROBERT....

VINCE. In a nursing home. 'Im can't even hold 'im piss, much less
put it in a pot. Yuh can tek life fi sport, Robert. Burn all yuh
money in which ever way yuh want, but when yuh start fi burn
bridge – game done... Excuse me.

VINCE *exits upstage-left.*

ROBERT *stands alone for a beat.*

LORRAINE *enters in her nightclothes, holding a candle.*

They are in separate scenes and cannot see each other.

*Simultaneously they turn and face the picture of Gloria on the
wall.*

ROBERT *exits.*

LORRAINE *stands a moment longer.*

Lights change.

Into:

Scene Six

Night Five.

The middle of the night. LORRAINE *and* SOPHIE *are sitting cross-legged on the kitchen floor.*

SOPHIE *sits upright with her eyes closed.* LORRAINE *is fidgety with her eyes open. She tries to mirror* SOPHIE*'s position.*

SOPHIE. Inhale. Exhale. Slowly.

> *They breathe.*

> Again. Inhale. Exhale. Keep that going. Inhale. Exhale.

> *They breathe.*

> Inhale. Oh God. Oh, fuck. Fuck. / Fuck.

LORRAINE. What? What? What?

> SOPHIE *cries.*

> Did you feel something?

> SOPHIE *cries.*

> LORRAINE *looks up to the heavens.*

> How the hell is that fair?

SOPHIE. I'm pregnant, Lorraine.

LORRAINE. What?

> *Beat.*

> You're forty-five.

SOPHIE. I know!

LORRAINE. Does Robert know?

> SOPHIE *shakes her head.*

SOPHIE. No.

Scene Seven

Night Six.

VINCE *sits alone in the kitchen, drinking rum.*

Music is blaring from the other room. It's distinctly louder than previous nights.

We hear the start of 'Sugar Bum Bum' by Lord Kitchener. The guests show their appreciation, we hear 'Wheel and come again', 'Tune!', etc.

MAGGIE *enters from upstage-left.*

MAGGIE. Come on nuh, Vincent, a we tune dis.

VINCE. Nah sah, Maggie.

MAGGIE. W'appen to yuh? Yuh vex cos George bus yuh ass at dominoes?

   VINCE *kisses his teeth.*

VINCE. Me tired, Maggie. Me tell yuh already.

MAGGIE. Is nuh tired yuh tired, is miserable yuh miserable.

VINCE. Is me always a complain bout me hip?

   Beat.

MAGGIE. Is not me hip a give me complaint tonight, Vincent Armstrong.

   VINCE *gets up.*

VINCE. Lard, Maggie, leave whe de argument.

   He puts on his coat.

   Mek we look fi go home.

   VINCE *exits upstage-right.*

   MAGGIE *refills* VINCE's *glass with more rum. She takes a mouthful and spits it out – deliberately allowing it to spray over the floor. She puts the glass down and looks up at Gloria.*

   She exits, following VINCE.

Scene Eight

Two days later.

Day Eight.

LORRAINE, ANITA, ROBERT, MAGGIE *and* VINCE *around the kitchen table.* ANITA *has an iPad.*

LORRAINE. Okay. Are we all clear so far?

ANITA. Yep. Ten-thirty.

MAGGIE. Yuh nuh just seh eleven o'clock?

LORRAINE. Ten-thirty, if you're meeting us here. Eleven, if you're making your own way to the church.

VINCE. You book de horse and carriage?

ROBERT. Horse and carriage? Since when?

LORRAINE. I did mention it.

ROBERT. She was scared of horses.

LORRAINE. It was her wish, not mine.

MAGGIE. Gloria a go gallop to de gates of Jesus!

When I go, I want two white horses. And I want my coffin to shine like when Charlton Heston grin him teet.

VINCE. Yuh better tell yuh dawta dat. I will be long gawn.

LORRAINE. The service starts promptly at eleven. The church organist will play as Mum / enters the church.

MAGGIE. Mek sure yuh cook enough food fi tomorrow night.

LORRAINE. I'm sorry?

MAGGIE. Nine Night.

LORRAINE. We're not discussing the Nine right now, / Auntie Maggie.

MAGGIE. Lord, people travel all de way from Brixton last night and when dem reach – not even a dry piece of bread left fi dem fi scratch dem troat / wid –

LORRAINE. I didn't / know –

MAGGIE. Dat can't happen tomorrow evening. Mek sure. Me already season me curry goat. Gloria spirit need plenty feeding. Curry goat was she favourite.

ANITA. No it wasn't. She found it too bony.

MAGGIE. Maybe when you cook it – (*To* LORRAINE.) you have any white candle?

LORRAINE.…?

MAGGIE (*to* VINCE). Whe me tell yuh? Dem don't know whe fi do. Remind me fi bring two white candle and a white tablecloth.

ANITA. For what?

LORRAINE. Can we please get back to the service? What's next, Anita?

ANITA. Pall-bearers.

LORRAINE. That's right. Robert's at the front. Winston and Patrick are at the back. Uncle Vince, we wondered if you'd like to be the pall-bearer next to Robert.

MAGGIE. Vince can't manage de coffin.

VINCE. Whe yuh a talk bout?

MAGGIE. 'Im legs long, but 'im arms too short.

VINCE. Tank you, Lorraine. Yes, I will.

ANITA. Readings.

LORRAINE. Anita's got the last reading, before I read the eulogy –

ROBERT. Why's that?

LORRAINE. Why's what?

ROBERT. Why are you reading the eulogy?

MAGGIE. Exactly what I was tinking. Trudy should read it. Trudy is de eldest.

LORRAINE. Yes, but Trudy's not going to be there.

ANITA. We could FaceTime?

ROBERT. Never mind Trudy, what about me?

ANITA. I'm serious –

LORRAINE. You?

ROBERT. Yes.

Beat.

LORRAINE. You didn't want to write it, so I didn't think you'd want to read it.

ROBERT. Did you ask?

Beat.

LORRAINE. Do you wanna read it?

ROBERT. Yeah. Yeah, I do as it goes.

LORRAINE. We're expecting a lot of people.

ROBERT. Yeah.

LORRAINE. It's a big church.

ROBERT. So?

LORRAINE. So, the words need to carry through to the back of the auditorium.

ROBERT. Just say what you're trying to say, Lorraine.

LORRAINE. You have a tendency to mumble.

ROBERT. What?

MAGGIE. Trudy / speak very clearly, and she 'ave a wonderful singing voice.

ROBERT. I don't mumble –

LORRAINE. Trudy's / not coming.

ROBERT. I make pitches to people all the time.

MAGGIE. She is coming.

LORRAINE (*to* ROBERT). It's not the same thing. (*To* MAGGIE.) No, she's not.

MAGGIE. I / speak wid ha last week.

ROBERT. I am gonna put one together actually.

LORRAINE. I spoke to her last night, and she hadn't even been to the Embassy.

MAGGIE. Suh?

LORRAINE. So, it wouldn't be possible to obtain a visa in time for the funeral next Thursday. We can't have two eulogies.

ROBERT. Who says we can't?

MAGGIE. What's de big rush anyway? Yuh can't wait?

ROBERT. Wait for what? Trudy's had ample time to sort out a visa.

MAGGIE. Yuh know how far she live from di Embassy?

ROBERT. So, how she gonna reach England, if she can't make the / forty miles to Kingston?

VINCE. I would like fi read someting.

MAGGIE. Dem road she haffi travel not easy-easy, yuh know.

LORRAINE. Finding a date that fits in with everyone's availability is, also, not easy-easy.

MAGGIE. Yuh hear dis, Vince?

LORRAINE. We also have to consider Mum. Every day that goes past, she's just lying there.

VINCE. A poem.

ANITA. Yeah, she wouldn't want that. It's really bad karma.

MAGGIE. Bad wha?

ANITA. Did anyone even ask her if she wanted to be buried?

LORRAINE. What?

ANITA. Because she was curious about cremation.

LORRAINE. Don't be / ridiculous, Anita.

MAGGIE. / A wha de?

ROBERT. Is she for real?

ANITA. She was. We discussed it. She read somewhere that cremations were better for the environment –

MAGGIE. We don't cook our people.

ANITA. You see? That's just ignorant –

MAGGIE. Whe yuh seh?

ANITA. You're gonna get nyam by maggots anyway.

ROBERT. Lorraine, I swear to God, speak to your daughter.

ANITA. She was very open to the idea.

LORRAINE. She's not being cremated, Anita. She's having a burial.

VINCE. I wouldn't mind it at all. Like de Indian Man. Burn de body, release de soul, ready to start over. A second chance.

Beat.

I want to read a poem at the service.

LORRAINE. A poem?

MAGGIE. What yuh know about poem?

LORRAINE. That would be lovely, Uncle Vince. What is it?

VINCE. Well…

MAGGIE. 'Im no know any poem.

LORRAINE. Have you got it with you?

VINCE. No.

MAGGIE. Wha me tell yuh?

LORRAINE. Do you know the title?

VINCE. No. Me a go write it.

LORRAINE. / Write it?

ANITA. A you dat, Uncle V?

LORRAINE. That sounds wonderful. Can I get back to you on that –

MAGGIE. Yes, Mr Shakespeare – gwan.

LORRAINE. I just need to check how we're doing for time, now that we're having two eulogies. What's next, Anita?

MAGGIE. Trudy! Me wan Trudy pon dis list.

LORRAINE. / Auntie Maggie –

ROBERT. Oh my God!

MAGGIE. Trudy is part of dis family. She clap eyes pon Gloria before oonuh even born. She have the right to see she madda before she end up inna de ground.

VINCE. Lard, Maggie. Yuh nuh hear wha dem seh? Dem can't leave Gloria coop up inna freezer like a damn fish. She need fi come off di cold ice and be lay to rest.

Silence.

MAGGIE. Well. Don't shoot de goose because di chicken never lay any egg.

ANITA. Do you mean – 'don't shoot the messenger'?

ROBERT*'s phone rings. He looks at it.*

LORRAINE. Can it wait? We're nearly finished.

He picks up.

ROBERT. Hello?

LORRAINE. Unbelievable.

ANITA. Do you want to move on to catering?

ROBERT. Speaking –

LORRAINE. No – that's taken care of.

ROBERT. Yeah, it's a good time… Just a minute…

ROBERT *gets up, exits downstage-left.*

(*Offstage.*) Go on…

VINCE. No Gloria fi cook de mannish water. Warm we up when we leave de graveside.

LORRAINE. Auntie Yvonne's going to do it.

MAGGIE. That woman gone senile. Yuh never 'ear wha she do at Pauline wedding? Season de chicken wid fish sauce. Blasted eediot.

Lorraine, yuh buy yuh madda stockings yet?

LORRAINE. Stockings?

MAGGIE. To put pon she foot. You need to get de nutmeg-coloured one. And she need a new wig. Dat one wheh she dead in look like any bird's nest. Yuh can't bury her in dat. She will frighten Jesus.

VINCE. Maggie.

MAGGIE. I'm meking sure she know what fi do.

Yuh want mi come wid you to dress her?

LORRAINE. No.

MAGGIE. Is not any and everybody know how fi do dem
someting. Yuh remember Pinky? Is me dress her fa she funeral,
yuh know?

Me grease up she foot good, help de stockings fi slide on.
People tink, because yuh dead, yuh don't need Vaseline.

Yuh never 'ear people seh dem never see her a'look so good.
Even she husband tek picture on WhatsApp to send back home.

LORRAINE. Right. That's it – meeting done.

MAGGIE. So quick?

LORRAINE *begins to gather their coats.*

LORRAINE. Yep – this one's yours, isn't it, Maggie?

MAGGIE. Why yuh always in a rush?

LORRAINE. I'm meeting the vicar in an hour. Anita'll drop you
home.

ANITA. What?

LORRAINE. Mustn't keep a man of the cloth waiting.

LORRAINE *takes money out of her purse.*

Put that towards the petrol.

ANITA. Mum?

MAGGIE. But we never get time fi discuss de Nine –

LORRAINE. Don't you worry, Auntie Maggie, we'll have candles
and tablecloths galore – you won't know if it's Nine Night or
Hallowe'en.

MAGGIE. Hallowe'en?

VINCE. Come on, Maggie. Lorraine 'ave business fi attend to.

LORRAINE *bustles them out of the upstage-right door and
exits.*

ANITA (*offstage*). Mum –

LORRAINE (*offstage*). Tell Rosa, Grandma's looking forward to seeing her tomorrow.

ROBERT re-enters from downstage-left.

MAGGIE (*offstage*). We can't mek it tonight. Yvette and Jonathan a tek us out fi dinner.

LORRAINE (*offstage*). Wonderful.

VINCE (*offstage*). See yuh tomorrow evening.

MAGGIE. Fi de Nine.

LORRAINE (*offstage*). Yes, Aunty Maggie. The Nine. See you then.

LORRAINE re-enters.

It's alright. You can go. The meeting's over.

LORRAINE pushes a chair in under the table. She allows herself to slump over it for a couple of beats.

She comes up.

Did you hear me?

She continues to push the chairs in.

ROBERT. I was being a dick. You do the eulogy.

LORRAINE ignores him. Goes to the fridge and takes out a bag of chicken wings.

I'll do that.

LORRAINE. What?

ROBERT. I'm at loose end this afternoon. Might as well help.

LORRAINE. Help? To season chicken?

ROBERT. I can cook, Lorraine.

LORRAINE. It's wings. They need plucking first.

ROBERT. I know how to prepare wings.

Beat.

She hands him the bag of wings.

LORRAINE. Alright.

ROBERT. You got any gloves?

LORRAINE. No. I use my hands.

ROBERT. Right.

He stands holding the bag awkwardly.

LORRAINE. I'll just carry on, shall I?

ROBERT. I normally use gloves.

LORRAINE *takes back the bag of wings and starts preparing them.*

ROBERT *watches her.*

I don't know how you're doing all this?

LORRAINE. Doing all what?

ROBERT. It's admirable, sis, but then you've always been like that. Busy. What was it Mum used to say? 'Lorraine come like bauxite. She inside everyting.'

LORRAINE *plucks.*

I keep thinking, any minute now, she's gonna appear at the bottom of the stairs. And give me that look. You know the one? Like if she hadn't seen me for a few days – dart me a frown before she'd crack a smile.

LORRAINE *plucks.*

I checked my phone today. To see if I had a missed call from her. Every lunchtime, the same conversation,

'Robert, yuh eat yet?'

'Whe Sophie cook fi yuh last night? – Yuh losing too much weight. Yuh nuh see how yuh neck string a stick out like marga turkey.'

LORRAINE. She called you every lunchtime?

ROBERT. One-thirty, on the dot.

LORRAINE....

ROBERT. 'Nuh stretch yuh basket to whe yuh hand can't reach – '

LORRAINE. Why are you still here?

ROBERT. What?

LORRAINE. Normally, you can't get out the door fast enough.

ROBERT. I told you. I'm at a loose end...

Beat.

Everything's happening so fast.

LORRAINE....

ROBERT. I need to talk to you, Lorraine.

Beat.

I know this guy. A property developer. He's interested in the house.

LORRAINE. Which house?

ROBERT. Come on, Lorraine –

LORRAINE. You're not serious?

ROBERT. He approached me –

LORRAINE. You bloody are / as well –

ROBERT. He's got several properties in the area –

LORRAINE. Robert, go home –

ROBERT. He'll pay properly –

LORRAINE. I'm not listening, / Robert –

ROBERT. We can get this done quite quickly –

LORRAINE. Have you no shame?

ROBERT. I'm not talking about selling tomorrow –

LORRAINE. She's still in here. Do you understand?

ROBERT. Where? Where is she? You keep saying that... I can't sleep in here like you do. It's not what she'd want –

LORRAINE. Don't talk to me about what my mum would want –

ROBERT. At some point, we've got to sell / the house –

LORRAINE. Don't you think I know that?

ROBERT. Property's gonna fall on its arse, this guy's / gonna –

LORRAINE. We're not having this conversation any / more –

ROBERT. We have to –

LORRAINE. This isn't property. This is her home. Our home. Three weeks ago she sat on that chair, laughing with Rosa and singing nursery rhymes, so don't / you dare –

ROBERT. She worked three jobs to keep this roof over our heads. And what? You wanna watch the value diminish, out of sentiment?

LORRAINE. Okay. You need to go now.

ROBERT. She's my mum too, Lorraine.

Beat.

LORRAINE. It was me that took voluntary redundancy to look after her. Every day for the last three-and-a-half months, I've been here, to hospital, to the chemist and back.

I can't talk about the house, Robert.

I can talk about anything else.

But not the house.

Not now.

Okay?

Beat.

So. Just go.

Beat.

Robert –

ROBERT. Thing is –

LORRAINE. If you really want to be helpful, fix the lock on the front door –

ROBERT. That was him / just now –

LORRAINE. I am so tired –

ROBERT. On the phone –

LORRAINE. So bloody / tired –

ROBERT. Lorraine –

LORRAINE. Yesterday, outside Sainsbury's, get this / there's this guy handing out vouchers for a free makeover –

ROBERT. Oh my God –

LORRAINE. – He takes one look at me, drops his gaze, waits for me to walk past before he starts handing them out again. / Can you believe that? –

ROBERT. I hate it when you do this.

LORRAINE. – His only task, all day, is to give those leaflets out and he decided to hang on to one rather than waste it on me. / I mean, I knew I looked rough, but – I've put more thought into what Mum should look like next Thursday than I have about myself. I bet you know what you're wearing? Don't you?!

ROBERT. Tell you what? Let me know when you've finished.

I need money, Lorraine – okay?!

LORRAINE. Ha! Of course you do!

ROBERT. If we get in with this developer now, it works out better for all of us.

LORRAINE. For you best. Come on then, why'd you need it? What have you done?

ROBERT. What have I done? Don't ask me what I've done like I'm some likkle eediot boy that arrived on the scene yesterday. Better to ask me what I do, who I am? –

LORRAINE. Oh, get over yourself.

ROBERT. The genius that's gonna hit the rich list in five years' time. That's who.

LORRAINE. Get on with it then. I'm not stopping you.

ROBERT. I can't!

LORRAINE. Why can't you?

ROBERT. Chris has fucked up! That's why he's not coming to the funeral, Lorraine. He's fucked up and now he's gonna walk away.

LORRAINE. He's fucked up how?

ROBERT. He's pissed off our main investor and now –

LORRAINE. What's that got to do with me?

ROBERT. How long is your redundancy gonna last? The market's at its peak now, Lorraine. You need to stock up every penny. When was last time you had to apply for a job?

Beat.

Let me take care of this now and in a year's time, you'll thank me. We're just expediting the process. Trust me, take a leap.

LORRAINE. That's where we differ. Even as kids. By nine months, you'd mastered walking. Didn't matter how many times you'd brock yourself up knocking into things, you'd jump up and crash on, with Mum in awe. Whereas, with me, she thought I was backward because I was nearly two before I took my first steps. I don't leap, Robert. I don't enjoy the feeling of falling.

ROBERT. You're not a kid now, Lorraine. You're a big grown woman. A grandmother.

LORRAINE. Leave me alone, / Robert –

ROBERT. I've lost her too, Lorraine, I'm not losing any more, do you understand me? I've lost her too, I'm not losing any more…

Silence.

ROBERT *makes to leave.*

I'm bringing him round tomorrow afternoon –

LORRAINE. Sophie's pregnant!

ROBERT. What?

Beat.

What did you say?

Beat.

Lorraine?

Scene Nine

The next morning.

Day Nine – Nine Night.

LORRAINE *asleep on the sofa.*

A black woman, dressed in her Sunday best, watches over LORRAINE *as she sleeps.*

LORRAINE *stirs and opens her eyes.*

She sees the woman and screams.

TRUDY. Dat's nice. After me travel all dis way.

　　Oonuh always leave yuh front door open?

Scene Ten

A few hours later.

LORRAINE, TRUDY, ANITA, MAGGIE *and* VINCE *in the kitchen.*

TRUDY *is in the middle of the sofa. From her suitcase she takes out gifts wrapped in newspaper and small black carrier bags.* VINCE *and* MAGGIE, *sit either side of her.*

TRUDY. Yam, plantain, dasheen, rum
　　Green banana, Bami, nutmeg – rum
　　Sweet potato, guinip – rum and chocolate tea
　　Callaloo, ackee and mango from mi tree!

VINCE. / Lard, Trudy, yuh nuh easy!

MAGGIE. Lard, Trudy!

LORRAINE. We do have markets in England.

MAGGIE. Is stale food dat.

TRUDY. Cerasee fi yuh, Auntie Maggie.

MAGGIE. Yuh shouldn't worry yuhself, Trudy – Tank yuh.

ANITA. How did you even get all of that through customs?

TRUDY. Dem too busy a study Al Qaeda fi notice me – Uncle Vinnie.

She hands VINCE *a carrier bag.*

VINCE. Tank yuh, my dear.

TRUDY. Niecey.

She gives a bag to ANITA.

ANITA. Oh, thanks, Auntie Trudy.

TRUDY. Lorraine.

She hands one to LORRAINE.

LORRAINE. Thanks.

TRUDY. And one fi Niecey Junior.

VINCE *unwraps a bottle of white rum and some energy tonic drinks.*

VINCE. Yuh 'ave me just right, Trudy!

TRUDY. Nuh drink dem all at once.

ANITA *unwraps a green-and-yellow, two-piece, skirt and blouse. The tops have short frilly sleeves. The skirts are floor-length with frills at the bottom.*

ANITA. Wow – these are really cool.

TRUDY. Yuh like it?

ANITA. I love it!

TRUDY. Me ask Maggie fi guess oonuh size.

MAGGIE. It beautiful, Trudy.

VINCE. Is yuh mek it, Trudy?

TRUDY. How you mean? A me mek it, yes.

VINCE. Yuh business doing good?

TRUDY. Business booming.

LORRAINE. What is it supposed to be?

ANITA. Oh, my God! – Rosa's gonna look so cute. I'm putting mine on now.

ANITA *starts putting her outfit on on top of her clothes.*

TRUDY. Me mek one fi Yvette tuh. A tank yuh fi di discount pon me flight.

LORRAINE. Yvette got you a discount?

TRUDY. Yes, man.

LORRAINE. So when you said, you hadn't been to the Embassy?

TRUDY. Lie, me a tell! Me did wan surprise yuh.

MAGGIE. Yuh surprise me tuh. Me tink seh a next week yuh a come.

LORRAINE. You knew, all this time?

MAGGIE. Me tell yuh seh she a come.

TRUDY. Maggie!

LORRAINE. You knew too, Uncle Vince.

VINCE. Nah, dawta… Is really Trudy dis?

MAGGIE. A Trudy yes, inna England, to rass!

TRUDY *and* MAGGIE *have a long hug.*

LORRAINE *watches them.*

Gloria wouldn't believe she eye.

TRUDY. Me dream seh me seh ha, yuh know? De night she pass.

MAGGIE. Me tuh.

TRUDY. She was inna pure distress. She di try fi talk, but, when she open she mout, she speech drown inna water – a river gush from she tongue, like a waterfall, and wash she away.

LORRAINE. That doesn't sound like Mum at all. I never knew anything that could stop her from talking.

TRUDY. How she did look?

LORRAINE. Sorry?

TRUDY. Gloria. When she pass.

Slight beat.

ANITA. Peaceful.

TRUDY. Yuh believe seh is ten years since me last see ha.

Silence.

ANITA *walks to* TRUDY *and embraces her.*

ANITA. Sorry. It's just – You standing there – it's like – it's like she's here – you know? Your mannerisms, the way you laugh… everything…

TRUDY. Save yuh eye water, niecey. Gloria inna betta place. Tonight, yuh fi hold up yuh head in celebration, nuh bow it down wid contemplation – let me look pon yuh in yuh dress.

TRUDY *spins* ANITA *around.*

Yes, Miss Ting. Yuh shall go to de ball. – It really fit yuh. She really look like a Kumina dancer.

ANITA. A what dancer?

TRUDY. A dance from we village. Now yuh just fi learn how it go.

VINCE. Is more dan a dance. Is a way of life.

TRUDY. Dance troupe travel over Jamaica wid it now.

VINCE. Dem can dance it all dem like but is only de people weh grow inna it, know de real Kumina.

ANITA. Show us how it goes, Auntie Trudy.

TRUDY. Is fi Uncle Vinnie, fi show yuh.

VINCE. Me?

TRUDY. Yuh remember yuh and Gloria? At Granny funeral?

VINCE. Wha?

TRUDY. De two of yuh nearly set de place a blaze wid dem fiery move dem – Remember, Auntie Maggie?

MAGGIE. I wasn't at de funeral. I was at home. Sick. Wid a chest infection.

TRUDY. Show 'nita some move, Vinnie.

VINCE. Me – me – can't –

ANITA. Come on, Uncle Vince.

VINCE. Is not someting, yuh do just suh –

ANITA *takes out her phone*.

MAGGIE. Lef 'im. 'Im tired. 'Im bawling fi tired, all week.

TRUDY. Lorraine, yuh nah open fi yuh present.

LORRAINE. I'll open it later, thanks.

ANITA *is looking at a video on her phone*.

ANITA. Oh my God! Is this it – that's wicked!

TRUDY *joins* ANITA.

TRUDY. Yuh hear de drum dem? Bam, bam, bam, bam, bam, bam, bam, bam, bam!

She moves her hips in time with the drumming.

ANITA *copies her.*

ANITA. Wah, wah, / wah, wah, wah, / wah, wah, wah, wah…

TRUDY. Pick up yuh foot dem – Bam, bam, bam – Dat's it! Bwoy, likkle English can move!

They laugh.

ROBERT *and* SOPHIE *enter.*

ANITA *turns off the video.*

A beat.

ROBERT *and* TRUDY *face each other. A stand-off like a Western.*

TRUDY. W'appen? Yuh nah go greet yuh big sister? Or, yuh fraid fi touch black 'ooman? – Joke, me a joke.

ROBERT. Hello, Trudy.

TRUDY *embraces* ROBERT.

TRUDY. How yuh buff, suh? Dem must put someting sweet inna de Queen water.

She turns to SOPHIE.

A Stephy dis?

LORRAINE. / Sophie.

SOPHIE. Sophie. Lovely to meet you at last.

SOPHIE puts out her hand.

TRUDY. A wha dat?

TRUDY embraces SOPHIE.

Good to meet yuh tuh. Yuh sure yuh know how fi manage im?

SOPHIE. I'm sorry?

TRUDY laughs.

TRUDY. Yuh soon get used to me.

Slight beat.

LORRAINE. Drink, Sophie?

SOPHIE. I could murder a glass of water.

TRUDY. Try de cerasee, Auntie Maggie. It pick fresh from me back yard yesterday marning.

VINCE. Me can smell de sunshine from 'ere suh.

MAGGIE. A true – Lorraine, put on a pot of water.

LORRAINE. You're going to boil that now?

MAGGIE. Is dat a problem?

LORRAINE. No. Just usually takes a while for the smell to go, that's all.

MAGGIE. Suh open de window.

ROBERT looks at ANITA.

ROBERT. What are you wearing?

ANITA. Auntie Trudy made it.

SOPHIE. Oh, wow!

TRUDY. Me couldn't mek one fi yuh – Maggie never know yuh size.

MAGGIE. She put on weight –

SOPHIE. I'm working on my black woman's arse.

TRUDY. She 'ave humour. We a go get along jus' fine.

She takes out two bags.

She hands one to ROBERT.

Robert.

ROBERT. Ta.

She hands a bag to SOPHIE.

TRUDY. Dis fi yuh, Stephy.

SOPHIE. Sophie – Thank you.

ROBERT *also has a bottle of rum.*

ROBERT. Cheers.

SOPHIE *unwraps a beautiful beaded necklace.*

SOPHIE. Trudy, it's beautiful. Thank you so much.

TRUDY. A blind woman from me village mek it. Me glad yuh like it.

SOPHIE *goes over to* LORRAINE.

TRUDY *goes to* ANITA.

Me can't wait fi see Niecey Junior in she outfit tonight.

ANITA. Me neither.

ANITA *gets her phone to show pictures to* TRUDY.

ROBERT *sits near* VINCE.

LORRAINE. I'm so, so, sorry / I –

SOPHIE. He nearly crashed the car.

LORRAINE. What?

SOPHIE. I'm still shaking.

LORRAINE. What happened?

TRUDY. What a beautiful baby!

ANITA. Nathan's taken her swimming, but you'll meet them tonight.

SOPHIE. He went straight through a red light...

VINCE. Yuh look rough.

ROBERT. I didn't sleep too well, Uncle V.

LORRAINE. Sit down.

TRUDY. Dat's Nathan? 'Im look like Denzel – yuh nuh fool.

MAGGIE. Lorraine, yuh put on de water?

MAGGIE *makes her way over to* LORRAINE *and* SOPHIE.

ROBERT. How was your flight, Trudy?

TRUDY. Murder. Me did tink seh we a go drop outta de sky.

MAGGIE *puts the bag of cerasee down and starts looking through cupboards.*

ROBERT. It can be full-on, if you're not used to it.

TRUDY. Me mek dress fi private client in Miami and de Cayman Island. Me travel all de while.

LORRAINE. What are you looking for?

ROBERT. How long are you staying?

MAGGIE. Honey.

TRUDY. Me only just reach.

LORRAINE. There isn't any.

MAGGIE. Suh why yuh never seh dat inna de first place.

TRUDY. Come – Lorraine. Is what kinda celebration dis? – Bring some glass.

LORRAINE. What?

TRUDY. Mek we toast Gloria.

MAGGIE. And Trudy! Tank de Farda dat she reach safe!

TRUDY. Uncle Vince, tek a bokkle – open it. Lorraine, move quick nuh man.

LORRAINE. It's the middle of the afternoon.

TRUDY. A Nine Night dis.

LORRAINE *gets some glasses*. TRUDY *hands them out.*
VINCE *opens a bottle of rum.*

TRUDY *takes the bottle and makes her way around the room, pouring.*

ANITA. Oh, a bit early for me, thanks.

TRUDY. Suit yuhself.

ROBERT. I'm in the car.

TRUDY. W'appen to yuh. A likkle can't touch a big man like yuh.

TRUDY *pours.*

MAGGIE. Splash likkle in me teacup, Trudy.

TRUDY *pours.*

Likkle more. Likkle more. Dat's it. Lorraine, stir de pot.

TRUDY. Yuh 'ave a glass, Sophie?

SOPHIE. I won't, thank you, Trudy.

TRUDY. Relax – 'im doing de driving.

SOPHIE. It's not that –

TRUDY. Yuh never taste rum till yuh taste dis –

ROBERT. She said no, alright?

TRUDY. W'appen? Yuh Christian?

SOPHIE. No, I'm not –

TRUDY. Yuh pon medication?

LORRAINE. / Trudy –

SOPHIE. No, it's –

TRUDY. Yuh pregnant?

SOPHIE. I...

Beat.

TRUDY. Me headside –

MAGGIE. Lard have mercy!

TRUDY. Lie, / yuh a tell!

VINCE. / A whe yuh a seh?

ANITA. You're shitting me.

MAGGIE. Me never tink me would live fi see de day!

ANITA. Don't be ridiculous. Sophie's not pregnant… Are you?

TRUDY. A double celebration to rass!!

VINCE. Robert! Yuh dark horse, yuh. Congratulations!

TRUDY takes centre stage.

TRUDY. Beg oonuh, tek up me hand.

She closes her eyes and holds out her hands.

MAGGIE. Come on, Vincent.

MAGGIE joins TRUDY, followed by VINCE. They go either side of her.

ANITA then joins, next to VINCE.

Oonuh. Come on.

SOPHIE joins and takes ANITA's hand. ROBERT rolls his eyes. LORRAINE reluctantly joins the other side of SOPHIE. They all look to ROBERT who closes the gap between LORRAINE and MAGGIE.

TRUDY. Raise up oonuh hand!

Slowly, awkwardly, still holding hands, they raise their arms.

Praise de Lard, and de blessing of Jesus –

MAGGIE. Praise im –

TRUDY. Almighty Farda, surveyor of Heaven and Earth, we tank yuh fi dis day –

MAGGIE. We tank yuh, Lord –

TRUDY. Me reach in time fi share Robert and Sophie blessed news. Bright beginnings de bout –

MAGGIE. Fresh / beginnings –

TRUDY. – precious is de life of all of yuh children. Farda, shine yuh light pon Gloria –

MAGGIE. Shine it!

TRUDY. Protect ha. Cleanse and bathe ha.

MAGGIE. Bathe ha, Farda –

TRUDY. You alone is de sole creator. Wash away all she sin! /
Amen.

MAGGIE. Amen!!

*The sound of drums beating quietly begins. As it starts, apart
from* VINCE, *everyone else peels away.*

The drumming grows louder. VINCE *dances. He undoes his top
two buttons as he moves. The drumming reaches a crescendo,*
VINCE *keeps up with the beat. Suddenly the drumming stops.*

VINCE *stands still – into:*

Scene Eleven

Late on in the same evening.

VINCE. What is man, If not a visitor pon God's earth. Some come,
enjoy dem stay, Others struggle fi find peace from day to day
We all need precious help along the way. I had a precious friend
in Gloria If I tap a rhythm She could fill the beat Me pulse run
fast Like a cat pon –

TRUDY *pops her head around the upstage-right door.*

TRUDY. Yuh seen Auntie Maggie?

VINCE. No.

She exits upstage-right.

Heat… Rest pon the other side, Gloria Me time soon come As
me visit soon done Greet me with that smile And a likkle white
rum. Vincent.

LORRAINE *and* ANITA *enter from upstage-left.*

LORRAINE *is holding a bin liner.*

LORRAINE. They're waiting for you in the car, Anita.

ANITA. I'm just saying, it was a bit abrupt. People were in the flow, mid-tune –

LORRAINE. I promised next door we'd finish by midnight.

ANITA. She was having a grand old time –

LORRAINE. You've changed your tune.

ANITA. Cos I get it now, Mum. When the church ladies started praying, for that half an hour, I believed in God. Or, the hope that comes from having one. Someone looking out for Grandma. If someone's looking after her then she can still take care of us… And Auntie Trudy knocking out those rhythms with the dutchie lids, the room just transformed… I've felt so disjointed, Mum. You've always said: stay true to who you are, Anita. I'm trying. All who've been before and all who've yet to come were jamming in that room and making space for me… Did you see Rosa's eyes? Have you ever seen them look so bright?

LORRAINE. It's late, Anita. Take her home.

ANITA gives LORRAINE a tight hug.

ANITA. Night, Uncle V.

VINCE. Night, dawta.

ANITA makes to go, stops and turns.

ANITA. She was here tonight, Mum. She's happy.

She exits upstage-right.

LORRAINE throws rubbish in the bin bag with vigour.

VINCE. Nobody mean fi upset yuh, Lorraine.

LORRAINE. Who's upset? I'm not upset. I just want things put back where they were. – Where's Robert?

VINCE. We only did wan fi mek Gloria feel good.

LORRAINE. All day, all night; laughing, barging, eating, pissing – Every time I've tried to use the bloody bathroom someone's been in there. Enough is enough. I'm putting the cabinet back, calling you a cab, then I'm going to bed.

VINCE. Yuh can't move dat cabinet by yuhself.

LORRAINE. Wanna bet?…

LORRAINE *exits upstage-left.*

VINCE. Lorraine!

He follows after her.

On the heels of their exit, MAGGIE *comes through the upstage-right door, tentatively.*

MAGGIE. Psst...

TRUDY *enters behind her.*

Without speaking they begin to rearrange some of the furniture, occasionally stopping to check that no one is coming.

They are in agreement as to where things should go, but MAGGIE *takes the lead.*

When MAGGIE *decides the room is ready, they stop.*

Yuh ready?

TRUDY. Yeah man.

From offstage we hear ROBERT *and* SOPHIE*'s voices.*

SOPHIE (*offstage*). All night, you've been avoiding me.

ROBERT (*offstage*). Now is not the time, Sophie.

SOPHIE (*offstage*). This has nothing to do with the business.

ROBERT (*offstage*). How can you say that?

SOPHIE (*offstage*). I couldn't care less.

MAGGIE *indicates for* TRUDY *to pick up a bottle of rum left on the kitchen worktop.*

They exit swiftly upstage-right.

SOPHIE *and* ROBERT *enter from downstage-left.*

I want this baby. Gloria wants this baby, did you not feel that tonight? I want it so much, you know what I did? I called my mother. This morning. I thought, fuck it. If I can tell her, I can tell anyone, and that'll make it real. And for all I know, she might say something nice. Something grandmotherly. Like Gloria would. She didn't. We exchanged a few words, then I hung up. Before the phone went down, do you know what she

said? 'Goodbye, dear. Good luck with your caffè latte'…
I thought that was quite witty, for her.

But that's it, isn't it? It's not the thought of becoming a father
that scares you. It's the idea of having a child with me. Isn't it?

ROBERT. Nothing's changed for me, I made it really clear, from
day one –

SOPHIE. The last time we set foot in my mother's house, the day
you stood up for me – the expression on her face, I can see it
now; I just remember thinking, 'My God, this man can do
anything.'

ROBERT. Like an animal.

SOPHIE. What?

ROBERT. That's how your mum looked at me. If someone were to
look at my child like that / it scares me what I might do to them.
I don't think you do understand.

SOPHIE. I understand, Robert.

We hear:

LORRAINE (*offstage*). Oh God! Are you alright? Somebody help!
Robert!… Robert!

VINCE (*offstage*). Lard, God…

LORRAINE (*offstage*). Can you stand up?

VINCE (*offstage*). Don't mek a fuss.

ROBERT *exits upstage-left.*

SOPHIE, *alone, looks up at Gloria*

ROBERT (*offstage*). I've got you, Uncle Vince.

LORRAINE (*offstage*). After three… / One, two, three.

ROBERT (*offstage*). One, two, three.

VINCE (*offstage*). Me alright, man.

ROBERT (*offstage*). Let me take him.

LORRAINE (*offstage*). Be careful.

SOPHIE *exits.*

ROBERT *and* LORRAINE *enter with* VINCE.

VINCE *is holding his back.*

VINCE. Me can manage.

LORRAINE. Let's put him on the – What's happened to the furniture?

ROBERT. Let's just put him down, Lorraine.

They sit VINCE *down.*

VINCE. God bless yuh.

ROBERT. What were you doing?

LORRAINE *looks around at the rearranged room.*

VINCE. Yuh sister seh, she wan fi move cabinet.

ROBERT. Not, the big one?

We hear a thump from upstairs.

They all look up.

What's that?

LORRAINE. Where's Trudy?

LORRAINE *exits upstage-right.*

ROBERT. Is it bad?

VINCE. Nah sah.

Slight beat.

Whe Sophie?

ROBERT. I think she might've gone, Uncle V.

A louder bang from upstairs.

We hear heated muffled voices of LORRAINE, TRUDY *and* MAGGIE.

What's going on?

LORRAINE (*offstage*). All now, you still can't answer the question.

TRUDY (*offstage*). Don't push her, Lorraine.

LORRAINE (*offstage*). I haven't touched her.

VINCE. Lard-'ave-mercy-in-heaven.

ROBERT *makes his way to the upstage-right door and is nearly trampled on as* TRUDY, MAGGIE *and* LORRAINE *come charging through.*

MAGGIE (*offstage*). Yuh wan me brok me neck?

TRUDY (*offstage*). Tek time, Auntie Maggie.

LORRAINE (*offstage*). Who said you could go in there?

TRUDY (*offstage*). Yuh tink seh yuh a de boss?

LORRAINE (*offstage*). Sneaking around de place like a damn teef.

LORRAINE *slams the door shut behind them.*

TRUDY. Is who yuh a call teef?!

MAGGIE. Outta order, she outta order.

VINCE. What's going on, Maggie? / Aigh…

TRUDY. A who wan fi teef any of dis ole brock?

ROBERT. Lorraine – ?

LORRAINE. I caught / the two of them up there –

TRUDY. / Catch what?

MAGGIE. Yuh 'ear she?

LORRAINE. Searching up the place –

ROBERT. What did I tell you?

LORRAINE. Caught red-handed. / Well, you're not leaving until –

TRUDY. / Seh yuh catch me more one more time and see if yuh can catch yuh teet when I box out every last one a dem from yuh mout?

MAGGIE. Jesus Christ!

LORRAINE. Come nuh!

VINCE. Oonuh stop it and calm down… (*Holding his back.*) Lard.

MAGGIE. Lorraine, apologise.

LORRAINE. Apologise for what!

MAGGIE. Yuh already mash up tonight proceedings wid yuh feisty self.

ROBERT. Why are you in cahoots with her, Auntie Maggie?

TRUDY *kisses her teeth.*

LORRAINE. What have you taken?

VINCE. Is not teefing dem teefing.

MAGGIE. Oonuh is just pickney to me. Me nuh answerable tuh any pickney.

LORRAINE. Alright then, you can answer to the police –

LORRAINE *moves from the door to find her phone.*

TRUDY. Yes! Yuh call dem!

VINCE. Yuh haffi explain yuhself, Maggie –

MAGGIE. Shut yuh mout. She lucky me lef ha standing after she a bawl out teef.

ROBERT. Explain what –

LORRAINE. Everything you've asked me to do tonight, I've done it. Put up with your, 'In Jamaica "we do it like this". In Jamaica "we don't do it like that".' Well, this isn't Jamaica – this is my mother's home, and all I've asked is that you respect it. I've let people in here, tonight, friends of yours that look like candidates for death row –

TRUDY. Yuh stuck-up –

LORRAINE. I told you to stay out of her room. / It still smells of her in there. I haven't even changed her sheets. Everything in there was exactly where she left it. It's not just about her stuff. It's a mapping of her routine. The dictionary under the Bible. The slippers next to the chest, that's where she left them. And, you two descend in there, like jankcrows –

ROBERT. You were in her room?

TRUDY. Is who yuh a call jankcrow? When is yuh a circle round Gloria like seh is only yuh a suffer –

MAGGIE. Of all of Gloria pickney, Trudy is de only one wid de intelligence fi know wha fi do. Is Gloria last night in she yard. A spirit never wan fi leave de family home. You have fi encourage dem out, disorientate dem, put dem mattress up against de bedroom door – if Gloria get trap inna dis house tonight – oonuh will fart!

ROBERT. What the hell are you talking about?

LORRAINE. Get them out, Robert. I swear to God –

MAGGIE. Mi nah leave dis yard before I see Gloria pass through wid me own two eye.

VINCE. Oonuh stop de argument. Gloria need fi mek she journey in peace. Travel back to Africa.

MAGGIE. Is Jamaica she come from, yuh blasted eediot.

LORRAINE. Get out. I'll call the police, I swear to God – Watch me get your arse deported!

TRUDY. Yuh can call de ratiid Queen, fi all I business. Who wan fi stay inna dis yard? Dis yard a suck out me blood! Gloria still inna it. The same pussy whe yuh spring from, is de same pussy whe trap me –

ROBERT. What did you say?

MAGGIE. Tek it easy, Trudy.

TRUDY. Yuh know weh it feel like, when de hole inna yuh heart carve out by yuh own mudda? Is like I spend my whole life stuck inside dat woman. Can hear she voice, but can't see, feel, touch. Is not botheration me a look. Is liberation. Liberation from de fuckeration, so I can draw breath, and fly free!

VINCE. Me beg yuh fi stop dis, Trudy.

TRUDY. Me was four years old when she look me dead inna de eye and tell me seh she a go to Ingland pon holiday –

ROBERT. Same old shit –

TRUDY. And me seh, 'But, Mummy, Ingland nuh freezing cold?'

LORRAINE. What do you think would have happened if she had brought you with her? She came with nothing –

TRUDY. See Auntie Maggie deh. Ask ha if she would abandon she own pickney.

LORRAINE. She wanted to build a better life –

TRUDY. A better life fi sheself!

LORRAINE. That's not true.

ROBERT. She wrote to you every month –

LORRAINE. Clothed and fed all of us, same way.

TRUDY. Year after year, mi long fi Mummy fi come back home. Finally, she reach. But, wid she two new pickney. Yuh remember? Granny seh, 'Suprise, Trudy! Meet yuh brudda and sista.' Oonuh look at me, coop up inna hell. Soak up de heat before you fuck off to your paradise.

ROBERT. You were the one she saved.

LORRAINE. We all had it hard, Trudy, but there wasn't a day, not one day, that she wasn't thinking of you. I know and he knows because we were here. Every year, September 12th, she'd wake us up to perform your birthday ritual. Do you remember, Robert? She'd make an enormous sponge cake, that we couldn't eat until bedtime, to fit in with the time difference, when you got home from school. And she'd take out the tablecloth –

ROBERT. That's right.

LORRAINE. That only came out / at Christmas.

ROBERT. Christmas Day.

LORRAINE . And we'd stand round the table and sing. Not 'Happy Birthday', cos that was too upbeat. – She'd make us stand with our hands clasped in the prayer position and sing, 'How Great Thou Art', as though you were God. She worshipped you.

TRUDY. September 13th.

LORRAINE. What?

TRUDY. Mi birthday is September 13th. Not the 12th. And me fucking hate sponge cake.

LORRAINE. She did the best she could.

TRUDY. She left me behind. She forsake me, like God forsake Jesus.

LORRAINE. Except you weren't pinned naked to a cross, were you?

Who was it that gave you the money to set up your dressmaking business in the first place?

ROBERT. Tell her!

TRUDY. Everyting for oonuh in Ingland is money, innit? Fuck up people life, and tink seh yuh Sterling can fix it.

LORRAINE. You didn't refuse it though, did you? Like you refused her. What about when you're flying off to Miami and the Caymen Islands –

ROBERT. That's right.

LORRAINE. Still feel abandoned then? –

VINCE. Dis is not how fi do it, children –

MAGGIE. Lef dem, Vincent –

ROBERT. She started dis, Uncle V –

TRUDY. Yes! And after de funeral me a go mek sure it done!

ROBERT. Really? So how much is it gonna take then, Trudy?

ROBERT *takes his wallet out.*

He starts to throw money out on the floor.

Let's cut the bull. How much? / So we can stop the pretence –

MAGGIE. / Damn disgrace –

VINCE. Gloria heart a bleed!

LORRAINE. This isn't about money, Robert. Look at her. I know exactly what she wants. But I don't know what she's going to do with it. All that bitterness, blistering inside of you. You sent her from this life to the next carrying shame. You can't do any more. She was sick for months. Where were you? She asked me over and over again, 'Trudy call?' 'Trudy coming?' I've always been rubbish at lying, but, my God, I got good at it by the end. Have you ever seen disappointment on a dying face? It's not

like she didn't try and make it up to you. When Alvin left. She
sent for you. Finally, she could have the family she'd always
wanted. She called you up. Begged you to come. Didn't she?
What? Can't you remember? We do – don't we, Robert? She
left us in the house and went to find a phone box. She was gone
for ages, I started to get worried. I went into my room and
started moving things around, thinking about where you would
sleep. As though you were going to walk through the door with
her. I didn't even mind sharing her, we were used to that. Half
of her was always tied up with you. When she got back in, she
didn't look at me. I didn't know how you'd said it but it was
clear. 'Trudy not coming.' You were right not to come. Mum
wanted you but England didn't. It didn't want her. It didn't want
them. It didn't want him. It didn't want me. So, you can stand
there, victorious, watch the rest of us grieve / but, I know –

TRUDY. When did she send fi me?

LORRAINE. What?

TRUDY. Name the day. The year, the hour, the second dat she send
/ for me.

LORRAINE. I remember it well, I was twelve –

TRUDY. She never!

LORRAINE. Yes, she did!

TRUDY. See Vince and Maggie a siddown deh. Yuh ask dem when
yuh mudda ever send fi me. Never, never, never, never, never,
never, ever, never, never!

LORRAINE. You're a liar!

TRUDY. Ask dem.

ROBERT. You choose to stay with your granny –

LORRAINE. Uncle Vince?

Slight beat.

Auntie Maggie?

Slight beat.

Answer me!

VINCE. I never hear of dat, Lorraine.

TRUDY. Fi oonuh madda was de liar. Not me. Me nuh business bout fi oonuh money. Every part of me, whe yuh see a stand up in front of yuh, well a Jamaica it mek. England nuh 'ave nuttin fi do wid it.

Mi come a Ingland fi bury de woman dat born mi. Mi grieve for me mudda already, de day mi granny dead.

Silence.

MAGGIE (*sings*). Precious Lord, Take my hand, Lead me on, let me stand I'm tired, I'm weak, I'm lone, Through the storm, through the night, Lead me on to the light, Take my hand, Precious Lord, Lead me home When my way –

MAGGIE *freezes. Stares out front.*

VINCE. Maggie?

Slight beat.

Maggie?

ROBERT. What's she looking at?

VINCE. Maggie?

TRUDY. Myal.

ROBERT. Uncle V?

MAGGIE. Gloria… Yuh reach.

ROBERT. Nah, nah, nah, not at all – fuck this –

MAGGIE. What a whe yuh look good, Gloria – Dead really suit yuh.

ROBERT. Uncle V, make her stop.

VINCE. Yuh can see ha good, Maggie?

ROBERT. This isn't funny –

TRUDY. Granny wid ha, Maggie?

ROBERT. That's enough. Lorraine – I'm gone!

ROBERT *turns to go.*

MAGGIE. Robert. Yuh madda seh she want fi see you.

Wherever ROBERT *has got to, he stops dead in his tracks, facing the door upstage-left. His back to* MAGGIE.

He buries his face in his hands.

ROBERT. Listen, Auntie Maggie –

MAGGIE. Move yuh hands from yuh face. She want fi see yuh good-good.

LORRAINE *and* VINCE *watch* ROBERT *as he slowly drops his hands, his back still facing* MAGGIE, MAGGIE*'s back facing his.*

Turn around.

ROBERT *doesn't move.*

Never turn your back pon a spirit.

ROBERT *reluctantly turns around.*

ROBERT. So. Now what?

MAGGIE*'s body bends and bolts.*

LORRAINE. Oh, my God.

When MAGGIE *speaks her voice is deeper.*

MAGGIE/GLORIA. Robert – When Crow look down from the mountain top / him see plenty food, but him wound him wing, so him 'fraid fi tek de chance. Him look up to de sky. Eagle a come. Crow seh, 'Eagle, beg yuh give me a chance. In a few hours I will surely be dead. Eat me if you must, but leave it till de mornin'. Mek me have one last meal.' Eagle lick im beak, and nyam Crow same way and seh, 'Crow, yuh shudda tek de chance when yuh did have it.'

LORRAINE. Mum?

MAGGIE/GLORIA. Trudy?

Mi leave off de heavy load me affi carry inna dis life. Every step mi tek forward, mi balance wid de step mi lef behind. One can't exist without de udda. Freedom have a rising motion. She stretch out she hand and invite every single one'a we. Latch on, but yuh haffi unclench yu fist.

Lorraine?

LORRAINE. Yes. I'm here, Mum.

MAGGIE/GLORIA. Lorraine, yuh – yuh –

MAGGIE*'s body jolts. She doubles over. She speaks as though she's in pain.*

Gloria, yuh need to pass now.

LORRAINE. What? No. Wait. She can't –

MAGGIE. Somebody open the door.

VINCE. Lorraine –

LORRAINE. No. She hasn't finished –

MAGGIE. Move from de path.

LORRAINE. No. Mum. Wait –

MAGGIE. Trudy, open it –

MAGGIE *groans.*

TRUDY *makes for the door.* LORRAINE *runs at* TRUDY *and pulls her down to the floor.*

LORRAINE. Leave it. Let her speak. What were you going to say, Mum?

TRUDY. Come offa me.

ROBERT. Lorraine. What the fuck are you doing?

LORRAINE *holds* TRUDY *down.*

VINCE *tries to get up but his back gives out.*

VINCE. Let her go, Lorraine!

ROBERT *stands, watches the chaos around him.*

LORRAINE *still has hold of* TRUDY.

LORRAINE. It's okay. You can speak to me now. Mum. I'm here. You can speak to me.

VINCE. Robert, get her off before she kill her.

MAGGIE *continues to groan.*

ROBERT *pulls* LORRAINE *off* TRUDY.

ROBERT. Get off her, Lorraine. Stop!

TRUDY *is on all fours, gasping for breath.*

MAGGIE. Pass, Gloria.

ROBERT. Shut up, Maggie!

MAGGIE. Open the door.

MAGGIE *begins to chant.*

TRUDY *crawls towards the door.*

ROBERT. Stop this now, Maggie.

VINCE. Gloria a go get trap in ya!

LORRAINE *runs to the kitchen drawer, pulls out a knife and holds it towards* TRUDY.

LORRAINE. I said, leave the fucking door alone.

ROBERT. / Lorraine!!

VINCE. Lard, Gad, Lorraine, put dat down!

LORRAINE. No! She needs to speak. Let her speak.

TRUDY *backs away from the door.*

MAGGIE *stops chanting and slumps on the chair exhausted.*

Mum? I'm here. What?

What is it?

I'm here now.

What do you need?

I'm here.

Have I done everything?

Do you like your dress?

I couldn't decide between the purple or cream.

Has the pain stopped now?

I said you were losing weight.

'Mi fine' you said.

You're not, Mum.

You're not.

We waited at the hospital –

'Whe dem seh?' You said. 'It a go kill mi?'

'I don't know, Mum. It might – I don't – I – Yes, yes, yes, It's going to kill you.'

'Me?' You said.

'Don't look so scared. I'll hold your hand. I'll rub your back.'

You faded so fast.

'The soup too hot.' You said, 'Mek it cool.'

I combed your hair.

'De room too hot,' you said, 'Open de window.'

I changed your sheets.

'Me foot feel heavy,' you said,

I massaged your feet.

I pulled up your blanket.

I notice you smile.

I notice you breathe.

'Mum?' I said.

'Mum?'

Yuh squeezed my hand.

Mum?

Mum?

Mummy??

Silence.

ROBERT. The knife, Lorraine?

Beat.

Lorraine?

LORRAINE *walks towards the door, the knife still in her hand.*

LORRAINE *stands in front of the door. She opens it.*

TRUDY *exhales.*

LORRAINE. She's gone.

LORRAINE *crumples to the floor and sobs.*

MAGGIE *begins to cry.*

ROBERT *watches on.*

VINCE. Gawn? She really gawn, Maggie?

MAGGIE. You tell me, Vincent Armstrong. You tell me.

ROBERT *goes to* LORRAINE.

Takes the knife out of her hand.

They hold each other.

Blackout.

The End.

PRINCESS & THE HUSTLER

Chinonyerem Odimba

Princess & The Hustler was first produced as a co-production between Eclipse Theatre Company, Bristol Old Vic and Hull Truck Theatre. It premiered at Bristol Old Vic on 9 February 2019, followed by a UK tour visiting seven cities. The cast and creative team was as follows:

PHYLLIS 'PRINCESS' JAMES	Kudzai Sitima
MAVIS JAMES	Donna Berlin
WENDELL 'JUNIOR'	Fode Simbo
WENDELL 'THE HUSTLER' JAMES	Seun Shote
LORNA JAMES	Emily Burnett
MARGOT	Jade Yourell
LEON	Romayne Andrews

Director	Dawn Walton
Designer	Simon Kenny
Lighting Designer	Aideen Malone
Composer and Sound Designer	Richard Hammarton
Movement Director	Victoria Igbokwe
Fight Director	Stephen Medlin
Voice and Dialect Coach	Joel Trill
Assistant Director	Emilie Lahouel
Dramaturg	Ola Animashawun
Casting Director	Briony Barnett

With respect to:

Princess Campbell
Paul Stephenson
Roy Hackett
Guy Bailey
Raghbir Singh
Owen Henry
Joyce Stephenson
Carmen Beckford
Barbara Dettering
Audley Evans
Prince Brown
Mary Seacole
George Odlum
Mrs Mavis Bowen
Alfred Fagon
Clifford Drummond
Delores Campbell
Tony Benn
Tony Bullimore & Family
And many many more…

C.O.

People

PHYLLIS 'PRINCESS' JAMES, *ten years old*
MAVIS JAMES, *thirty-eight years old*
WENDELL 'JUNIOR' JAMES, *seventeen years old*
WENDELL 'THE HUSTLER' JAMES, *forty years old*
LORNA JAMES, *nine years old*
MARGOT, *forty-two years old*
LEON, *nineteen years old*

Places

1. Mavis's front room. A small front room with an even smaller kitchenette in the corner of the room. Decorated sparsely with pictures of the Caribbean and family members on the walls. There is one small sofa and a dining table where a sewing machine sits occasionally. A wireless radio sits on a small mantelpiece.

2. Cupboard room. A large cupboard big enough to stand and walk in – not big enough for a bed. This room is only lit when Princess is in it.

3. The other room. The room Wendell Junior and Princess share. Also becomes the room Wendell Junior shares with Wendell.

4. The Docks, Bristol.

Things

...indicates a trailing off at the end of a sentence or a pause.

/ indicates an overlap in speech between two characters or within a character's dialogue.

A new paragraph indicates a natural pause/change of thought in dialogue.

VOICE-OVER – indicates pre-recorded news pieces.

ACT ONE

Scene One

Christmas Day. St Agnes, Bristol. 1962.

The stage opens like a big box – as though opening the front of a doll's house.

PRINCESS, *eyes closed, stands in the cupboard room.*
She is wearing a swimming costume and a sash around her.
She raises her hands in the air and places a crown made of cardboard and tinsel on her head.

VOICE-OVER. *Ladies and gentlemen, I present to you the winner of the year's Weston-super-Mare Beauties of the West Contest – (Voice booming.) Princess James.*

PRINCESS*'s eyes open wide.*
The cupboard room explodes into a world of pageantry – scenes of people jumping into a swimming pool, Union Jacks, music and fireworks – fill the stage.
PRINCESS *approaches a microphone.*

PRINCESS. My name is Phyllis Princess James. I will wear this crown every day. I will never take it off even when I am asleep.

I want to thank my mummy, my friends, Margot and Junior...

Even though he is so annoying!

I will use all this money to help the poor...

After I have bought my mummy a new coat and...

I might buy a new bicycle for me and...

MAVIS*'s voice can be heard shouting above the noise –*

MAVIS. Princess James did you hear what I said?

Princess!

If I have to carry on with this hollering at you then the next thing you hear will be my hand against your backside.

You hear me chile?

Phyllis!

PRINCESS *steps into the front room –*

PRINCESS *stands, crown on, sash falling off, dejected –*

PRINCESS. Mummy!

MAVIS. Don't you 'Mummy' me! Been calling you for the last ten minutes. Sometimes I do wonder where your head is at /

PRINCESS. Beauties of the West /

MAVIS. What you say?

PRINCESS. Nothing Mummy /

MAVIS. Good. Now go wash your hands and come help me with the beans. Not going to be eating until five o'clock if you children don't fix up.

Where's your brother?

Junior. Come here now.

Wendell Junior!

PRINCESS. I heard the door go this morning.

Or maybe I only think I hear it.

MAVIS. What you think you're saying?
You two thick as thieves in the night /

PRINCESS. I think I hear something…

The sound of footsteps heavy, climbing stairs –

WENDELL JUNIOR *enters.*
A camera swings around his neck –
He casually walks across his mother and sister towards another door –
He places his hand on the door handle –

MAVIS. You turn the handle of that door and it will be the last thing you do on this God-given earth.

WENDELL JUNIOR *releases his grip on the door handle –*

Beat.

I am done waiting for an explanation as to what reason you
might have for leaving this house this early today of all days.
You better having a conversation with the leather of the belt
instead.

MAVIS *moves to a cupboard. She opens it and pulls out
a man's leather belt –*

WENDELL JUNIOR. No! Mummy! Hold on a minute /

MAVIS. Oh you find the power of speech now?

WENDELL JUNIOR. It was some of the guys…

They were meeting up you know…
Gotta be there or be square!

MAVIS *flexes the belt –*

I should have told you but didn't want to wake you. I was
thinking better let you /

MAVIS. So you were doing it for me? Looking after your mummy
by sneaking out the house to Lord-knows-where at Lord-knows-
what-time for me. That right son?

PRINCESS. God doesn't go where he's been /

WENDELL JUNIOR. Shut your face!

PRINCESS. Mummy is going to beat you and you gone cry like a
baby.
Cry baby.

WENDELL JUNIOR *moves to grab at* PRINCESS –

WENDELL JUNIOR. If I beat you first then you gon' cry louder
than me.

MAVIS *raises the belt high above her head –*

WENDELL JUNIOR *backs off –*

MAVIS. You done explaining yourself?

And now you have the nerve to be all sorts of cruel to
your sister?

WENDELL JUNIOR. Mummy. I am really sorry.
We're doing nothing bad. We just hang by Queen Square with
our cameras…

MAVIS. So let me get this right. You sneak out of my house at whatever time on this particular day to choose to go posing in the street /

WENDELL JUNIOR. Not posing Mummy.

Leon and some other guys wanted to take photographs by the docks. And you know I'm trying to learn everything I can...

I'll be an apprentice one day in one of them photography studios /

MAVIS. You're not an apprentice yet. Right now you are about to get another kind of education /

WENDELL JUNIOR. I split from those guys so I could come back and do portraits of you...

Mummy...

Gon' use some of my savings to get them developed in that place Leon goes. Over by Fishponds...

Going to take real pretty pictures of you.

MAVIS *puts down the belt –*

You gon' shine like a queen!

MAVIS *pats her hair –*

MAVIS. Pictures you say?

WENDELL JUNIOR. Yes Mummy. Right there in front of the...

WENDELL JUNIOR *looks at the sad withering Christmas tree in the corner of the room –*

MAVIS *shakes her head –*

By the wireless.
You just listening to the radio all casual like...
A movie star!
You going to wear your pearls?
They always make you look so ladylike.

WENDELL JUNIOR *lifts the camera to his face, and circles his mother, pretending to be taking photos –*

MAVIS. You think so Junior?
Maybe...

You know when I iron out this wig and add a little colour on my face, you wouldn't even recognise your own mother.

MAVIS *preens herself* –

PRINCESS. What about me? You going to take a photograph of me Junior?

WENDELL JUNIOR. No! Wasn't planning to break the glass of my new camera with your face.

PRINCESS *bursts into heartbreaking sobs* –

MAVIS *remembering the hundred and one things she still has to do, turns on her heels and heads for the small kitchenette* –

MAVIS. You stop that way of talking to your sister.

Princess you stop your noise and get started on those beans.

Junior you make sure you tidy up the bedroom, this room, and the washroom.

WENDELL JUNIOR *stomps his foot in frustration* –

WENDELL JUNIOR. That is so uncool.

MAVIS. You got something else to say Junior?

WENDELL JUNIOR. No Mummy.

WENDELL JUNIOR *exits* –

PRINCESS. Mummy?

MAVIS *is busy at sink washing up* –

Mummy.

MAVIS. I hope when I turn round you're busy on those beans Princess. I just as easily pick that belt up again /

PRINCESS *busies herself with the pile of beans* –

PRINCESS. Doing it Mummy.

Doing it quicker even...

I need to ask you one question. Just one...

MAVIS. Go on then Princess.

PRINCESS. Why don't we have any presents under the tree?

MAVIS *turns to face* PRINCESS –

MAVIS. Nothing you really want beyond your family and this roast chicken I have in the oven.

PRINCESS. But they made me do the list at school. I was writing it in my best handwriting…

Even Miss Turner give me a gold star for how good my Gs and my Ys were /

MAVIS. Gave me /

PRINCESS. She said it was best in the class and '*considering my ability*' /

MAVIS. And what exactly is wrong with your ability?

MAVIS *kisses her teeth* –

I did read your list baby. I did. Every single word of it…

It's just…

Nobody ordering curtains at this time of year.

MAVIS *packs away the sewing machine* –

PRINCESS. Who needs presents all wrapped up in the sparkly paper and a pink ribbon? Who needs any of it?

When we have beans and pumpkin!

PRINCESS *bursts into a dance routine with the vegetables she is meant to be cutting up* –
MAVIS *starts to dance and laugh as she exits with the sewing machine.*

PRINCESS *is still doing her dance routine* –

WENDELL JUNIOR *enters.*

WENDELL JUNIOR. What you doing peahead?

PRINCESS. Mummy!

WENDELL JUNIOR *runs to put his hand over her mouth* –

PRINCESS *wriggles away from him* –

WENDELL JUNIOR. Why you always got to tell tales?

Princess you just need to grow up some time soon.
Most girls your age not so...

One day when you want to sneak out of the house /

PRINCESS. I am never going to be sneaking off to no place.
I am a good girl /

WENDELL JUNIOR. Course you are!

PRINCESS. And I'm big and grown enough /

WENDELL JUNIOR. Too big to still be dreaming of beauty
pageants and crowns /

PRINCESS. Beauty pageants *are* for big girls.
Women. Grown girls and women.
Not little girls.
You know nothing Junior.

WENDELL JUNIOR. I know that if you tell tales on me again I'm
going to make sure you never get to Weston-super-Mare. I'm
going to tell Mummy about some of the ungodly things that go
on there. They say at night boys and girls go on the pier there to
do sin. If I tell Mummy that then she will never let you go.
Ever!

PRINCESS. You can't!

WENDELL JUNIOR. Then you better keep *that* shut /

PRINCESS. Margot says that they even give you free ice cream if
you're really good. She is going to take me for my birthday.
Margot says we can watch them all day. Watch all those women
with perfect straight shiny hair all down to their waist /

WENDELL JUNIOR. Well none of that is going to happen when
Mummy hears that Weston is worst than the devil's playground.
And Margot she says all sorts of things but none of them seem
to ever happen so /

PRINCESS. I hate you Junior. I hate you and /

MAVIS *enters*.

MAVIS. We do not say such things in this house especially on *this*
day.

PRINCESS. Junior was /

WENDELL JUNIOR *gestures a 'shush' at* PRINCESS *behind* MAVIS*'s back –*

Sorry Mummy.

PRINCESS *stomps off back to preparing the vegetables –*

WENDELL JUNIOR *slumps onto the small sofa –*

MAVIS. You tired son? You rest up. Put your feet up. You want me to bring you a cold glass of something? Or maybe put a blanket across your knees?

WENDELL JUNIOR. Thanks Mummy. Thinking of having a little shut-eye before food /

MAVIS *picks up a cushion and jokingly swipes* WENDELL JUNIOR *across the head –*

MAVIS. You wan ar lickle shut-eye is wha' ya say?

MAVIS *swipes at* WENDELL JUNIOR *with the cushion again –*

PRINCESS *giggles –*

Which food yuh gon' nyam?

Which table yuh gon' sit down 'pon?

PRINCESS *picks up another cushion and throws it at* WENDELL JUNIOR –

Yuh two children fool fool fram mawnin' till night!

PRINCESS *and* WENDELL JUNIOR *start to play/cushion fight –*

You watch yourselves and don't bring no mess to my house you hear me.

A loud knock at the door –

PRINCESS *and* WENDELL JUNIOR *don't hear the door –*

How many of them undercook mince pie I have to eat before these neighbours leave us alone?

MAVIS *walks to the door and opens it –*
She shuts the door quickly and goes back to clearing the table.

Scene Two

Ten minutes have passed. The knocking at the door is persistent now.

WENDELL JUNIOR *and* PRINCESS *are motionless, watching their mother. Watching the door.*

Beat.

PRINCESS. Mummy I think there's someone at the door /

WENDELL JUNIOR. You want me to get it? /

MAVIS. You stay where you are!

  Beat.

  Must be children from upstairs.

  You see how they've been running up and down the street since morning like they don't have mothers. And what kind of mother let their children run wild like that.

  Beat.

  Princess you lay the table.

  Another knock –

  This chicken smells so good and the potatoes nearly done roasting.

WENDELL JUNIOR. You hear my belly?

MAVIS. Chile when you finished talking to your belly /

  Knocking gets louder –

PRINCESS. Mummy /

  MAVIS *wipes her hands on her apron –*

MAVIS. You make sure you lay those knives and forks straight and neat.

PRINCESS. Yes but Mummy /

WENDELL JUNIOR. One time when we at Deejay's house
  the police came to ask him a few questions about some business
  he say he never heard of. They come knocking in this same way.

  The police have anything to talk to you about Mummy?

PRINCESS. The police!

MAVIS. You lost your mind?

PRINCESS. They're going to take you away Mummy?

MAVIS. No one taking anyone any place!

MAVIS *turns to open the oven door –*

PRINCESS. I won't let them take you!

PRINCESS *stomps to the door, and before* MAVIS *can stop her, she opens the door wide to reveal* WENDELL 'THE HUSTLER' JAMES *standing tall and handsome on the other side –*

MAVIS *and* WENDELL JUNIOR *freeze in shock –*

You can't take my mummy away! She hasn't done anything /

MAVIS. Move away from that door Princess!

WENDELL *bends down to face* PRINCESS –

WENDELL. Well hello Princess /

MAVIS. Now Princess!

PRINCESS *backs away from the door slowly – never taking her eyes off* WENDELL –

WENDELL *straightens himself out –*
Looks further into the room –

MAVIS *gathers her children in her arms –*

WENDELL. Blouse an' skirt is dat Junior?

MAVIS *pushes them towards the door of the other room –*

MAVIS. You children go to your room /

PRINCESS *and* WENDELL JUNIOR *remain still – frozen by curiosity –*

You gone deaf? Your room now!

PRINCESS. Mummy.
Do you know him?

MAVIS. You stop with the questions Princess /

WENDELL JUNIOR. You want me to stay?

WENDELL. An' hear dis! De bwoy gon' broke 'im voice.

MAVIS *points at* WENDELL – *warning him –*

MAVIS. You / you…

(*To her children*.) I won't tell you again /

PRINCESS (*groaning*). We haven't eaten our lunch yet.

We haven't done Christmas /

MAVIS *turns and slaps* PRINCESS *across the face –*

PRINCESS *squeals and cools the stinging with her hand –*

WENDELL JUNIOR *and* PRINCESS *exit.*

MAVIS *stands staring at* WENDELL –

Scene Three

A few minutes have passed. WENDELL *moves further into the room.*

MAVIS *holds a cautionary hand out to stop him –*

WENDELL. Mavis /

MAVIS. No.

WENDELL. Lissen /

MAVIS. No.

WENDELL. I /

MAVIS. You /

WENDELL. Long time /

MAVIS. Ha! What kind of thing Satan bring to my door today. Unless you his ghost?

WENDELL. No.

MAVIS. Yes must be that /

WENDELL. It mi far real!!

MAVIS. No… No… No!

Take yourself fram mi house duppy.

WENDELL. Nuh be like dis Mavis.

Let mi juss come in an' tark…

Far ar lickle while…

Mi an' you…

Dat's all mi arsking.

MAVIS. If you don't take yourself out of my house, I will call the police on your backside.

WENDELL. Mavis mi know it ar shock.

Mi tink twice before mi come 'ere.

Tree times even. Mi tink real hard 'pon dis one.

Beat.

WENDELL *moves closer –*

MAVIS *walks to the kitchen, opens a drawer and pulls out a knife –*

WENDELL *backs off –*

Look at dis.

Let mi juss talk wit yuh ar lickle.

Juss ar lickle time far mi. Mi beg yuh Mavis.

MAVIS. Listen to me now Wendell. I don't have the time nor the inclination to abide your foolishness today.

If yuh nuh wan' to be lock up today, I beg you take yourself back to whatever ol' an' mess yuh juss crawl fram /

WENDELL. Yuh vex. Mi sees dat. Yuh vex in ar way an' yuh 'ave every right to be /

MAVIS. Vex? Vex? You come say *vex* like someone come and take my purse from my handbag.

Or eat too much from the Dutch pot.

Mi nuh *vex* Wendell. Mi beyon' vex.
Mi angry.
Mi angry nuff to kill yuh right 'ere an' den go tell yuh modder why.
Mi angry nuff to go to jail far dem years, an' still be laughing.

WENDELL. Tink of de children /

MAVIS *laughs out loud – hysterical – dangerous –*

MAVIS. Children?

MAVIS *waves the knife wildly –*

WENDELL. Wait wait /

MAVIS. Wait 'pon what?

We done talking now Wendell. You best step from mi door before I do something you going to regret /

WENDELL. De thing is Mavis /

MAVIS. Wendell mi nuh 'ave business wit you /

WENDELL. Mi kyaant go nuh place else /

MAVIS. Thank you for your visit.

WENDELL *backs out the door –*

You go duppy 'pon somebody else.

MAVIS *slams the door behind him –*

MAVIS *puts the knife away –*

Beat.

A knock at the door again –

Beat.

WENDELL. Mavis!!

Mavis.

You still mi wife yuh hear.

MAVIS *picks up the knife again and marches towards the door –*

MAVIS. Forgive me Father.

Mi gon' cut 'im rass throat!

MAVIS *jerks the door open –*
She lifts the knife up –

WENDELL *is standing at the door holding the hand of*
a girl barely younger than PRINCESS –

MAVIS *lowers the knife slowly and hides it behind her back –*

Beat.

WENDELL. Mavis. Meet mi darter. Lorna.

Scene Four

Meanwhile…

WENDELL JUNIOR *and* PRINCESS *in the other room. It has two*
single beds – a small wardrobe against one wall and a small chair.

WENDELL JUNIOR *is at the door – listening hard.*

PRINCESS *sits on one of the beds – face hardened – holding back*
tears.

PRINCESS. Mummy hates me now doesn't she?

WENDELL JUNIOR. Princess…

PRINCESS. Junior…

WENDELL JUNIOR. Hush!

WENDELL JUNIOR *goes back to listening at the door –*

PRINCESS. She hates me Junior. She hates me and she's going to
give me away to the Salvation Army like them old jumpers from
when I was a baby.

PRINCESS *lets out a small sob –*

WENDELL JUNIOR. No one hates you Princess.

PRINCESS. But Mummy /

WENDELL JUNIOR. She didn't mean it.

Beat.

Is it still hurting? You want me to blow on it?

PRINCESS. No...

WENDELL JUNIOR. You want a lollipop?

PRINCESS *nods –*

WENDELL JUNIOR *hands her a bright-orange lollipop from his pocket –*

PRINCESS *unwraps it eagerly and pops it into her mouth –*

PRINCESS. Junior?
What did I do that was so bad?
She looked meaner than the headteacher when she's walking down the corridor holding her ruler. She looked meaner than that...

WENDELL JUNIOR. She's trying to...
She wouldn't do it if she didn't have to...
Don't think she will again...
She only did it because she's needing to protect us /

PRINCESS. From what? She hit *me*! That's not protecting!
If I wasn't locked in here, I'd run away.
Next time I *am* going to have to run away. Sneak out in the night /

WENDELL JUNIOR. I told you! She didn't mean it...

She wouldn't if it wasn't because...

Try to grow up Princess. It's important because some things...

You're going to have to start understanding things different soon.

At that moment, the door is opened and LORNA *is shoved into the room –*
Door closes –

Beat.

PRINCESS. Hello.

LORNA. –

PRINCESS. My name is Princess.

What's your name?

LORNA. –

WENDELL JUNIOR. Sit down if you want.

LORNA *moves to sit on the other single bed –*

PRINCESS. That's Junior's bed. It smells of feet. Dirty feet and sweaty socks and –

LORNA *stands back up again –*

WENDELL JUNIOR. You see what you've done!

WENDELL JUNIOR *goes back to listening through the door –*

PRINCESS. Your feet do smell!

LORNA. I like standing.

PRINCESS. What you doing in here? Did you get a slap too? Do you want Junior to give you a lollipop too? It doesn't make the pain go away but it helps.

WENDELL JUNIOR *reaches into his pocket – without looking at* LORNA *pulls out a lollipop – holds it out towards* LORNA *–*

WENDELL JUNIOR. Here…

LORNA. Daddy says I can't take anything from strangers.

WENDELL JUNIOR. –

PRINCESS. If you don't want it I can /

WENDELL JUNIOR. Princess!

LORNA *snatches the lollipop from* WENDELL JUNIOR*'s hand –*

Beat.

LORNA. I'm Lorna.

PRINCESS. Where did you come from?
How old are you?
Do you go to school?
Why do you speak like that?
Where's your daddy? /

WENDELL JUNIOR. Stop!

WENDELL JUNIOR *slumps on the bed – lies down and closes his eyes –*

You don't have to know everything. Some things are secret.

PRINCESS. Mrs Turner says it's not good to keep secrets. She says that they are like a bad bellyache. They won't go away until you let it out. She says secrets are the devil's work. Not a good thing ever comes of secrets she says /

WENDELL JUNIOR. You just going to keep on talking?

PRINCESS *throws* WENDELL JUNIOR *a dirty look –*

PRINCESS. I don't have any secrets.
I don't want to have any secrets.
Secrets can eat you up. From the inside like a zombie or a /

WENDELL JUNIOR. You don't know what you're talking about so why don't you just pipe down.

PRINCESS. I do know. I do. Secrets are bad things. They make people do bad things. They make people ugly.
I have never seen anyone with a secret who is beautiful or smiling.

When George wet himself in class and he tried to keep it a secret. Everyone could tell. He is funny-looking so that's not why. He just didn't smile for the whole day. Like his face forgot how to smile and he looked like he was in pain.

Cos that's the thing with secrets sometimes they show anyway.
No need to keep them.
Secret.
No need to keep your mouth all tight like George had to.
No point.
Cos we can see your wet trousers and we can smell it too.

LORNA. Do you ever stop talking?

PRINCESS *moves to the door –*

PRINCESS. Who is that man talking to Mummy Junior?

PRINCESS*'s hand rests on door handle –*

I want to see his face again /

WENDELL JUNIOR. Only if you're after another hard slap on your face.

PRINCESS. You said she wouldn't do it again /

WENDELL JUNIOR. Mummy is...

She wouldn't if it wasn't *him*.

PRINCESS. Why? Why you not being right Junior? I wish I could start today again! All over again!

Beat.

And Christmas is never going to happen now!

PRINCESS *marches to the bed and throws herself face down on it –*

WENDELL JUNIOR *sits back down on the bed next to* PRINCESS –

WENDELL JUNIOR. '*Not even de devil himself going to stop Christmas inna dis country.*'

PRINCESS *lifts her head from the bed –*
WENDELL JUNIOR *tickles her a little –*
PRINCESS *giggles –*

Beat.

PRINCESS *catches sight of* LORNA *sitting alone. She jumps up and walks over to where* LORNA *sits –*

PRINCESS (*to* LORNA). You're pretty. And your eyes are almost blue...

LORNA. They're green.

PRINCESS. I wish my eyes were blue or green or...

Do you want me to show you my dance for the pageant. It's good isn't it Junior? Want to see...

PRINCESS *doesn't wait for an answer – she takes a place in front of them and starts her dance routine –*

Scene Five

Half-hour later.

MAVIS, WENDELL JUNIOR *and* PRINCESS *sit tightly together on the small sofa.*

WENDELL *sits in the single armchair with* LORNA *perched next to him.*

Long beat.

MAVIS. This chicken can't cook no more.

Let's eat.

Nobody moves –

Nobody hungry now?

WENDELL. Well one ting hard to forget is yuh cooking Mavis.

WENDELL *moves to the small table –* LORNA *following quickly behind him –*
They sit themselves at the table –

MAVIS *watches* WENDELL JUNIOR –

WENDELL JUNIOR *watches* WENDELL –

PRINCESS *watches* LORNA –

PRINCESS *moves to sit at the table –*

MAVIS. Junior I don't want to tell you again.

PRINCESS. You sit next to me Junior.

Will you?

WENDELL JUNIOR *moves to the table –*
He scrapes the chair noisily away from the table and sits as far away from WENDELL *as possible –*

The chicken is carved up and vegetable distributed in the same way it is being done in homes across the land.

LORNA *picks a fork up –*

WENDELL. No Lorna!

WENDELL *puts a hand on* LORNA*'s arm before the first mouthful goes in –*

MAVIS. We still do this the old-fashioned way.
Our people way.

WENDELL. Yuh wan' me to /

MAVIS. Not your place /

WENDELL. Mi try Mavis /

WENDELL JUNIOR. Feet well and truly under the table.

MAVIS. Hush Junior!

Princess you want to say grace?

LORNA. But Daddy I'm hungry /

PRINCESS. Heavenly Father.
Thank you for this delicious chicken that Mummy has cooked.
Thank you for our Christmas tree that Margot find for us.
Thank you for making Junior not so annoying today.
And thank you…

Beat.

And thank you for giving us more people to feed today.

Beat.

Amen!

A chorus of 'Amens' chime around the table –

MAVIS (*to* LORNA). You can eat now chile!

Long beat.

LORNA *eats ravenously –*

The others eat in silence –

WENDELL. Mavis dis chicken…

WENDELL JUNIOR. Mummy this is the best…

Beat.

LORNA. What's for dessert?

PRINCESS. Eh?

MAVIS. Pardon.

PRINCESS. What?

MAVIS. Phyllis James!

No *dessert*.

Apple and spice cake cooling. And I made some custard...

WENDELL. Yuh behave now Lorna.

(*To* MAVIS.) Juss de way har modder bring har up.

MAVIS. I'm sure.

'*Manners tek yu thru' di worl'*.'

Chile...

Lorna...

LORNA. Yes.

MAVIS. You want any more to eat?

Plenty of steam vegetable left in the pot.

LORNA. No thank you.

LORNA *jumps to her feet and leaves the table –*
She flops onto the small sofa –

PRINCESS *gasps –*

WENDELL. Tanking yuh Mavis.

MAVIS *kisses her teeth –*

MAVIS. So...

WENDELL. Yes /

MAVIS. Can you let me /

WENDELL. Yes. Sorry /

MAVIS. I want to /

WENDELL. Look how grown you two ar /

MAVIS. Please don't speak.

WENDELL. Of course /

WENDELL JUNIOR. Yes.

WENDELL. Junior.

MAVIS. Hold your tongue.

WENDELL JUNIOR. It's just /

MAVIS. It just what? /

WENDELL. It nuh easy.

MAVIS. You didn't hear me?

WENDELL. Yes.

MAVIS. No. I mean it Wendell.

PRINCESS. Wendell? But Junior your name is Wendell.

MAVIS. Yes Princess /

WENDELL. Princess /

WENDELL JUNIOR. So what?

MAVIS. If you don't let me speak /

WENDELL JUNIOR. Mummy /

PRINCESS. Mummy why you call him Wendell?

MAVIS. Because he is your father!

   Beat.

PRINCESS. –

WENDELL. Yes Princess.
  Mi yuh daddy /

WENDELL JUNIOR. Whatever you call it /

MAVIS. Junior!

WENDELL. All of yuhs daddy.

   All eyes on LORNA –

   PRINCESS *cannot take her eyes off* LORNA –

PRINCESS. My daddy?

MAVIS. Yes.

WENDELL JUNIOR. It takes more than a word to make a father /

MAVIS. Junior!

WENDELL JUNIOR. How long are they staying for?

MAVIS. Princess you done eating?

Or you going to keep chasing them peas round your plate all day and night?

PRINCESS. I can't catch not one of them…

MAVIS *almost laughs watching her daughter –*

PRINCESS *gives up and rests her fork on the plate –*

These peas are too slippery…

MAVIS. Not the only slippery things still here today my dear.

You go and sit with Lorna and…

You want to show her the pictures of beauty queens Margot been giving to you?

PRINCESS. My pictures?

MAVIS. You know everything about them beauty pageants.

Maybe she wants to know too.

PRINCESS. She can never know as much as me. Margot says I have an encyclo… encyclocdo…

I know a lot!

MAVIS. Yes and today you have someone to talk to about them things without bothering me or your brother…

PRINCESS *leaves the table – exits.*

WENDELL JUNIOR. How long are you planning to stay?

MAVIS *puts a finger to her lips to silence him –*

PRINCESS *enters – and sits silently/awkwardly next to* LORNA *on the small sofa –*
She is holding a large folder/book under one arm –

Beat.

The two girls become engrossed in the pictures – whispering excitedly –

The action at the table becomes more focused – speaking in hushed tones/whispers –

MAVIS. Junior you watch your mouth now /

WENDELL JUNIOR. I'm too big to stay quiet /

WENDELL. Yuh big enuff to be ar man dat's far true.

MAVIS. That is no good reason for rudeness.

WENDELL. Mi understand how de bwoy feeling still.

    MAVIS *walks towards the girls on the sofa –*

MAVIS. Why don't you two girls take them photos and lay them down on my bed. See them better that way.

    PRINCESS *and* LORNA *exit – still engrossed in the book of photos –*

    You sit here for all of ten minutes, and now you feel you can tell me about my own children?

WENDELL. Juss sayin' Mavis.
Mi ar growing bwoy once.

    Dese tings take ar lickle understanding.

    Particula' overstanding.

MAVIS (*turning to* WENDELL JUNIOR). We're giving them food for today.

    All my Christian duty can stretch to.

WENDELL. We 'ave no place to go Mavis /

MAVIS. I can make a bed up for the little one…

WENDELL JUNIOR. Can I leave the table?

MAVIS. I can't turn away the child…

    WENDELL JUNIOR *exits.*

    WENDELL *and* MAVIS *stare each other down –*

    Long beat.

WENDELL. It really very kind of yuh to take mercy on us. Yuh know only so much ar man kyaan do when it come to looking after children dem.

    You will be rewarded in heaven Mavis.

    You nuh hear me breathe till wi get to sekkle somewhere /

MAVIS. No!

I did not say *you* could stay Wendell.
And you do good to remember I am only doing this for that little one.
If not for pity for the child, I would happily cut out your dirty tongue from your mouth!

WENDELL. Mi kyannt wander street. Where mi gon stay?

MAVIS. Wendell. I don't care.

You come get the child when you find somewhere. And if you don't come back in a matter of days, then I hand her over to Salvation Army themselves /

WENDELL. What 'appen far yuh to get so cruel Mavis? De Mavis I remember never tark like dis. De woman mi 'ave dem children wit /

MAVIS. Wha' ya say? De Mavis you wha?…

MAVIS *stands up and slaps* WENDELL *across the face –*

De Mavis you leff you mean? She dead!

WENDELL *jumps to his feet – backing off all the time – whilst* MAVIS *walks towards him – pushing him –*

An' today dis cold-heart woman… she born de day mi wake and find my husband gone!

Mi nearly starve my children waiting 'pon you. Walking street fram Southmead to Hotwells looking far yuh.

MAVIS *points in the direction where her heart should be –*

Nothing here for *yuh*! An' only nuff far the bastard child you choose to have!

WENDELL *grabs his jacket –*

De girl will be here waiting for you tomorrow.

WENDELL *opens the front door –*

MARGOT *enters/bursts in.*

WENDELL *jumps back –*

MARGOT. Someone say my name?!

MAVIS. Margot!

What are you doing here?

MARGOT. Not much.

Just passing in the corridor.

And heard voices…

Voices like I never heard before…

MARGOT *stares directly at* WENDELL –

And you know I'm not one to poke it where it's not wanted but…
Well it looks like I was right.

Voices…

MARGOT *glides over to* WENDELL –
Her voice like butter-wouldn't-melt –

Faces I never heard or seen before.

MAVIS. You're back? /

MARGOT. My name is Margot Barker.

Named after Margot Fonteyn /

MARGOT *holds a hand out to* WENDELL –

WENDELL *nods politely and puts his coat down on the chair –*

WENDELL. Good to meet you.

MAVIS. Thought you still away for next two days at least /

MARGOT. So did I Mavis!
So did I.

MARGOT *pulls up a chair very close to* WENDELL *and takes a seat –*
Crossing her legs seductively –

But turns out my sister-in-law's nothing more than one of the witches from that play…

What 'em call it? The one by Shakespeare…

MAVIS. *Macbeth*?

MARGOT. Yeah that's the one.

MAVIS. You can't talk like that about family.

MARGOT. If you had the displeasure of her face you would have a few choice words too.

Had barely got through the pleasantries before she started on her high-and-mighty speeches about them living with less. The *damned poor* as she likes to call 'em.

Calling each and every one something mean. Scums she would say in between mouthfuls of porridge. Horrible and mean. And well I'm choking on my cuppa. Right mare!

And as we all know I'm living here purely by choice, and well the working-class blood don't quite run through these veins, and I'm no socialist, but couldn't sit there and listen to 'nuffer minute of it.

MAVIS. You walked out?

MARGOT. Well I would of walked out.

If only the silly cow dinned start throwing all my stuff out the door first. Dinned have much choice. Asking me to keep my filthy language to myself. Well she hadn't even heard all I had to say before she threw my best.

You know that fur I'm always promising little Princess? Nearly lost that in the scrap.

Where is my Princess? Missed that little chicken.

And what's for Christmas dinner then?

MAVIS. We've eaten Margot.

MARGOT. Will have to be a sherry and a mince pie then /

MAVIS. No mince pies /

MARGOT. Well many a sailor have done good with sherry alone /

MAVIS. We are a little busy.

MARGOT. Right.

Nowhere else to go and spending Christmas alone it is for me then.

WENDELL. Mi an' yuh both /

MAVIS. We are just *discussing* a few things…

Be no fun for you to be hanging around /

MARGOT. Don't mind me!

MARGOT *throws herself on the armchair* –

Anything going on in these four walls none of my business mind.

WENDELL. Mi nuh say no to ar lickle something hot mi self /

MAVIS. I have no sherry!

MARGOT. Not like you Mavis. Always have everything a guest could ask for in your cupboards.

WENDELL. She de kindest woman mi know. If yuh like it so mi kyaan go buy something. Be good to sit ar lickle an' meet some of dem good people inna yuh life.

MARGOT *gestures a prayer to* MAVIS –

MAVIS. If it keep you quiet!

WENDELL *slaps/rubs his hands together* –

WENDELL. Mi an' de bwoy kyaan go to ar liquor store.

MARGOT. Offie?

WENDELL. Yes dat's de one. Buy dis woman a drink.

Be good to take ar walk. Get to know how de land lie ar lickle.

MARGOT. I can get this one…

MARGOT *reaches into her handbag and pulls out some notes* –

MAVIS. No!
There is no drink in the house because I was not expecting any guests. If any guest turn up on their own accord, then they should bring a bottle as a matter of *respect*.

MARGOT *stifles a laugh* –
Beat.

WENDELL. Maybe mi kyaan find ar lickle someting in dis old coat pocket…

WENDELL *walks towards his coat –*
Puts it on –
Searches pockets briefly –

WENDELL *cocks his head at* MAVIS *and* MARGOT *–*

WENDELL *exits.*

MAVIS (*shouting after* WENDELL). Only when he has something to run from!

MAVIS *busies herself clearing the table –*

MARGOT *watches* MAVIS *intently –*

MARGOT. Well…

Christmas a day for joy and good tidings…
And we just the picture of 'em Christmas cards sat here.

Nice tree. …

MAVIS *pulls out a bottle of rum from a cupboard –*
Holds it out to MARGOT *–*

Mavis James!

MARGOT *helps herself to a glass on the table and quickly pours a drink –*

Beat.

Saw Mrs Bowen day before. She was chirping away at your handiwork for all to hear in the grocer's mind. Said you gone and made better curtains than 'em in Marks and Sparks. Every pleat exactly where it should be.

MAVIS. She's always very good to me.

MARGOT. Well she would be!

MAVIS. Why?

MARGOT. Well you're one and the same so be a bit odd to be against your own /

MAVIS. Not this again!

MAVIS *stops clearing – holds her head in her hands –*

Beat.

MARGOT. You feeling okay Mavis?

Things seem very strange in 'ere.

And your face reminding me of someone who might have just seen a ghost in the flesh...

Dinned know you had a brother. Seems nice /

MAVIS. He is not my brother.
Can't you see?

MARGOT. Barely know my nose is there most days.
You're going to have to give me a bit more /

MAVIS. Even after all these years, and that ridiculous moustache...
Him still the same man.
Nothing changed on his face.

MAVIS *traces the contours of her face –*

And me...

MARGOT. Wait!
You mean...

MAVIS. Yes.

MARGOT. No!!

I mean he is a good-looking fella.
But I'm with you,
Moustache a bit off if you asks me.

PRINCESS *enters –*

PRINCESS. Margot!

PRINCESS *runs towards* MARGOT *and wraps her arms around her as high as she can reach –*

MARGOT. Princess!

PRINCESS. You got any more pictures Margot?

LORNA *enters –*

MARGOT. Who's your friend Princess?

PRINCESS. She's not my friend. She's my sister /

MAVIS. Princess! /

MARGOT. Your what?

> Ark at ee!
> A sister eh?
> Bets that's the best Christmas present you ever had.

> Hello.
> My name is Margot.

PRINCESS. Her name is Lorna.

MARGOT. Hi Lorna.

> (*To* MAVIS.) I mean look at that!
> She must be half half /

MAVIS. Ssshhh…

PRINCESS. Margot can we come to your room and look through your dresses?
And you can tell Lorna all about Weston. And the beach and the donkeys and /

MAVIS. Not today Princess /

MARGOT. Got nothing better to be doing with my time, and
I reckons you could do with having a bit of time to yourself…

> Maybe tidy yourself up a little?

MAVIS. You spoil her.

MARGOT. We'll be just down the corridor if you need us.
Stop worrying.
Put on a nice dress.
You look lush when you give yourself a bit of time in
the mirror.

> MARGOT *pushes her cleavage up* –

> Need a whole half-hour just to get these puppies looking right
> most mornings.

MAVIS. Margot!

MARGOT. That's more like it. The Mavis I know and love.

> Come on mi babbers. Let's be having some dressing up!

> MARGOT *exits – quickly followed by* PRINCESS *and* LORNA.

MAVIS *moves to stand at a mirror –*
She looks closely at the lines on her face –

MAVIS *exits into the bedroom.*

Scene Six

Three days later.

PRINCESS *and* LORNA *sit on a couple of crates – looking extremely bored.*

PRINCESS. Daddy!

    Daddy!

LORNA. I'm hungry.

PRINCESS. I'm tired.

LORNA. We've been waiting for ages.

PRINCESS. You said we were going to the park…

LORNA. It's been a long time now…

PRINCESS. You said we could feed the birds…

LORNA. And have chocolate.

PRINCESS. We haven't had chocolate…

LORNA. Or been to the park.

PRINCESS. We haven't done anything actually…

LORNA. For a long time now…

PRINCESS. Just been sitting here…

LORNA. Waiting…

PRINCESS. And waiting…

LORNA. And I want to go home now…

PRINCESS. And I'm going to tell Mummy!

WENDELL *enters full of cheer – a bundle of money in his hands. He stands with his back to* PRINCESS *and* LORNA. *He carefully folds the bundle, and puts it into his pocket – leaving a single note out.*

WENDELL. Yuh girls nuh appreciate ar single ting. Yuh know where unu stay?

PRINCESS. We are at the docks. There's nothing special here and it smells.

WENDELL. Of steel an' de sweat of hard-workin' men.

LORNA. They don't look like they're sweating.

WENDELL. Dem shipbuilding. Hard work. Good hard-workin' people.

PRINCESS. They don't seem to be working that hard. They're sitting around playing cards with you.

WENDELL. Everybody need ar break!

WENDELL *whips his fingers together – in victorious mood. He waves the single note in front of the girls.*

So now mi going take mi darters out far ar lickle chocolate an' ting. Then maybe buy my Princess – es – some toys. Unno wan' far nothing yuh hear!

PRINCESS. Can we go now?

WENDELL. Mi juss 'ave to tark to one man dere…

Yuh girls stay right 'ere. You nuh move fram 'ere! I juss need to tark to one man 'bout ar dog.

WENDELL *exits.*

In unison –

PRINCESS *and* LORNA. Puppies!!

Beat.

PRINCESS. What was Liverpool like?
Is it the same?
Or is it different?
It must be different because you speak different. Have you been speaking different since you were a baby Lorna?
I like how you speak…

LORNA. –

PRINCESS *leans in* –

PRINCESS. Do you like living in Bristol?

Beat.

Bristol is nice and all but really I think we should move and live in Weston-super-Mare.

Would you like to live in Weston-super-Mare Lorna?

LORNA. I don't know it. I only know home.

PRINCESS. Don't worry when we go to the pageant with Margot, we will see Weston. You will see it really is magic. It has a beach and sand. Golden sand. And they don't have just ice cream, Margot says they have *choc ices*. And donkeys. And everyone there is beautiful that is why they have the pageant there. But don't worry Lorna we won't talk to any boys. Boys get you into trouble Mummy says. Did your mummy ever say that?

LORNA. No. She never really said anything like that.

PRINCESS. Where is your mummy Lorna?

LORNA. Having a rest Daddy said.

PRINCESS. Everyone needs a rest…

Beat.

LORNA. Princess do you want me to stay here forever?

PRINCESS. If you stay here forever I will be happier than the sky Lorna.

But I understand if you have to go away. I missed my daddy even though I couldn't remember him. If you miss your mummy too much, then I will understand. But I will be sad…

Will you be sad Lorna?

WENDELL JUNIOR *and* LEON *enter – cameras in hand.*

PRINCESS *and* LORNA *run towards him. He hugs them tightly.*

Junior!

LEON. Is this…?

WENDELL JUNIOR. Yeah.

LEON. You didn't say she…

WENDELL JUNIOR. Lorna this is my good friend Leon.

Say hello.

LORNA. –

LEON. Hello Lorna.

PRINCESS. Hi Leon!

LEON. Is this a real-life Princess talking to me?

PRINCESS. Yes.

LEON *bows – picks* PRINCESS *up and spins her around – puts her down again –*

WENDELL JUNIOR. Why you here?

Princess answer me!

PRINCESS. We're… we're…

LORNA. Waiting for my daddy /

PRINCESS. Our daddy!

WENDELL JUNIOR. He brought you here? Where is he now?

Why are you waiting for him all alone like this?

PRINCESS. He said he needed to talk to a man about a dog.

LORNA. We're getting a puppy!

LEON (*to* WENDELL JUNIOR). Your mum won't like that!

WENDELL JUNIOR. Right.

WENDELL JUNIOR *grunts with frustration – takes a deep breath –*

Think you two should go back and tell Mummy all about it.

PRINCESS. Daddy said we are not to move.

LEON. This is no place for young girls. There is grown men and dirt and machinery.

WENDELL JUNIOR. Leon can you take them home for me. I'll wait for him to come back.

LEON *tries to grab hold of the girls' hands. They struggle with him.*

LEON. Guess you don't want to pass by the sweet shop on the way back then?

PRINCESS *and* LORNA *stop their fuss – and obediently hook their arms together and follow* LEON *– exiting.*

WENDELL JUNIOR *takes a seat on one of the crates – and waits!*

WENDELL JUNIOR *takes pictures as he waits.*

Time passes at the docks.

WENDELL *enters.*

WENDELL. Junior!

WENDELL *goes to pat* WENDELL JUNIOR *on the back –* WENDELL JUNIOR *flinches and moves away –*

Where yuh sisters?

WENDELL JUNIOR. They went home.

WENDELL. Yuh leff dem to walk all de way back on dem own?

WENDELL JUNIOR. No. But you left them here waiting in this place on their own.

WENDELL. Mi juss leave dem far ar minute. Mi nuh gone long.

Yuh did ar good thing sending dem home anyways /

WENDELL JUNIOR. Don't bring them here again. The docks is not a place for them.

WENDELL. Okay. Okay. Mi hear yuh loud an' correct.

Where you passing through fram? De way you boys move round de city dese days…

WENDELL *produced a pack of cards from his pocket –*

Yuh wan' run ar game of cards?

WENDELL JUNIOR. No.

WENDELL. What 'bout ar run of Cut-Throat?

Yuh looking at de champion of champions.

Beat.

WENDELL JUNIOR. Only thing I want is for you to go!

WENDELL. Wah?!

WENDELL JUNIOR. You heard me. You want to be down here playing cards then go ahead but keep us out of it.

We're doing fine without you.

WENDELL. Son...

WENDELL *reaches out and grabs* WENDELL JUNIOR*'s arm –*

WENDELL JUNIOR *jerks away from* WENDELL*'s grasp – stands up –*

Mi come to make good son. Make right /

WENDELL JUNIOR. Make trouble more like.

WENDELL. Why yuh say dat? Dat wha' yuh modder tell yuh?

WENDELL JUNIOR *turns his back to* WENDELL –

Beat.

Mi know mi do wrong in de past. Yuh 'ave ebbry right to be angry.

Mi spirit troubled since de day mi leff yuh an' yuh modder but ebbryone deserve ar second chance. Yuh nuh say so?

WENDELL JUNIOR *turns to face* WENDELL –

WENDELL JUNIOR. You're a liar! Everyone knows it.

WENDELL. Dis stink-up attitude 'ave to end some time mi son. Some time cus only so long mi put up wit dis kinda disrespect yuh know.

WENDELL JUNIOR. So? So what you going to do about it?

WENDELL. Mi nuh business wit yuh son /

WENDELL JUNIOR. Yeah I know. You're not here for me. Or for Princess or even for Lorna. You've come back just so you can leave again. That's what you want isn't it? To break us all over again.

I won't let you...

Quicker than imaginable, WENDELL JUNIOR *grabs* WENDELL *by the neck, they struggle with each other until* WENDELL *has* WENDELL JUNIOR *pinned up against the wall –*

WENDELL JUNIOR *doesn't resist –*

WENDELL. Inna yuh shoes mi too be ready to break ar man but yuh kyannt put yuh hand 'pon yuh fadder Junior. Yuh kyannt do it nuh matter what pain yuh.

WENDELL *lets go of* WENDELL JUNIOR *and straightens himself up –*

Mi juss wan' talk to you son. Mi know mi 'ave ar long way to go before yuh look 'pon mi like ar fadder again. An' wha mi do to yuh modder...

Mi proud of yuh far protectin' yuh modder an' sister but yuh 'ave to tell mi wha' mi do 'bout dis business.

Mi here to do what mi kyann to be ar good fadder and ar 'usband. Nuthing yuh kyaan do to change dat. So yuh need to fix up yuh attitude Junior. Cus yuh see son, no matter how yuh carry on, De Hustler back!

WENDELL *fixes the hat on his head and moves to leave –*

An' when mi start making big big money yuh soon be telling everybody in dis Bristol who yuh daddy be. Yuh be proud son. Mi nuh leave till mi make yuh proud as ar peacock. Yuh hear mi?

WENDELL JUNIOR *slumps back down on the crate – and cries hard hot tears –*

Scene Seven

St Agnes, Bristol. January 1963.

PRINCESS, LORNA *and* MARGOT *sit at the table – the girls busy drawing –* MARGOT *is reading a magazine.*

WENDELL *enters.*
He is wrapped in blankets and shivering a little.

PRINCESS *and* LORNA. Daddy!

    Both girls run to throw their arms around WENDELL –

MARGOT. Oh!

    I wasn't expecting any visitors…

WENDELL. Mi juss come far ar lickle something hot /

MARGOT. There's a caff down the road /

WENDELL. Mi 'ave juss pennies in mi pocket /

MARGOT. That right?

WENDELL. Mi 'ave every right to come see mi children an' mi wife /

MARGOT. She's not here mind so…

    WENDELL *sits –*

WENDELL. Mi wait…

MARGOT. If you want!

PRINCESS. You're cold Daddy.

WENDELL. Yes mi know Princess. Still sleeping where mi kyaan find.

    Juss need ar lickle coffee fi warm up my flesh an' bones /

MARGOT. Alright mi babbers you go in your room now and clean up that mess we made earlier cos I don't want to be here if your mother sees it like that.

WENDELL. Bible or belt.

    WENDELL *laughs at his own joke –*

    PRINCESS *and* LORNA *exit.*

MARGOT. Yes but she got a lot of heart too. Looks after everyone. And I look after her.

WENDELL. Dat very good of *yuh*.

MARGOT. You ask anyone on this street, they'll tell you Mavis and me are always together. I help her out and she…

She looks out for me. And not one of *'em* messes with me because they know I'm with Mavis. That's how it works round 'ere.

That's what you do for family. You look after *your* family. You go out. You get a decent job /

WENDELL. Fram where?
I take mi self down to dat job exchange every day. Standing in dat line far hours in dat smelly, smoky, crowded office room. An' after mi come out of dere, walk de whole ar de street knocking on shop daw an' factory askin' far any employment. Still nutting!
If rumours true den dem nuh wan' us far any work!

MARGOT. Well it has been a long time since you been here…

Things changing. They've changed in here. And they're changing out there too.

WENDELL JUNIOR *enters with* LEON *in tow –*
WENDELL JUNIOR *stares at* WENDELL *–*
He walks silently to chair, sits and plays with his camera –
LEON *stays standing awkwardly –*

Junior? You alright handsome?

WENDELL JUNIOR. What's he doing here?

LEON. Hello Mrs…

Margot…

MARGOT. Leon you growing into a real man too I see. Guess you two have the young girls all after you.

LEON. No time for girls. Want a real woman.

LEON *moves closer to* MARGOT *–*

MARGOT *moves closer to* LEON *–*

I'm working now. Got income. Enough to take a woman out dancing /

MARGOT. And which woman you think you're going to be dancing with chicken?

LEON. Well…

LEON *attempts to casually lean on a wall and slips –*

MARGOT *moves back to* WENDELL JUNIOR *–*

MARGOT. Junior you not yourself these days.

WENDELL JUNIOR. Things not so right *here* any more.

LEON. Things are looking good from where I'm standing!

MARGOT *throws* LEON *an exasperated look –*

WENDELL. Yuh 'ave nowhere you 'ave to be Margot now Junior 'ere?

MARGOT. I do actually!

MARGOT *walks over to* WENDELL JUNIOR *–*

You alright to keep an eye out for your sisters? I have to go help out with that am-dram lot again for an hour or so. Don't know why I signed up now. When a charitable deed must be done, well it seems I always ends up being called in. It's like people can see all that kindness and goodness pouring out of me. When you've got a face like this, you have to be careful people don't take advantage…

Even though I wouldn't mind the caretaker taking advantage once in a while /

WENDELL. Watch yuh words, dem juss boys.

LEON *coughs –*

WENDELL JUNIOR. I'm not a boy! You think I don't know about the world. About what it means to be a man… a Black man /

MARGOT. Anyways *Junior* make sure your ma don't get upset about nothing when she gets back in.

MARGOT *squeezes* WENDELL JUNIOR*'s cheeks –*
She smiles a dry smile at WENDELL *–*
She saunters past LEON *and exits.*

Long beat.

WENDELL. Junior…

WENDELL JUNIOR. –

WENDELL. Junior. Mi come to talk far true.

LEON (*whispering*). Look I better be going…

LEON *stands –*

WENDELL JUNIOR. You said you show me that thing with the aperture again /

WENDELL. You hear mi?

LEON. It's just /

WENDELL JUNIOR. Leon you said!

LEON. Told my dad I've go help him set up for this meeting thing.

WENDELL JUNIOR. At the boys' club?

LEON. You know what his 'disappointed in you' face is like.

WENDELL JUNIOR. Yes.

LEON. Sorry.

WENDELL JUNIOR. Think there's still talk about a colour bar /

WENDELL. De rumours true den? About dem stopping upright men fram working?

LEON. Likely.

WENDELL JUNIOR. Wish I was coming with /

WENDELL. Mi nuh see you far ar few days…

WENDELL JUNIOR. It's just… I can't… leave my sisters /

WENDELL. If yuh wan' step out, mi stay wit dem girls /

WENDELL JUNIOR. I wouldn't trust you with a dog!

LEON. Junior!

WENDELL. Yuh wan' fight mi every time bwoy?

WENDELL JUNIOR *jumps to his feet –*

WENDELL JUNIOR. Why not!

WENDELL *moves towards* WENDELL JUNIOR –

WENDELL. Just trying to be a father /

WENDELL JUNIOR. Don't need you! Leon's daddy looks out for me fine. Lent me this camera. Said I could have it as Mummy dinned have enough… And gave me the paper round in his shop so I could save up. A man should have saving he said. Dinned he Leon?

Leon's daddy been more of a daddy to me than you!

WENDELL. Dat so!

WENDELL JUNIOR. He's a good man. Does for other people not just himself.

WENDELL. Is it? You wan' hear some good things mi do too. Mi used to cut a man's hair good back in de day.

Beat.

What 'im do so impressive?

WENDELL JUNIOR. Getting involved in the protests. Standing up for good things.

WENDELL. Protest? Here in Bristol?

Dis true Leon?

WENDELL JUNIOR *stares hard at* WENDELL –

LEON. Yes. If people start making noise, they will take notice. That's what my dad says anyway.

WENDELL. Dat true!

If yuh daddy involve maybe mi kyaan /

WENDELL JUNIOR *laughs hard and loud* –

WENDELL JUNIOR. I already warn Leon not to believe anything you say!

WENDELL *kisses his teeth and moves to pour himself another drink* –

LEON. I have to go.

WENDELL JUNIOR *stands* –
He shakes his head at LEON *to try to make him stay* –

LEON *grabs* WENDELL JUNIOR *by the shoulders and pulls him towards the front door – out of* WENDELL*'s earshot –*

Cool it Junior.

You dig?

WENDELL JUNIOR. It's just /

LEON. He's your daddy. He deserves a little…

Stay cool.

Yeah?

WENDELL JUNIOR. Yes yes!

You think my photos are getting better Leon?

LEON. Maybe!

WENDELL JUNIOR *and* LEON *laugh – and touch hands –*

LEON *exits.*

WENDELL JUNIOR *moves to go to his room –*

WENDELL. Come talk to me /

WENDELL JUNIOR. I need to read.

WENDELL *reaches to grab* WENDELL JUNIOR –

WENDELL JUNIOR *shrugs him off –*

WENDELL. Junior yuh gon' 'ave tark to me man to man
some time?
Mi need to explain some tings to *yuh* /

WENDELL JUNIOR. You know what they call a boy without
a father round here?
Do you?
Bastard!
A bloody bastard! /

WENDELL. Mi beg yuh stop!

When mi come to dis country I was ar good man.
Ar soldier.
Fight far King an' country.
But it never make far respec'.

Fram dis Englishman.
Dem just throw mi out of the army, and expect mi to live
on air.
Mi try to make it work for all af us.
Truly.
But here...

Beat.

Even now everywhere mi go looking far work, dem look at mi
so so...
An' grown men wit ar family scratching around far even ar
paper round.
Wha' kinda world?!
Wha' kinda world put men in de same sentence as dogs?
Supm 'ave ta change fram de days of mi ancestors.
'Ave ta!

WENDELL *pours himself a large drink –*

WENDELL JUNIOR. Why have you come back? It still the same.
Nothing is different /

WENDELL. Mi trying to tark to yuh straight...

WENDELL JUNIOR. Sounds like excuses to me.

WENDELL. Excuses?

WENDELL JUNIOR. Lots of excuses.

WENDELL JUNIOR *gets up to leave –*

WENDELL. Yuh nuh live yet.
Yuh young'un still.
One day yuh understand.

Lorna's modder...
She kind.
Give mi time an' ar roof over mi head when de squat got raided.
Wi juss living together for ar while.
No-ting more.
But den...
Well wit de right music an' drink...
An' ar lickle moonlight...
Tings 'appen.
Den odder tings 'appen nine months later.
An' I could've leff it at dat.

Yes I could've gone den an' dere.
But mi remember unu.
'Pon mi modder's life mi never forget yuh.
Yuh an' ya sister an'...
Tink only ar fool make ar mistake like dat twice.
Leave anodder chile?
Nuh mi kyannt do it.
Mi juss kyannt do it.
And ting is...
Lorna modder not well.
In de head.
Yuh understand?
She start show signs.
Har heart good, but har mind trouble beyon' help.
After she done screaming de street down 'bout de black devil
who come an' possess her.
Rape har.
So dey take har arway one day.
'Ave to hold har firm all de way to de hospital.

People start writing all sort of nonsense 'pon mi door.
On de house.
Windows break every day till one day mi come back to find ar
rope hanging fram de tree outside de house.
An' I never plan to be nuh strange fruit.
Yuh understand son.
Never plan dat.

WENDELL JUNIOR. Well at least you didn't leave in the middle
of the night this time.

Beat.

WENDELL. I leave in de mawnin'. Juss as yuh waking /

WENDELL JUNIOR. I didn't know the difference between early
morning and night.
I didn't know the difference between another day and goodbye.
(*Shouting.*) Why are you even talking to me about these things /

MAVIS *enters.*

MAVIS. Junior! You want to get us the reputation of being like
them angry Black people?

WENDELL. It not 'im fault Mavis. Wi juss 'aving ar lickle man till man.

Beat.

Why yuh always 'ave to be de prettiest gyal 'pon de street?

MAVIS *kisses her teeth loudly –*

MAVIS. The girls eat yet? Princess! Lorna!

PRINCESS *and* LORNA *run out of the other room –*

WENDELL JUNIOR *exits.*

PRINCESS. Mummy! It's the best thing in the world having a sister. We were holding hands all through the market, and everyone wants to talk to us.
Everyone was saying we must be sisters because I tell them everything Lorna likes and /

MAVIS. Princess James you going to let Lorna speak for herself? Lorna you like the market?

WENDELL. Sound like de girls 'ave a busy day /

MAVIS. We can't all be idle.

You come to collect her then?

LORNA. Are we going home Daddy?

WENDELL. No.
Mavis. Mi looking everywhere far some place decent to put mi head down but only manage to find ar few old friends who 'ave ar chair or two. Mi kyannt be moving ar young girl dis way an' dat /

MAVIS. Well it take as long as it take. She safe and happy here until…
You like it here Lorna?

Beat.

WENDELL. Answer when yuh been asked ar question Lorna.

LORNA. Yes Daddy. I like having a sister.

WENDELL. I juss come to warm up an' check on mi girls…

I better be going…

WENDELL *gets to his feet – feebly and unsteady –*

PRINCESS. Mummy!

MAVIS. Yes Princess.

PRINCESS. If someone is cold all the time, you wouldn't let them stay out in the cold would you? You're too kind like that aren't you Mummy?

And you always say that '*God watch the devil in people all the time.*'

WENDELL *stifles a laugh –*

Daddy could share a room with Junior.

And then we would all be together, and Lorna wouldn't cry at night so much…

MAVIS. Why didn't you tell me she been crying?

Long beat.

WENDELL. Yuh nuh worry Mavis. Yuh already done good by us dese last few weeks…

MAVIS. Go tell Junior to make up the beds while I cook. You girls will have to come in with me.

PRINCESS. We can help Junior make the beds. I'm good at making beds.

PRINCESS *hooks her arm into* LORNA*'s – they exeunt.*

MAVIS. The rules simple.
You sleep only in that room.
You never walk around the house half-dressed /

WENDELL. Mi know de temptation dat come over woman when mi inna small vest.

MAVIS *gives him the coldest stare imaginable –*

MAVIS. You use the bathroom only after we all done getting ready for school and work. You wash every plate and spoon you use. You never bring no woman into this house. You never bring no friend into this house. And you have just two weeks to find somewhere else to take yourself and that child.

WENDELL. Mavis mi kyannt tank yuh enuff. All mi want is to be here with mi family /

MAVIS. You listen to mi good Wendell. If you so much as look or do mi or mi children de wrong way, mi call de police on you. An' mi personally tell dem to lock you up far good. Still things I remember that can put you an' your backside inna police cell. You remember dat!

MAVIS *exits.*

WENDELL *sits back down at the table and smiles wryly to himself –*

ACT TWO

Scene One

St Agnes, Bristol. May 1963.

MAVIS *sits at the table.*
Her sewing machine tapping rhythmically.

PRINCESS *and* LORNA *enter.*

PRINCESS *is dressed in school uniform.*

PRINCESS *has her head down.*
She runs to the sofa and throws herself across it sobbing loudly.

LORNA *stands holding a school bag.*

MAVIS. What happen *today*?
    That teacher saying meanness to you again?
    Those teachers need to realise they can't keep putting my
    children on some dunce table.

    Tomorrow I'm going /

    Another loud sob from PRINCESS –

    Beat.

    Phyllis James are you not going to answer me?

    Beat.

LORNA. She was crying hard all the way home.

MAVIS. Why?

    WENDELL *enters.*
    He is holding a big box –

LORNA. Daddy!!

    LORNA *runs to* WENDELL –
    Hugging him –

    WENDELL *puts the box down –*

MAVIS *doesn't take her eyes off the box –*

WENDELL. Hello Princess…

I mean…

All mi favourite girls inna one room.

LORNA. Daddy when are we going home?

WENDELL. I tell yuh already 'bout asking dat.

MAVIS. What you bringing in my house Wendell James?

WENDELL. Just a little something I pick up fram ar man…

For Junior!

MAVIS *gestures at* WENDELL –

An' how is my Princess today?

Beat.

WENDELL *stands over* PRINCESS *who is still motionless –*

How school go Princess?

WENDELL *kneels down –*
He taps PRINCESS *gently –*

Baby girl?

Yuh know mi go by dat shop with all dem princesses dress today. De real pretty ones /

LORNA. I know why she is crying.

MAVIS. Someone saying mean things on the way home?

LORNA. No.

MAVIS. She fall and hurt herself?

LORNA. No.

MAVIS. –

LORNA. I think it was…

She wasn't crying before. But then she started to cry.
Or maybe she was crying before but I only hear it after /

WENDELL. After what Lorna?

LORNA. After Barbara invited me to her birthday party.

Says there's going to be a big cake and a clown.

A real-life clown!

MAVIS. Why would that make her cry?
That girl love cake like people love Jesus!

LORNA. She didn't invite Phyllis.

MAVIS. She invite only you?

LORNA. Yes…

WENDELL. Children!

PRINCESS *jumps up suddenly and exits to the bedroom –*

LORNA. And she started crying. Crying all the way home…

I want to go to Barbara's party Daddy. Barbara says that I can even wear my hair like hers if I like /

WENDELL. Did *she*?

MAVIS. No one going to no birthday party with such a mean girl /

LORNA. But she asked *me*.

Daddy I can go can't I?

WENDELL. It nuh dat simple Lorna.

Yuh sister /

LORNA. But Barbara says she can't invite Phyllis!

MAVIS. And why is that?

WENDELL. Mavis!

Lissen Lorna. Dere is nuh talking on dis. If yuh sister nuh good nuff far har party den yuh not good nuff far har party. Dat simple.

LORNA *stomps off in a huff – exits.*

Beat.

MAVIS. You don't think to educate that girl?

She is going to learn the hard way one day.

WENDELL. Where she come fram dese things nuh spoken 'bout Mavis /

MAVIS. But she half come from you so /

WENDELL. Why yuh always on mi?

MAVIS. Maybe because I have more than enough experience of you not doing what you're suppose to do for your family.

WENDELL. Yuh nuh see mi trying?

WENDELL *starts to undo his shoes –*

MAVIS. Once a hustler always a hustler!

WENDELL. Mi show yuh Mavis!

Yuh juss 'ave ta give mi ar lickle chance.

Ar lickle chance to be ar better man.

MAVIS. For what? So you can go running back to Liverpool?

WENDELL. Lissen 'ere. Dat business over. Over.

MAVIS. I don't care to hear about it.

Beat.

WENDELL. Yuh de woman far me.

Remember how it used to be?
Remember how wi used to laugh. Like children ourselves.
Yuh sitting on mi knee.
Drinking rum.
Yuh face all bright…
Still is…
Yuh lips always juss de right shade of pretty.
An' yuh legs Mavis…
Still…

MAVIS. Right now you're talking like a madman.

WENDELL. Mi juss saying yuh legs enuff to drive ar wild man 'alf outta 'im mind /

MAVIS. You want to talk about my legs?
What about these hands that been doing the work of two people? /

WENDELL. Mavis /

MAVIS. Wendell how you think we have food? When mi nuh here sewing till my fingers turn blue, mi out there asking every woman if she need a new dress. Then I come back and sew them ones too!

MAVIS is close to tears –

WENDELL. One day dem hands nuh work no more mi promise.

It only ar matter of time before I find mi ar lickle pay packet. Den mi buy ar house – ar 'hol' house far mi wife. Ar house wit ar staircase, ar garden, inna better street. Nuh dis place where everybody live on top of everybody.

WENDELL stands, walks towards MAVIS and pulls her to a small window –

Yuh look out de winda Mavis. What yuh see? Juss de backa more house. Nuh trees. Nuh hills like back home. Yuh nuh worry.
Only ar matter of time before mi start to give yuh de best in life an' take yuh out ageen. No worries mi whine yuh off dem feet...

WENDELL in one quick movement grabs MAVIS and spins her fast in a dance –

MAVIS. Wendell!
You lost your mind?

They spin faster –

You nothing more than a jack – ass!

MAVIS laughs out loud –

WENDELL. Like dem first dances in ar Monty's.
Remember?

MAVIS. I remember.

WENDELL. An' den slow dance when mi pull yuh up close...

WENDELL pulls MAVIS close by the waist –

An' wi push up 'pon each other till de last person leave /

MAVIS. –

WENDELL JUNIOR enters.

MAVIS jumps out of WENDELL's embrace –

WENDELL. Son /

MAVIS. Where you been Junior?

WENDELL. I find something far yuh /

WENDELL JUNIOR. I'm going to my room /

WENDELL. If yuh juss give mi ar minute of yuh time…

> WENDELL JUNIOR *moves towards the other room* –

> WENDELL *moves to pick up the box* –

No wait! Junior! It ar piece of equipment…

He hands it to WENDELL JUNIOR –

WENDELL JUNIOR *tentatively opens it* –

WENDELL JUNIOR. Oh!

WENDELL. You like it son?

MAVIS. What is it? Junior? It junk?

> WENDELL *kisses his teeth* –

WENDELL JUNIOR. No.
It's a Tully flash.

MAVIS. What?

WENDELL JUNIOR. A light. I've been reading about it and now…

MAVIS. Well education is never a bad thing.

> WENDELL JUNIOR *goes towards his room* –

Junior you forget your mind. I haven't heard thank you yet.

> WENDELL JUNIOR *turns to face* WENDELL –

WENDELL JUNIOR. Thank you.

WENDELL. How yuh paying far dose books den Junior?

WENDELL JUNIOR. Got more hours at the shop delivering. And more hours work cleaning at the pub…

MAVIS. Him saving.

WENDELL. Saving far wha'?

WENDELL JUNIOR. I got go see Leon about this /

MAVIS. No. Not for now Junior. You going out too much these days. I never know where to find you /

WENDELL JUNIOR. Me and my boys have ar squat.
That's where we spend most of our days.

But today we were mainly at the boys' club because today they held a press conference…

Five days from now, the students are holding a march in support. They've got people behind them now.

MAVIS. Who and what?

WENDELL JUNIOR. The bus boycott! They've officially called for a boycott. Today May 1st. Today it has happened. We can't ride the buses no more until they win.

MAVIS. Who *we*?

WENDELL JUNIOR. Black people. *Us*.

MAVIS. How am I meant to get up the hills by Totterdown?
I tried it once, and had to sit down halfway up.

Anyway none of these people forget the days that we have to walk a whole hour to get to school. The bus system here like a dream compared to that /

WENDELL JUNIOR. But Mummy you have to support. They're doing it for us too.

MAVIS. Is it?

WENDELL. Mi kyaan support son.

Junior wha yuh say?

Yuh an' yuh father united in the struggle?

WENDELL JUNIOR *exits*.

Scene Two

St Agnes, Bristol. June 1963.

PRINCESS, *eyes closed, stands in the cupboard room.*
She is wearing a swimming costume and a sash around her.
She raises her hands in the air and places a crown made of
cardboard and tinsel on her head.

VOICE-OVER. *Ladies and gentlemen, I present to you the winner*
of the year's Weston-super-Mare Beauties of the West Contest –
(Voice booming.) Princess James.

PRINCESS*'s eyes open wide.*
The cupboard room explodes into a world of pageantry – seems
less alive… still there… but somehow subdued.

PRINCESS *approaches the microphone.*

PRINCESS. I…

    I…

    My name is Phyllis Princess James. I want to wear this crown…

    I want to be the prettiest girl in the whole of Weston-super-Mare
    and Bristol…

    But everyone in school says I can't be…

    PRINCESS *picks up a small round mirror –*
    She stares at her reflection in it –

    Because…

    PRINCESS *touches her lips –*

    And my hair? And my skin is…

    Beat.

    Maybe I don't want to look like everyone else…

    PRINCESS *hears a noise –*
    The sound of a key turning in the door. The door opens –
    PRINCESS *opens the door of the cupboard quietly –*
    A light is switched on.

    MAVIS *and* MARGOT *enter –* MARGOT *is shrieking with*
    laughter.

MAVIS *tries to shush her quiet.*

WENDELL *follows quickly behind.*

They all seem a little bit tipsy.

MARGOT *almost falls over a large stack of packaged toilet rolls.*

MAVIS. You trying to wake the whole building up Margot?

MARGOT. What are those?

WENDELL. What they look like?

MARGOT. Where you get those from Mavis?

WENDELL. Actually I bring them. I have a friend /

MARGOT. Just the one then!

MARGOT *laughs hard –*

MAVIS. Margot!

WENDELL. Mi providing far mi family anyway mi choose to.

MAVIS. My feet hurt so much. I'm sure they about to drop off.

MARGOT. But that was so much fun.

MAVIS. You gave them something to look at for certain.

MARGOT. Nevers seen Mavis enjoy herself so much.
And those dance moves?
Didn't think you had it in you.

MAVIS. These hips do more than push baby /

MARGOT. I nevers seen pushing like that before.

MAVIS. You want me to show you how?

MAVIS *starts to whine her hips to imaginary music –*

MARGOT *tries to imitate – badly –*

WENDELL *sidles up to* MAVIS *– dancing close behind her –*

WENDELL. You see wha' dese Black wimmin kyaan do t'yuh!
Dat's it baby /

MAVIS *moves him away from him –*

MAVIS. All women know how to get a man to do things /

WENDELL. Is it?

MARGOT. I think I was getting plenty of attention myself.
Dint you see?
All sorts of attempts to you know…

WENDELL. Yuh making plenty attempts yuh self.
No place safe fram de white woman *attempts*.

MARGOT. What you say?

WENDELL. De club welcome everybody for sure.

Only inna Bristol yuh see so many different different people in
same place.

MARGOT. Nearly danced until I broke my back mind /

WENDELL. I'm surprised yuh mout nuh pain yuh too.
De way yuh chat chat to every person like…

MARGOT. Like what?

WENDELL. Well like yuh nuh know how to behave round people
sometimes.

MAVIS. We had a nice evening.
Let's not spoil it /

MARGOT. I am a very friendly person if you must know.

WENDELL. Especially with de Black man it seem /

MARGOT. That being the only men available in there.
I play with the hands I got if you gets what I mean like.

WENDELL. No mi nuh *gets* it.

MARGOT. Well you clearly not shy with the white woman…

WENDELL. Dere go dat mouth again.

Wan-time fool no fool, but two-time fool damn fool!

MAVIS. Wendell!

Another drink Margot?

WENDELL. Tink *she* might need to be getting back.

MARGOT. No ways.

What you got?
More of that dark rum?
Might help to loosen these hips mind.

MAVIS. You going to make it back upstairs?

MARGOT. Might pass out on your sofa /

WENDELL. Mi carry yuh out if mi 'ave to.

MAVIS *hands* MARGOT *a glass of rum* –

MARGOT. You got enough of them eyes on you in there too
Mavis.
A few men in there who wouldn't have minded having
a dance /

WENDELL. *She* ar married woman!

MARGOT. Lighten up Wendell.

MAVIS. I don't care who's watching.
Since that place open last year, I just put it down as a place of
sin.
But you know I might actually go back.
How you get to hear about that place Wendell?

WENDELL. Mi kyaant tell yuh dat…

WENDELL *taps his nose* –

MARGOT. Hustler by name.
Hustler by nature /

WENDELL. Wha' yuh know 'bout dat?
Yuh see mi in de days when mi hustle proper?

Take de clothes fram ya back an' yuh still be standing dere
naked askin' how dat come t'be.
Slicker dan oil.
Faster dan lightning.
Hustle ar man outta 'im own witout breaking ar sweat!
Enuff story to tell.

MARGOT. Don't sound like nothing to be proud of if you asks me.
Taking what's not yours. Got another word for that /

MAVIS. That's the old Wendell /

WENDELL. Mi nuh play like dat no more.

Beat.

MAVIS. Been a long time since I dance like that.
And with *my* people.

WENDELL. It juss make mi happy to see yuh like it Mavis.

MARGOT. We could go back now.
It's still going.
Come on Mavis.
You know you wants to.

WENDELL. Mavis got ar lot to be doing tomorrow so /

MAVIS. Tomorrow is Sunday.

WENDELL. Yes an' de struggle nuh 'ave nuh days off.

MARGOT. What struggle?
No one going to be hiring tomorrow.
A day of rest.
For me head anyways.

WENDELL. Mi involved inna bigger fight now.
Bigger dan five pounds of Queen's money.
I tink dem boys wit de buses got something 'bout right /

MARGOT. You mean that silly bus-boycott lot?
In the papers making all sorts of accusations.
It's not like that here.
No reason to take it personal like.
You just have to accept how things are.

WENDELL. Nuh reason?

Nuh eberyting dat 'ave sugar sweet.

Yuh mean to tell mi when even ar Boys' Brigade officer nuh get
ar job cus 'im colour is far no good reason?

MAVIS. Margot don't mean it like that /

MARGOT. Yes I do.
There are some good people here.

You want things to change then you do it peaceful and all.
People trying to get along with each other.
Nobody wants that kind of trouble round here.

WENDELL. Wi see 'bout dat.
Yuh know de man running things in de boycott Paul
Stephenson?
'Im born here.
Dis country belong to alla us.

MARGOT. Hold on a minute.
People haves to be accommodated that's for sure, and many
people round here doing their best to be tolerating of youse, and
your West Indian churches, and you've got to be mindful of *us*.

WENDELL. Wi done being mindful /

MARGOT. Not sure that's a good idea.
And no one going to be thanking you when you start taking
away their overtime by giving work to them who never really…

Well…

My brother Dan. Other brother. Not that one married to that
mouthy cow. The other one. Lives down by Bedminster. He
been working on them buses since he come out of school. He's a
good sort. A proper worker. Fixed your door lock dinned he
when you couldn't find your keys 'member? Good laugh too.
He works on them buses. I don't want to see him out of work
cos of all this raucous…

Beat.

You got any more of this rum. Bloody delicious it is /

MAVIS. You want to drink me dry?

Anyway my legs feel like two piece ar dead wood. I'm going to
go…

Margot you let yourself out.

WENDELL. Mavis wi only juss start…

MAVIS *exits*.

Beat.

MARGOT *pours herself another large glass of rum – which she
downs in one mouthful –*

Tink yuh need to slow down.

MARGOT. Don't worry about me love.
Margot Barker not your average woman.

Can drink and talk anyones under the table.

WENDELL. Like yuh an' dat mouth running all over tings you
know nuffin 'bout?

Beat.

MARGOT. Look 'ere!
Don't get me wrong.
You're alright.
I mean I know you.
I knows many of your lot.
Makes no difference to me.
But some of them men depend on those overtime hours.
And you start giving those hours to other people, foreigners
like, then well it's not going to go down well is it?

WENDELL. An' what 'bout de men dat need to feed deer children
too?
Do right far deer families.
Make deer women proud.
Have enuff spare change to treat dem like queens once in
ar while.

MARGOT. Queens?!
There's only one Queen in this country.

MARGOT *laughs out loud –*

There's other jobs.
Better suited to them /

WENDELL. It driving damn buses.
Who nuh suit dat?

Yuh tink it juss de buses? De police, de fire brigade, de NHS
dey all discriminating. When de last time yuh see somebody
brown inna senior position inna hospital or classroom?

MARGOT. Don't shoot the messenger.

WENDELL. Yuh nuh messenger. Yuh juss anodder white woman
trowing herself where she nuh wanted.

MARGOT. Them Liverpool ladies certainly got you all riled up.

WENDELL. Wha' yuh know 'bout Liverpool?

MARGOT. Mavis tells me everything. Like family I am.

And they abouts the only family I've got so…

And I gets to walk in parts of the city others can't cus everyone round here knows how close we are. Walk into any church I like on any Sunday. I don't. But I could if I ever wants to.

WENDELL. Mi see it all before Margot.
Yuh nuffin special.
As stale as de week's bread.
Happy to be seen wit ar nigger.
Even do de missionary ting for ar nigger but when it come down to it Margot, yuh always stand by yuh own.

Yuh think mi lie?

MARGOT. Suit yourself.
Only trying to say it as it is.

We'll all be using the buses next week as usual.

But I tell you what Mavis don't need none of this. She has taken to walking everywhere. Like she hasn't got enough on her plate, now she's walking back and forth to show *support*.

She could do without the troubles you lot bringing. She's a good sort and not one to rock the boat that brought her here.

And you do good to remember that Wendell James.

WENDELL *kisses his teeth* –

Now to top up that beauty sleep!

MARGOT *grabs a pack of toilet roll – and exits.*

WENDELL *stands shaking his head after* MARGOT –

MAVIS *enters.*

WENDELL. Dat woman!

If speech wort shillin, silence worth pound!

MAVIS. Quiet down Wendell! She's just got a big mouth, but she innocent really.

And my head paining real bad now /

WENDELL. Saying what everybody else tinks.

Mavis, mi kyaant leave dis alone.

Now dem man Roy Hackett an' Paul Stephenson announce de bus boycott it all going to get very interesting. Wi 'ave to do everything wi kyaan.

Tomorra mi knocking on every door an' church of every Black person inna Bristol telling dem 'bout dis situation. Giving leaflet. Tarking 'bout the real struggle.

Educate dem.

MAVIS *moves to stand close to* WENDELL –

Dis is serious tings Mavis.

De unions, all of dem dey 'ave to answer far dis colour bar. Dey 'ave ta answer to us far taking food outta children mouth.

Dey 'ave ta!

Beat.

MAVIS. You make me proud *'usband*.

WENDELL. It sweet to hear yuh call mi yuh *'usband* again. Yuh mean dat Mavis?

Beat.

MAVIS. Yes.

WENDELL. An' mi get all de rights of ar husband too?

MAVIS. I can't think what rights you talking about?

MAVIS *and* WENDELL *are now playing a game of cat and mouse around the table* –

WENDELL. I mean de rights ar man might 'ave if 'im find 'imself inna de marital bed.

MAVIS. Who say anything about a bed? Not everything 'ave ta happen inna bed.

WENDELL *bites his hand with frustration* –

WENDELL. Where?...

Mi mean...

How...

Yuh playing wit mi Mavis James?

MAVIS *stops running* –

WENDELL *moves to stand face to face with* MAVIS –

Beat.

MAVIS. Why don't you turn off the lights and I tell you?

WENDELL. Sweet Jesus.
Tank you!

WENDELL *slaps* MAVIS *on backside again* –

MAVIS *giggles* –

PRINCESS *closes the door to the cupboard again* –
She sits with her back firmly against the door –
Sighs heavily –

Scene Three

St Agnes, Bristol. June 1963.

The room is filled with boxes labelled – 'Broken Biscuits'.

MAVIS, WENDELL, PRINCESS *and* LORNA *are sitting on the sofas and armchairs.*

MAVIS *is plaiting* PRINCESS*'s hair.*

WENDELL *is reading a newspaper.*

LORNA *is playing with a doll.*

WENDELL. Dem really showing themselves up now.
Can't believe wha' my man here saying 'bout de bus boycott.
Wait…
Let mi juss read yuh ar lickle section of dis –

Beat.

'*It is true that London Transport employ a large coloured staff…
As a result of this, the amount of white labour dwindles steadily
on the London Underground. You won't get a white man in
London to admit it, but which of them will join a service where
they may find themselves working under a coloured foreman? … I
understand that in London, coloured men have become arrogant
and rude, after they have been employed for some months.*'

Yuh hear that? Arrogant and rude 'pparently.
Wha' good enough far London Transport nuh good nuff far de
Bristol Omnibus Company.

Even when Tony Benn an' Harold Wilson 'emselves speaking
against dere actions, dey still feel to tark like dis? Dey fine far
our cricketers to come 'ere to de County Ground an' play
Gloucestershire but no one wan' to be giving deer bus change to
nuh Black man.

MAVIS. I pick up something today…

MAVIS *reaches for a folded newspaper in her bag –*

This one woman write…
Wait let me find it…

A Bristol woman, Mrs Margaret Batt, write to the newspaper, all
the way from Jamaica just to say –

'*Is this the example which Britain is set to other Commonwealth
countries and to the rest of the world?
Is our criticism of South Africa's policy, in these circumstances,
not merely a case of "the kettle calling the pan sooty"?*'

You see how people supporting? /

LORNA. Daddy can I go and see Margot?

WENDELL. Dat woman ignorant!

MAVIS. Not now Lorna.

LORNA. I want to say thank you for my doll.
She gave it to me yesterday.
Because my hair is as pretty as a doll's she said /

WENDELL. She 'ave ar lot to say 'bout ar lot of tings.

PRINCESS. Is my hair pretty too Mummy?

LORNA. She said she's going to do them into ringlets for me.
Nice like t' other girls at school.

WENDELL (*to* MAVIS). You still tink she *juss tarking*? Mi feel ar
way 'bout how she talk an' mi nuh sure at all 'bout giving har
any time wit mi darters.

PRINCESS. Mummy!

MAVIS. Wendell!

WENDELL. Wi tark 'bout dis already Mavis.

> WENDELL *stares hard at* MAVIS –

> It decided. Yuh girls nuh go to har place. She nuh look after dem again. Fram now if mi or yuh modder not here, den she nuh allowed inna dis house. She nuh welcome yuh hear?

> PRINCESS *slumps in a sulk* –
> WENDELL JUNIOR *enters. He is bleeding and hurt – stumbling –*
> WENDELL *jumps to his feet – runs to catch him –*
> MAVIS *runs to the kitchen to grab a towel –*

> Wha' 'appen Junior?
> Wha' dis?

WENDELL JUNIOR. –

MAVIS. Junior say something? You been fighting?

> WENDELL JUNIOR *shakes his head –*

What then?

WENDELL. Yuh badly hurt son? It hurting anywhere in particular?

> WENDELL JUNIOR *shakes his head –*

MAVIS. Who do this?

> PRINCESS *runs to hold* WENDELL JUNIOR *tightly around the leg.*

PRINCESS. Poor Junior. I have plasters Junior.
You want my plasters?

> WENDELL *bats* PRINCESS *away – She stands close –*

WENDELL JUNIOR. They jumped us in town. There was another march. For the boycott. A bigger one for students. We were running late and couldn't make it up to the Suspension Bridge so met them at the bottom of Park Street. So many people. Walking proud. Students all shouting – '*No to the colour bar. Not in our name.*' It felt good. No trouble really. The bus crews were there. All shouting too. But they were outnumbered. Fair and square. More of us than them this time. People tearing up their bus tickets. Then on the way back to the squat...

MAVIS. I don't like this squat business /

WENDELL. Dat nuh matter far now.

WENDELL JUNIOR. We see four white boys. Big. Ugly. Standing on the corner by the Chocolate Factory. They follow us. We try to pretend they're not there but by the time we get to the cemetery, they're real close. Come right close up to us. Then they start pushing and shoving. And then more of them turn up. Pushing harder...
Saying their daddies work for the buses and don't want no coloured bastards working with them.

WENDELL. Dey do dis to yuh? Laid ar hand 'pon mi own?

WENDELL JUNIOR. They got as good as they gave. If it weren't for the bicycle chains /

WENDELL. Bicycle chain! Dat nuh right at all. Beat up like dis far standing up far good? Far de right ting?
Mi going to find de devil chile an' give dem ar beating. Mi done wit dese bakra!

WENDELL *exits*.

MAVIS. Wendell!

MAVIS *runs after him – only as far as the door –* WENDELL JUNIOR *walks dejected to his room –* MAVIS *anxiously follows him –*

PRINCESS. Will we get beat up too?
Maybe we won't go out again.
We'll have to hide in here forever.

LORNA. I'm not going to hide.
I'm not like *you*.

PRINCESS. If I get beat up so do you!
Let's hide!

PRINCESS *attempts to take* LORNA*'s hand –*

LORNA *pulls away hard –*

LORNA. I won't get beat up.

PRINCESS. But we're sisters /

LORNA. I'm not Black like you.
I'm only half.

Half of everything.
Half-sister.
Half-caste.
Everyone says so.

MAVIS *looks up* –

I don't want a sister.
I want my mum.
I want to go home!

LORNA *runs off – exits.*

MAVIS *runs to* PRINCESS *who is standing in the middle of the room. Holds her tighter than she's ever held her before.*

Scene Four

St Agnes, Bristol. July 1963.

MAVIS, *with music in the background, folds clothes. Meditatively taking them from the clothes dryer precariously standing in the middle of the room, folding them, and placing them in a basket next to her.*

MARGOT *enters. She stares hard at the boxes that seem to be taking up more space in the kitchen.*

MARGOT. There you are!

MAVIS. Yes.

MARGOT. Haven't seen you for while…

   Beat.

   Starting to think you're avoiding me.

MAVIS. I've been busy.

   Beat.

MARGOT. New radio?

   MAVIS *turns music off –*

MAVIS. Yes. Wendell knows a man at the market who gets the latest models /

MARGOT. He bought it did he?

MAVIS. It was a gift. He knows how much I like to listen to the wireless.

Beat.

MARGOT. I've been round asking after you /

MAVIS. What they do to Junior...
He's just a boy!

MARGOT. There's a lot of bad feeling at the moment. If Wendell hadn't brought all this talk /

MAVIS. People looking at me a bit stranger in those houses these days. I see something different in them eyes.

MARGOT. That's what's I'm saying. Wendell and those *others* stirring it. Stirring it up and /

MAVIS. It's not Wendell's fault that the world look at us like we lesser. Look at us somehow as second-class citizens. This country call upon us to work. Call us! And now we're here they're telling us only certain work suit us. Who do you think runs the hospitals and schools in the Caribbean?

MARGOT. This is what I mean. He has everyone singing out of his songbook now.

I need a cuppa!

MARGOT *moves to the kitchen to fill the kettle –*

MAVIS. I'm busy Margot...

MARGOT. He wormed his way into your bed again is that it?

MAVIS. Margot! You know that I don't discuss things like that /

MARGOT. I just want to know Mavis. I wants to know if I'm no longer welcome here now...

It's no secret that my life isn't exactly a shining example of anything worthwhile. A woman in her... widow even... in her early thirties... living independently with the best curves this side of Bristol... is something *rare*. I know. But it gets lonely up there in that flat. And if it weren't for them babbers... cos you know I sees them as my own... if it weren't for them and you...

I mean I don'ts like to be where I'm not wanted...

MAVIS. It's...

Things get a little complex...

Wendell he is...

MARGOT. Why is he still here Mavis?

Why you listening to all his speeches about this bus and that union and...

And I've been hearing things around...

MAVIS. We have never exchanged a bad word between us Margot but you have to stop talking like this.

Certain things I never told you Margot about my life with him before. Sometimes I don't recognise the woman wearing these clothes. Most days in fact...

MAVIS *takes a seat –*

MARGOT *busies herself with making a pot of tea –*

You know something Margot? All those years ago, we were young and happy. I knew from the beginning what he was. My mother said it. His mother said it. The whole town was saying it –

Dat bwoy ar hustler! 'Im nevar earn ar honest day's money in 'im life!

But then he goes into the service. And whenever I see him on leave, he look so sharp. Uniform straight. Hair combed. Taking me out proper.

After a few years, he was discharged after an incident because as they examine him they find he have a condition. Something on his lung they said. Well he come back to Jamaica but they promise him a desk job. A good job in *Hingland* if he want it. We get married on April 1st 1945. April Fools' Day. Imagine! But I was already carrying Junior by the time we arrive in England.

MARGOT *places two cups of tea on the table –*
She sits too –

I feel so lucky Margot. A husband with a job, a baby and this new land of Hope and Glory. 'Cept you see when we move here to Hingland we didn't find no hope that for sure.

Wendell arrives at the place to work, they tell him to start as a junior clerk. He was a second lieutenant back home, and had never done an office job in his life. He didn't understand why they invite him to come here if all they want to do is make him feel invisible.

So just like that things change. He give up on the job. Take to staying out all hours of the night. And I was stuck here with Junior. And no way of knowing what he was doing. But people start talking…

I nagged. I controlled. I made sure he didn't make a move without me knowing. I used to have people report on 'im if they see him where he shouldn't be. I thought I was getting through.

But The Hustler was back. Lying. Scheming…

And when he left. Disappeared just like that one night. I cry of course! Cry like I never cry before. Then…

MAVIS *takes a sip of tea –*

I start to feel something different. Like a kind of… like something lift off my shoulders. Like a kind of freedom.

MARGOT. And now? You still got that feeling Mavis?

MAVIS. All I know is everything harder when you try to change a man.

MARGOT. So you're going to just let him get away with anything he wants to?

MAVIS. He is trying to make good with this bus action.

MARGOT. You really believe that?

MAVIS. Only so many battles I can fight Margot.
I want to survive long enough for my children to feel like this their home too.
That's all I have the strength for these days.

MARGOT. And what if nothing comes of the bus boycott? What then Mavis? Think he's still going to be a changed man?

MAVIS *looks away from* MARGOT –

MAVIS. If a whole city can try to change, why not one simple man?

MARGOT *puts her cup down* –

MARGOT. So that's it is it? That's the way /

MAVIS. Yes.

Beat.

MAVIS *puts the radio back on –*
The radio signal crackles and then cuts out –

MARGOT. I'll see you then. Mavis…

MAVIS *doesn't look up –*

MARGOT *exits.*

Scene Five

St Agnes, Bristol. 24 August 1963.

WENDELL JUNIOR *is sitting at the kitchen table in front of*
a dismantled camera, meticulously cleaning it.

PRINCESS *lies on the sofa – a blanket almost covering her entire*
head and face.

WENDELL *enters from the front door –*
He moves to kitchen sink –

WENDELL. Mawnin' son.

Mi an' yuh modder take ar lickle early-morning walk up to
some big house in Clifton. She nuh take de bus now. Mi an' she
walk all dat way juss to measure up dem curtains.

Yuh see dem houses? Mi kyannt imagine any amount of fabric
big enuff far dem windows. Yuh modder say it simpler – '*Dem*
need to be sure dey kyaant see de poor fram dem big winda.'

Beat.

Yuh doing ar fine job wit dat camera.

WENDELL JUNIOR. Princess sick with something…

WENDELL. Still?

WENDELL *walks over to the sofa and peers at* PRINCESS *who lies motionless –*
He moves to kitchen cupboard, pulls out bottle and pours himself a drink –

Medicine.

WENDELL *takes a seat at the table opposite –*

Yuh make mi proud son.
Prouder dan ar cockerel.
De way yuh focus so hard on yuh photography.

WENDELL JUNIOR. So you're not going to get a job?

WENDELL. Yes yes! Once mi give everything mi got to dis boycott action /

WENDELL JUNIOR. Most people managing to keep a job, and help out with the boycott /

WENDELL. Most people nuh mi! Mi put mi heart full into everything. Mi hundred per cent committed to see dem men dere inna bus-company uniform looking sharp like razor blade!

Yuh nuh let ar few bruises stop yuh! Wi 'ava fight far equality. Nothing come far free /

WENDELL JUNIOR. Mummy works every day for things to be free /

WENDELL. Mi de man of dis house an' dat de way it stay now!

Yuh do better to adjust yuh attitude Junior. Make it easier far all us to be ar family again.

WENDELL JUNIOR *moves towards his room and exits –*

PRINCESS *who has had her eyes open, listening, quickly shuts them again –*

Junior! Dis bwoy testing every inch of mi soul!

WENDELL JUNIOR *enters. He is holding a bag. He puts the bag on the table and pushes it towards* WENDELL.

WENDELL JUNIOR. Have it!

WENDELL *peers into the bag –*

I know you think you're going to *stay*. That things are different and that you are different...

WENDELL. Where yuh get dis?

WENDELL JUNIOR. There's enough there for you and Lorna to find somewhere to live. Outside Bristol. Back to Liverpool or... anywhere! Twenty pounds all yours.

I can get more. Or borrow some from Leon /

WENDELL. Junior think straight /

WENDELL JUNIOR. All you have to do is leave. Just leave.

WENDELL. You really think? /

WENDELL JUNIOR. I'll leave it here. For you. I've got to go to work now...

WENDELL JUNIOR *extends his hand waiting for a handshake –*

Have a good life!

WENDELL JUNIOR *heads towards door –*

WENDELL. Yuh feel real hate far mi like dis?

WENDELL JUNIOR. I remember hearing her crying. Every day and every night after you left. It was like some kind of sad song, no more could turn off. It went on forever and I thought it was never going to stop. But it did. One day it did. That one day Princess was walking around the kitchen with a pan on her head, hitting it with a stick and dancing to her own music like she didn't know it was her making it. And I remember Mummy laughed. For the first time, I heard her laugh. We all laughed. It was like a new song being played for the first time.

I don't hate you. I just love them more. And Princess...

WENDELL. Dat girl love me. An' she love har sister same way /

WENDELL JUNIOR. She wouldn't have recognised you a few weeks ago /

WENDELL. Yuh wan' do dat to dem? Yuh baby sisters?

WENDELL JUNIOR *exits.*

WENDELL *stands looking at the bag on the table. He puts his hand in and holds up a single note to the light. He looks harder inside the bag. He shuts the bag tight and throws it into a corner of the dresser.*

WENDELL *exits to other room.*

PRINCESS *opens one eye but before she can move,* WENDELL *appears out of the bedroom without the bag.* PRINCESS *quickly closes eyes again.*

WENDELL *puts his hat and coat on – exits.*

PRINCESS *sits up immediately –*

PRINCESS. Baby? I am not a baby!

PRINCESS *moves a drawer – opens it and takes out a pair of tailor's scissors – too big for her small hands.*
She walks to her cupboard – but now her world of pageantry doesn't come alive. Instead we see it for just what it is.
A dark room, strewn with mop and bucket, brooms and other rejected items from the household. On the walls and ceiling hangs a variety of handmade art and decorations.

I am Phyllis. I am Phyllis James.

PRINCESS *stands for a beat, feeling more alone than ever. She picks up costumes/dress from her box and starts to cut up them up. She kicks and screams – and destroys her cupboard world.*

PRINCESS *leaves the cupboard – she walks to where* WENDELL's *hat is hanging and picks it up. She exits into the bedroom – hat and scissors in hand.*

ACT THREE

Scene One

St Agnes, Bristol. 24 August 1963. Evening.

MAVIS *stands in the middle of the living room, clearly distressed.*

WENDELL JUNIOR *and* LEON *enter.*

MAVIS. Junior! Where you been till this time?

WENDELL JUNIOR. Sorry Mummy. I was just…

I got some extras shifts at the warehouse.

MAVIS. Is your sister with you? Have you seen your father?

WENDELL JUNIOR. No. What's happened?

MAVIS. Your sister's gone. I've been up and down those streets twenty times /

WENDELL JUNIOR. Have you tried Margot's she's always there dressing up if she's not here /

MAVIS. She's not there! I've been knocking on Margot's door every half-hour since I come back and found Princess gone /

LEON. What about Mr James, won't she be with him?

MAVIS. He wouldn't take her out, she's sick. She's barely moved off that chair for the past week. And I find this…

MAVIS *pulls out several locks of* PRINCESS*'s hair from a waste bin.*

I've got a bad feeling about this.

Leon, will you stay here and mind Lorna for me?

LEON. Yes Mrs James of course.

MAVIS. She won't be any bother, she's fast asleep, tired out from all that marching up and down with me all afternoon.

MAVIS *heads for the door –*

LEON. I'm sure Princess is fine. She's probably someplace playing her Princess thing.

MAVIS. Thank you Leon. Junior we've got to find her. You walk towards the city centre and I'll go and try Margot again. Oh Lord, please look after my baby.

WENDELL JUNIOR *doesn't move –*

Junior! What are you waiting on? Your sister needs you!

WENDELL JUNIOR. Daddy. I told him to go. I gave him all my savings and I told him to go.

MAVIS. What you say? Why would you do such a thing? Junior?

WENDELL JUNIOR. I told him to take Lorna I didn't think he'd…

MAVIS. You didn't think! And now your sister gone someplace and /

WENDELL JUNIOR. But he's showed his true colours now hasn't he?

LEON. Junior! Mrs James, Junior doesn't mean it.

WENDELL JUNIOR. Yes I do. He's gone like I said he would /

LEON. Mr James could come back with Princess any minute. He's probably out collecting signatures for the petition again, you know what he's like. You'll see.

MAVIS. Yes, I know what he's like.

MAVIS *turns and looks at the hat stand, and sees* WENDELL's *hat has gone.*

WENDELL JUNIOR. You've still got me. I will never leave you.

MAVIS. We have to find your sister. I can't lose my Princess. My joy.

MAVIS *exits.*

Scene Two

St Agnes, Bristol. 24 August 1963. Even later that evening.

MARGOT *enters her small bedsit room. It is dark until she fumbles and finds a light.*
She closes the door. She leans against the door for a beat. She moves to a dresser a few feet away, looks at herself in the dresser mirror, and slowly peels off her earrings, rings and eyelashes. She takes off her bra – expertly doing whilst keeping her dress in place, and slides a wig off her head. Her limp and lacklustre hair underneath falls to her shoulders. She looks at herself again. Pauses. She hears something. Pauses. Picks up a shoe.

MARGOT. Someone in 'ere? Someone trying to play games with me? I've got a gun 'ere mind and I can use it. I'll use it to blow your blimming head off. I'm not some scuttler youse hear?

Come out!

A rustle by the side of the bed –

Beat.

PRINCESS *slowly appears from her hiding place –*
Her hair is cut short and uneven –

Princess!

MARGOT *throws shoe back on the floor –*

Babber what you think you're doing sneaking in 'ere?
Did you get the spare key outta the kitchen drawer? Your ma's going to flip her lid.

You nearly gave me a blimming heart attack. You want to have that on your conscience for the rest of your life? How you get in 'ere?

Beat.

What the bloody hell's happened to your hair? Princess?

MARGOT *turns on another side lamp –*

Say something then!

Beat.

Your ma know you're 'ere Princess?

PRINCESS *shakes her head –*

Sit on the bed. Sit there whiles I put my wig back on and get you along to yours /

PRINCESS. No! I want to stay with you Margot.

I have run away!

MARGOT. Run away? Ark at ee!

What's there to be running away from? And where's you planning on going? Your escape? Where's that to then?

PRINCESS *bursts into tears –*

MARGOT *runs to hug the sobbing* PRINCESS –

Princess no one's running anywhere!

MARGOT *places* PRINCESS *back on the bed, and sits down next to her –*

MARGOT *goes to a small cupboard/wardrobe and starts to rummage –*

MARGOT *emerges with a bright-blue dress in her hands –*

How do you fancy wearing a ball gown to bed tonight? It's an old one. Don't wear it any more what with it reminding me of my Fred.

Tomorrow you will be back at school running around the playground with your friends playing Hopscotch /

PRINCESS. They say mean things to me.
They only like Lorna now.
They tell me to go away.
Go back to where I came from.

What does that mean?

MARGOT. Is that what all this is about Princess?

PRINCESS. I don't want no beauty pageants or Weston-super-Mare. I don't care if I don't see the donkeys or eat choc ices… but I can imagine they are delicious… but…

Please run away with me Margot. Lorna says she won't tell anyone.
Will you? If you don't I'll have to go on my own and /

MARGOT. And how am I going to go to Weston-super-Mare without my Princess? Without the prettiest girl in all of Bristol.

PRINCESS. Mummy won't be happy now /

MARGOT. All your ma wants is for *you* to be happy. You've got lots of growing up to do before you need to worry /

PRINCESS. I thought if I was a beauty queen, and I won the prize money then I could buy anything I wanted. And I would buy my mummy a big house. That will make her happy. A big house with the best curtains. But I can't be can I… I can't win!

MARGOT. Everything will be just fine Princess.

PRINCESS. I want her to have her big house and happiness now!

MARGOT. *Now* is bedtime.

Beat.

PRINCESS. You look different Margot.

What happened to *your* hair?

MARGOT. I'm old. That's what. Old with all sorts of new tricks…

Now you gets to sleep…

No more of this running-away talk.

PRINCESS *slips out of her dress and into the oversized ball gown –*
MARGOT *then tucks her up in her bed –*

PRINCESS. Are you not going to sleep too Margot?

MARGOT. Yes I am. And I'm going to be sleeping right next to my Princess and keep her safe.
First I've just got a little errand to run before I gets in. So you just close your eyes…

PRINCESS, *exhausted, closes her eyes happily – and goes to sleep –*
MARGOT *watches* PRINCESS *for a moment, making sure she's really asleep –*

(*Whispering.*) Poor little chicken! Think I'm going to have to pop upstairs and let 'em know where you are… Mavis will be at her wits' end by now. Everything will be right as rain tomorrow.

Everything will be right as rain tomorrow. I promise you
Princess.

MARGOT *exits*.

Scene Three

St Agnes, Bristol. 25 August 1963.

MAVIS *sits, pretending to be sewing some curtains.*

WENDELL JUNIOR *is hanging developed pictures on a string
across the room.*
LORNA *is reading a book.*

Music is playing.

A key turns in door.

PRINCESS *and* MARGOT *enter.* PRINCESS *is wearing
a wide-brimmed hat.*

MARGOT *takes a look round – sighing at the thought that what
was once familiar no longer feels like hers.*

MAVIS *jumps up out of her seat and wraps her arms around*
PRINCESS.

MAVIS. Princess!

WENDELL JUNIOR. Princess what were you thinking?

PRINCESS. Mummy. I'm sorry I ran away /

MAVIS. Why would you want to do that Princess?

MARGOT. She's been helping me out /

MAVIS. Margot…

MARGOT *straightens up –*

You alright Mavis?

Beat.

MARGOT *spots the pictures hanging up –*

MARGOT. Always knew you was talented Junior but these…

Beautiful people.

There's one of you here Princess. 'My Sister, The Beauty Queen'.

PRINCESS *walks to stare at the image of herself. Sash on. Crown on –*

Beat.

Princess is just fine.

MAVIS. I need to talk to *my* children Margot.

PRINCESS. But Mummy it was Margot that looked after me /

MARGOT *heads for the front door –*

MARGOT. It's alright Mavis. I gets it.

PRINCESS. Don't go Margot!

MARGOT *stops – stands awkwardly by the door –*

LORNA. Am I in any of them Junior?

WENDELL JUNIOR *points at another one of the images hanging up –*

WENDELL JUNIOR. That one's called 'My Other Sister'.

LORNA *smiles a big smile –*

LORNA (*to* PRINCESS). Where's my daddy?

PRINCESS *shrugs –*

MAVIS. It doesn't matter for now. We have each other /

LORNA. When's he coming back?

MAVIS. Your daddy might be gone somewhere /

PRINCESS. Is Lorna going to have to go away too?

MAVIS. No Princess. We are all going to stay right here. This is where we belong and your daddy… he's got to find where he belongs.

PRINCESS. Margot here's your hat back.

PRINCESS *takes the hat off –*

MAVIS. Princess James!
Lawd a mercy! What 'appened to yuh hair?

WENDELL JUNIOR. That is really…

MAVIS. Which devil throw scissors 'pon yuh head dis way?
Margot you do this?

PRINCESS. I…

LORNA. I think I like it Princess /

WENDELL JUNIOR. I mean it's a look!

WENDELL JUNIOR *tries to hide his laughter* –

MAVIS. None of this is funny! Let me go get some kind of comb to
do something with this…

MARGOT. Mavis. I don't like to speak out of turn because well
I'm brought up proper, and ladies like me, we know how to stay
well out of things…
Anyways I just wants you to be happy… remember that. You
know where I am if you need me.

You keep the hat Princess…

I've got a couple of errands need doing.

MAVIS. Thank you for bringing Princess back home safe to me.
And you're always welcome here. Any time. Girls say bye to
your Auntie Margot.

The girls turn to MARGOT –

PRINCESS *and* LORNA. Bye Auntie Margot!

A tear runs down MARGOT's *cheek – she wipes her eyes – and
exits quickly.*

MAVIS. Lorna, Princess you two go wash your hands ready for
food. Think we all need a good meal after all these *surprises*.

PRINCESS *and* LORNA *exeunt.*

MAVIS *moves to the kitchen and starts to cook dinner for her
children.*

Scene Four

St Agnes, Bristol. 28 August 1963.

WENDELL *staggering – enters.*

WENDELL (*shouting*). Mavis!
   Mi 'ave tings to be celebrating… get some news …
   Mavis!
   Today is ar new day!

MAVIS *enters.*

   WENDELL *staggers towards her –*

MAVIS. Shhhh!!…
   So you're here…

WENDELL. Where else?

MAVIS. You haven't come home for a whole two days Wendell!
   What you think we all doing here? And what you think Princess
   and Lorna thinking now?

WENDELL. Exactly! Two 'hol' days mi missing in action! But
   lissen to mi now Mavis /

MAVIS. No you listen! You cannot start this… this… disappearing
   act with me again you hear!

   Take your bag and stay out. Get out Wendell James. Get out for
   good!

   PRINCESS *opens the door from the bedroom –* LORNA *and*
   WENDELL JUNIOR *follow –*
   WENDELL JUNIOR *holds his sisters close –*

   MAVIS *and* WENDELL *do not see them standing there –*

WENDELL. Dat wha' mi wan' tell yuh Mavis! Dem two days mi
   have some serious things 'appen /

   WENDELL JUNIOR *lets go of his sisters – moves towards*
   WENDELL –

WENDELL JUNIOR. Why are you back?
   You said /

WENDELL. I never say anything /

WENDELL JUNIOR. You're not wanted here /

WENDELL. Dat between mi an' yuh modder son.

WENDELL JUNIOR. You thief!

WENDELL. Hol' up! Who yuh calling teef? Mi nuh teef any ting in mi 'hol' life!

WENDELL JUNIOR. You took that money and you're still here! I told you to take it and leave but you're still here and now you're /

WENDELL. Mi nuh take nuh money. Mi never touch it! In fack /

WENDELL JUNIOR. That was my money! My money for when I get an apprenticeship! I've been saving that for nearly two years! You're the worst father any family can ask for.

WENDELL JUNIOR *bursts into full tears* –

WENDELL *grips* WENDELL JUNIOR*'s arm hard* –

WENDELL. Hush up! Yes yuh leff dat money on de table. But mi put it right back where it belong. In yuh room. In it rightful place /

MAVIS. You don't touch *my* son.

WENDELL *lets go of* WENDELL JUNIOR*'s arm* –

WENDELL JUNIOR. See you're lying. You don't even know where I keep it.

WENDELL. Yuh sure 'bout that? Dey never call mi Hustler far nuh good reason.

WENDELL JUNIOR. So where is it then!

PRINCESS. It was Junior's money!

WENDELL. What yuh know about it Princess? Yuh lissenin' inna business nuh yuh own?

PRINCESS. I heard it all. You're going to take Junior's money, and run away from us… from me again. And you did run away, and Mummy has been crying, because, because…

PRINCESS *bursts into tears* –

WENDELL. Be quiet! Nuh more cryin' like a baby /

PRINCESS. I am not a baby! Junior is right about you. You're nothing but a hustler!

MARGOT *enters*.

MARGOT. Can hears youse all the way down the corridors /

WENDELL. Dis family business Margot so go home!

MARGOT. Rather wait… if alright with Mavis /

MAVIS. This my house and Margot stay as long as she want!

MARGOT. Actually Mavis. Not sure I've got time for tea or 'em
dumpling thingies…
I'm going to the pictures. With a man!
Found this in my room and not ever seen it before so…

MARGOT *puts bag on the table –*

WENDELL JUNIOR *grabs the bag –*

You can thank me later.

WENDELL JUNIOR. How did it end up your room Margot?

MARGOT *exits.*

WENDELL. Well well. Mi nuhn out dat money dere so there must
be another hustler in dis family here.

All eyes turn to PRINCESS *–*

WENDELL JUNIOR. Princess? Why?

PRINCESS. I…
I thought we could use it for the bus to Weston-super-Mare.
Then we can all go /

WENDELL. That's what mi tryna tell you…

Beat.

Yesterday when mi leave 'ere, mi head over to one house where
alla us boycott people gathering. Plenty of us dere. Nuh body
really talking. Yuh see wi all dere waiting far de news. It quiet.
Nuh body knowing wha' t'say. Dem bus workers 'ave ar
meeting. Union come to tark.
Five hundred of dem all gathered inna some place tarking far
hours…
The whole place filled with hope. Someting big coming. Mi feel
it in mi bones. Something bigger than all our hopes. Dat where
mi been. Dat what mi trying to say…

MAVIS *stands and moves over to an open window – she leans
out – takes a deep breath –*

Yuh hear dat Mavis?
Wi might actually win dis ting.
Far once.
Wi take on de system an' it look like wi might beat dem.
Mi no lie Mavis.
And well mi 'ave ta 'ave ar lickle drink to celebrate dat, and
well night turn till mawnin'...

WENDELL *takes a handkerchief from his pocket and wipes his
eyes –*

Beat.

Nobody 'ave anything to say?

WENDELL JUNIOR. Wild...
Unbelievable...

MAVIS. Them actually going to let Black men work on the buses?

WENDELL. Yuh see dem men dat make dis happen, dem heroes. If
this come off, it ar victory far de Black man. De brown man.
Every kinda man dem.

PRINCESS. And girls and women!

WENDELL *goes over to the radio and turns it on loud –
He dances to the music blaring out of it –
The children watch bemused but do not join in –
WENDELL suddenly turns the music off –*

WENDELL. Lissen Mavis.
Mi an' yuh got tings to discuss /
Some tings kyannt wait yuh hear.

WENDELL *moves towards* MAVIS –
*He circles her with one arm and plants a long kiss on
her mouth –*

Dere supm mi 'ave ta say Mavis.

MAVIS. Children go to your room!

PRINCESS. But Mummy /

MAVIS *gives her a hard look –*

PRINCESS *and* LORNA *exeunt.*

MAVIS. You too Junior. Go now...

WENDELL JUNIOR *stares at* WENDELL *hard –*
WENDELL JUNIOR *exits.*

MAVIS *turns her back on* WENDELL –

WENDELL. Yuh right Mavis…
Mi have plenty to explain mi know dat…
It juss …
Mavis lissen up.

WENDELL *slowly lowers himself until he is on one bended knee –*

MAVIS *turns to face him –*

MAVIS. What are you doing?

WENDELL *reaches into his pocket and pulls out a ring –*
He holds it out towards MAVIS –

WENDELL. Mavis.
God muss 'ave known what 'im doing when he create yuh.
Yuh de best woman any man kyaan arsk far in 'im life.
Mi marry once but it feel to mi dat yuh ar woman dat need to be respected so I juss wan' know if yuh do mi enuff honour an' be mi wife far anodder time…

MAVIS *kisses her teeth –*

Wha' yuh say Mavis? Yuh going to make mi de happiest man on dis God-given earth? Mi nuh take nuh far answer Mavis /

MAVIS. All this time I was thinking you…

Beat.

Mi 'ave dreams too Wendell. Small quiet dreams but dem still alive in 'ere…
And every day, mawning and night mi fall on my knees and pray that dis country Hingland truly see de possibilities of our children… dat dem juss see dat…

WENDELL. Our children? You see mi involve in dem dreams Mavis?

MAVIS. You just hear what you want to hear Wendell James.

Beat.

What you done to us cannot easily be forgiven Wendell and you
see these children, they the ones that need you to change.
Princess needs you to know all of her dreams, because they are
important. She needs to know that even when the world out
there ready to break her heart, we in *here* never let it happen that
way. And Junior… you need to teach him what a good man look
like. If you can't do that, then better to leave now.

WENDELL. No mi hear you good. Because yuh see my children
teach mi good. Something far mi to look up to. 'Im know if yuh
wan' it den yuh 'ave ta work far it.
Mi see all our dreams coming together Mavis…
Hustle nuh win anything far mi. Mi see dat…

Beat.

Tomorrow morning mi heading straight to docks to ask
far work.
Now mi 'ave ar family to look after…
Let mi go take ar wash. Den we kyaan tark…
Or yuh kyann tark an' mi juss lissen…

MAVIS. Hmm…

WENDELL *exits to bedroom.*

Scene Five

St Agnes, Bristol. 28 August 1963.

A short while later.

MAVIS *is dressed, ready to go out.*

MAVIS. Girls hurry up with putting your shoes on!

LORNA *enters.*
She is dressed elaborately in a dress from MARGOT*'s –*

Where's Princess?

I want us to be out there!

LORNA. She got dressed and went somewhere.

MAVIS. That girl stranger every day!

Where's your brother?

I don't have time for no dilly or dally from you children today.

Go get Junior!

LORNA *exits.*

Beat.

Come out of there Princess.
Princess Phyllis James do not make me come to look for you!

The cupboard door opens –
PRINCESS *pops her head from round the door –*

PRINCESS *watches her mother intensely as she steps out of the cupboard –*

MAVIS. Princess...

I can feel that thing you always talking about...

PRINCESS. Mummy...

MAVIS. Like someone take a whole hive fulla honey and pour it into me!

PRINCESS. Like when my dreams fill me up. Fill everything up...

MAVIS. Yes just like that...

PRINCESS. I don't feel it any more Mummy. I don't think I can be pretty again. Ever. Now my hair is like this and /

MAVIS. What you say? Phyllis James you listen, and you listen good!
Whether your hair long or short. Skin good or bad.
Us...
Us... girls and women with our skin dark as the night, every shade of brown, glowing like fresh-made caramel, or legs spindly like a spider, we are everything that is beautiful on this earth.
And *you...* you the prettiest of them all because you are *my* girl.
And your mother...

MAVIS *stands and struts in an exaggerated manner around the room – wiggling and dancing –*

Your mother can still turn heads...
My crown invisible but it there...

MAVIS *adjusts an imaginary crown on her head –*

And like any queen I can do anything I want!

You remember if you come from a queen then you must be a...

PRINCESS. A princess!

PRINCESS *starts to copy her mother's exaggerated posing around the room –*

MAVIS. So you take that pretty and you never let anyone tell you what or who you can be.
You free to be *anything*.
That freedom.
You never ever forget you have that freedom Princess.
So many princesses before you fight for our right to that freedom.
In here.
Up there.
It all yours.
You hear me Princess?

PRINCESS. Mummy you think I can win the beauty pageant and have ice cream?

MAVIS. Yes! And if anyone ever try to tell you any different you just show them your crown!

But ice cream will have to wait until Margot takes you to that den of sin Weston-super-Mare.

PRINCESS *hugs her mother tighter than she has ever hugged her before that day –*

Dance for me my little Princess...

PRINCESS *dances and as she does the room comes alive –*

MAVIS *watches her daughter with joy –*

WENDELL *enters.*
He is looking clean, smart and sober. He holds out his hand for
MAVIS –
MAVIS *takes his hand –*
They dance – together – joyfully –

WENDELL JUNIOR and LORNA *enter. He is also dressed smartly wearing a sharp suit –*

Junior!

WENDELL. My son!

MAVIS. The James family going to celebrate this win today!
Into the sunshine.
Into the streets.
We all going out there to stand with our people.

WENDELL JUNIOR. Wait! Let me take a picture of us. All of us…

WENDELL JUNIOR *picks up his camera –*

PRINCESS *arranges the family for the photograph –*
She stands proudly in the middle holding her sister's hand –

A big flash envelopes the room –

Beat.

MAVIS. Come!

'*Di hotta di battle, di sweeta di victory!*'

FAMILY. Di hotta di battle, di sweeta di victory!

The family walk out of the room – except for PRINCESS *who stands centre –*

PRINCESS. This is just as I dreamt it…

All fruits ripe.

PRINCESS *laughs and exits – towards the sunshine outside, head held high, knowing that just for this one day, they won –*

Beat.

Radio crackles back on –

VOICE-OVER. *Breaking news! Today it was decided that the colour bar on Bristol buses is over. The company has already promised to interview ten coloured men who had previously applied for positions on the bus. The lead campaigner of the bus boycott Paul Stephenson of the West Indian Development Council said today –*

'*Bristol coloured immigrants are grateful to the many Bristolians who gave support and sympathy in their struggle against racial discrimination.*'

Scene Six

St Agnes, Bristol. September 1963.

PRINCESS *waits with her ear to* WENDELL JUNIOR*'s bedroom door. She is dressed in a swimsuit with a makeshift cloak.*

PRINCESS. Come out!
Come out!

Beat.

You want me to help you?

The door opens –

WENDELL *appears – he is wearing make-up and has a skirt over his trousers – a shawl around his shoulders, and a makeshift headdress/turban –*

PRINCESS *claps excitedly.*

Daddy! Daddy you really look like a real woman…

PRINCESS *circles* WENDELL, *admiring her handiwork –*

WENDELL. Yuh better not tell any body 'bout dis.
Yuh hear?

WENDELL *catches a glimpse of himself in a mirror –*

Lord! Give mi strength!

PRINCESS *pulls* WENDELL *by the arm –*

PRINCESS. Come on then.
Let's go.

PRINCESS *points to the door of the cupboard room –*

WENDELL. In dere?

Okay.

PRINCESS *and* WENDELL *walk into the cupboard hand in hand –*

The cupboard room is now bigger than it ever looked. The pageantry starts slowly –

WENDELL *stands speechless –*

PRINCESS. I told you Daddy.
I told you it was just like a pageant.

WENDELL. Yes yuh did.

Yuh do dis?
Mi never in mi life see any ting like dis Princess…

WENDELL *looks up – around him –*

So what do wi do now?

PRINCESS. You have to crown me the winner.

First you have to put the crown on my head…

WENDELL. I see. Every princess need to be crowned far true.

PRINCESS *jumps with joy –*
She searches a box until she pulls out the crown of the most wonderful sparkles –

PRINCESS. Then you have to say it like this…

'*Ladies and gentlemen, I present to you the winner of the year's Weston-super-Mare Beauties of the West Contest, Miss Princess James.*'

WENDELL. Juss like dat?

WENDELL *gently places the crown on* PRINCESS*'s head –*

PRINCESS. And now watch everything beautiful in the world come alive…

The room explodes into a world of pageantry – scenes of people jumping into a swimming pool, Union Jacks, music and fireworks – fill the room – and as PRINCESS *watches her world come to life, for the first time she imagines a pageant where all the beauty queens look like her.*

And as if the room knows just what she is thinking, a line of the most beautiful Black women of all sizes and nations appear before her. A line – a parade of women dressed in the finest gowns, with the most coiffured hair, assemble around PRINCESS.

PRINCESS *puts on her sash and her crown, stands right in the middle of the line and takes a bow with her fellow queens.*

The End.

BURGERZ

Travis Alabanza

*Dedicated to all the trans people, all the gender
non-conforming people, all the outsiders and the others
that have had their life stopped, halted, ended,
constrained due to violence.*

You / We / I deserve more.

Burgerz was first performed at Hackney Showroom, London, on 25 October 2018. The cast and creative team was as follows:

TRAVIS   Travis Alabanza

Director   Sam Curtis Lindsay
Designer   Soutra Gilmour
Associate Designer   Isabella Van Braeckel
Lighting Designers   Lee Curran & Lauren Woodhead
Sound Designer   XANA
Movement   Nando Messias
Dramaturg   Nina Lyndon
Production Manager   Shaz McGee
Assistant Production Manager   Cat Ryall
Stage Manager   Beth Lewis
Assistant Stage Manager   Vita Ingram-Anichkin

Foreword

At the point of first publication I'll be twenty-three. I have no university degree. And I didn't really know what an artist was until I moved to London when I was eighteen. What I mean to say is: I don't really know how any of this works. What I do know is that *Burgerz* needed to be written, it needed to be performed, and it needed to be heard.

This play could be described as something that is looking at one incident, but instead I believe it is more accurate to say that *Burgerz* has become an emblem for so many other incidents, deaths, acts of violence and harm, that the trans and gender non-conforming community have to face every single day. *Burgerz*, for me, is about archiving the pain in our reality. It is about complicating the narrative. It is about writing down that these things exist, and that we cannot keep pretending they do not.

So many other trans people could have written this truth. So many other members of our community mentioned how they have had food thrown at them, dodged insults, faced beatings, been harmed – and so many of those mentioned the deathly silence surrounding their attacks. In this current moment, in 2018 in Britain, the public are being consulted on the Gender Recognition Act. Trans people are having to withstand countless attacks from media, public, and private sectors. The news is filled every day with debates about whether or not trans people are a danger to society – but no one is talking about the dangers we face from the rest of society.

I conducted a series of dinners called 'Tranz Talkz' across the country. I sat around a table with strangers, bonded only by our transness, eating burgers and chips and asking them questions about their life. Every single person said they were anxious outside. Most said they edit themselves before they leave the door. Almost all said they were harassed. My Facebook feed has at least one status a day from a trans and/or gender non- conforming friend detailing their attack. I check in with my trans friends and hear weekly about the struggles they faced from their transphobic doctor, or boss, or family. This has the power to fill me with sadness and remorse, but more often I think about how this reminds me of our resilience as a community. A resilience we should not have to harbour, yet still manage to.

Burgerz is about the violence. It is about the hurt. It is about telling you that this pain and that hurt exist and that society is complicit in this.

But also, with that, I hope it is a text that reminds you of our resilience.

With love, and a call to action,

Travis
2018

Character

TRAVIS

A warehouse with a giant box centre-stage. The doors of the box
open to reveal TRAVIS *wearing overalls and boots.*

TRAVIS. A burger was thrown at me in broad daylight in April
2016 on Waterloo Bridge whilst someone yelled the word
tranny. I think over one hundred people saw and I know no one
did anything.

Pause.

If I become obsessed with how the burger works, how it flies,
how it smells and how it lands then maybe I will have some
agency over it. Maybe I will feel like I was once in control.

Imagine that burger now. Imagine it in front of you. The most
typical burger you see. The emoji. The archetype. The original.
The real burger.

Pause.

The burger bun. A piece of dough.

A piece of dough is just a piece of dough until you figure out it
is supposed to be part of a burger, to make the bun. Then, there
are many things you must do to it to make it right. Make it
work. Turning flour and yeast to whole things, heating things,
changing things. Altered to circles through knives and cuts.
Kneaded and poked, stretched out and pinched, moulding and
ploughing the dough, prodding it into shape to eventually be the
bun, that will eventually hold the burger.

The burger bun must be round. Top heavy, bottom light, one
bigger than the other. Always one bigger than the other, big
holding small in place. Top to bottom. We are not aiming for
equal.

Imagine that burger now. Imagine it in front of you. The most
typical burger you see. The emoji.

The archetype. The original. Real burger.

The burger bun.

Once made, cut into half, burger in mind, always burger in
mind, bread cut, cursed for not being quite right. A patty placed
in. We imagined beef, do not pretend you did not. Or moreover
that it would be weird if I placed chicken in there now. Sure, we
accept a veggie patty, or even aubergine in high-end food places
in East London served in old car parks – but do not lie that you
imagined that first. You saw the patty. Real burger equals real
patty equals real beef equals real... burger. Placed inside.

Pause.

This is where people believe the burger has some freedom.
We've got the bun, the beef, the patty – and now, we finally feel
we have a choice. That the burger becomes your liberal
playground, toppings are where you can make you... You! The
burger that liberals want. Now it's your turn to jazz it up, place
whatever on top, go wild, it's your burger, it's your life! But
let's not pretend we didn't all have ideas for how this burger
should look. Expectations. Lettuce, green. Tomatoes, sliced, I
guess red. Cheese, thin. Mayo over the top. Onions, maybe.
Some other garnish. Sure, some freedom – but we did know
what to expect. We had this burger planned, and imagined. All I
see now is the dough that is the burger bun, attached at the waist
to the patty, to the salad, to the expectations. And if I change too
much about how this burger was imagined, it will be ridiculed.
Sent back to the kitchen.

Pause.

'HOT DOG OR BURGER?'
'HOT DOG OR BURGER, LOVE?'
'HOT DOG... OR BURGER, LOVE?'

I can't remember what I chose or I do not want to mention it,
partly because I'm not sure it was a choice.

'You often have to choose between burgers and hot dogs in life,
Travis – it would be odd to have both.'

'But, Mum, last time I saw a burger stall was at that tacky
Christmas fair with you, they sold hot dogs there, and you didn't
find it odd.'

'Yeah, you're right. But they were in separate containers.
Clearly labelled.'

Pieces of the same dough could be made into a bun for a burger or a bun for a hot dog, but once it's made into another it's very hard to change back. People would still know it was always a hot-dog bun first.

People might only see buns as something to hold burgers, that is until they hear about hot dogs, and then there is this whole other world where you had hot dogs as your priority; your archetype, your emoji – and figuring out about hot dogs meant that you looked at burgers completely differently. My mum never really cooked or made hot dogs in the house, so all we ever knew was how to choose burgers, but if I grew up with my dad then I'd pick hot dogs every time, without question. Then twenty years or so down the line I'd be making some show called *HOT DOGZ* with a Z.

Pause.

It's ridiculous that we place two things next to each other and expect ourselves to be able to make a choice, or to lie and tell ourselves it is a choice when there are two things placed next to each other. As if something containing only two could ever be a choice. That is not a choice. That is rather jumping to which death you think may be less painful.

HOT DOG OR BURGER?

Die quietly or die loudly? Splitting things up into two arbitrary categories has never worked ever since the beginning of time.

Then you went there with your fucking utensils, your fucking cutlery, your fucking recipe books with no fucking seasoning and decided that we all had to choose between a fucking burger and a fucking hot dog, but it wasn't a choice, because you looked at me, and you said in one minute this person is a fucking person that eats burgers. As if I couldn't be that and more, as if I couldn't catch my breath, for a minute.

As if burgers isn't something that happens violently after it, as if burgers isn't violence in its definition. As if the burger isn't violent in its creation. As if violence doesn't happen to hot dog and burger-choosers, as if it scares you when you are choosing between hot dog and burger, as if choosing…

TRAVIS *realises they are losing composure. They pause. Regain poise.*

They get out a very large box and get inside, changing out of their overalls and into a dress and heels.

The first time I tried on a dress...

I was young, even younger than now, not embryonic, but you know, not this time. I was ten years old, at my gran–

TRAVIS *looks out into the audience.*

What am I doing?

I don't remember the first time I tried on a dress. Oops, that's it, go on, remove my trans card. I don't remember.

A pause as they look out into the audience.

Well look:

Tried on a dress at nine, black sparkly; seven years later beat up for wearing one exactly like that.

Played a witch in a school panto, found a bit of my gender, football team made fun of it, got an A-star.

Can't tell you the first time I got called a faggot but can tell you every time I've ever been called beautiful by a stranger. Didn't base my gender off of female celebrities, was more interested in emulating aliens.

A recipe book falls from the ceiling and slams onto the floor.

I need to make this burger.

TRAVIS *pushes out a kitchen island, currently hidden in a box.*

Maybe it is about knowing when you need help. Recognising when you could continue to struggle on your own, but would breathe lighter with someone else. It feels weird because I do not know you, but I do not think that is a prerequisite for help. I've never made a burger from scratch before. I'm not a very good cook, in fact, I rarely ever cook.

I need to do this, I just know it will be hard.

They look out to the audience.

So I'm wondering if there is anyone here that would help me? Cooking experience helps, but isn't required, a lot of us learn on the job.

You do not need to have brought your own ingredients, or utensils, or kitchen, I've done all that.

They reveal the kitchen.

You would have to come up here, for a while, be okay with sticking around. You'd have to be okay with talking in front of strangers... I'm still getting used to it.

I could get you a drink, we'd give you a cushion for your chair.

(To themselves.) Wow, look at all these things I think I have to bring in to get someone to help.

(To the audience.) Just bring yourself, all of it.

So, who will help me make a burger... anyone?

TRAVIS *waits for some people to put their hands up.*

I never thought I'd say this, but I need a man. I think we have some shit we gotta work through. I need a white man.

I need... a cis white man... to help me. Make a burger.

They identify a volunteer.

This feels scary, you... I think I want your help. Can you take my hand? Commitment is scary, right? How do you feel?

TRAVIS *brings them onstage and gives them the recipe book.* TRAVIS *then brings out a stool and a cushion from a box at the back. They get out their own stool. They go into a drawer and get out an apron and hand it to the* MAN. *They sit down together.*

Would you like a drink? I can get you white wine, red wine, rosé wine, G&T, vodka Coke (diet as well), water, sparkling or still, Heineken, Carlsberg or... an orange Capri Sun.

TRAVIS *serves the requested drink.*

I need to do some of this on my own, but it's just nice to know that you could be here to help. I can't cook, so, it helps to know someone is there.

Could you tell me what the first page says?

MAN *reads from the recipe book.*

MAN. Wash your hands.

TRAVIS pauses. Looks round for a sink. Realises/remembers there isn't one.

TRAVIS. Budget for a sink would've been...

Then goes into the drawer and gets out some hand sanitiser. Squirts twice on their hand. Gestures to the MAN, squirts it on theirs, and rubs it together. When they have finished they put the sanitiser away and gesture to turn the page. The page will have instructions for the MAN to read.

MAN. Travis, before you can make the burger, it is important you decide the type of box the burger must go in.

TRAVIS. Type of box? Hold on, I thought I'd start cooking now, what do you mean?

MAN. Travis, before you can make the burger, it is important you decide the type of box the burger must go in.

TRAVIS. I'm sorry. But... but how do I pick a box for something that isn't even made yet? That doesn't seem right.

MAN. Travis, before you can make the burger, it is important you decide the type of box the burger must go in.

TRAVIS. But... I mean, even with that logic, this seems unfair. I mean, say even if I pick the beef burger, which I know I will, it's the most typical one, then I do not know what shape it will come out. I do not know if I will change my mind whilst cutting it, spontaneously pick a different shape last-minute, or... or what if in the pan it changes shape, or my knife slips. Do I then still have to try and squeeze it in the box I've already picked? Like, a reminder that I really can't cook so to predict a shape of anything at this point feels really beyond my skill set.

MAN. Travis, before you can make the burger, it is important you decide the type of box the burger must go in.

TRAVIS pauses and looks at the many boxes. They find a box containing boxes and the text is spoken as they explore this.

TRAVIS. What came first? The Burger or the Box for the Burger. Man or woman. Or the cages made for man or woman. The person free from man or woman. Or the person in charge of capturing the person free from man or woman. Gender or violence? The last one was the same thing. When I think about boxes I think about order, about containment and the need we have to tidy things. I think about how when things are tidy, it is always those that are messy that are punished. Colouring outside the lines was never rewarded, only shunned.

Do you feel boxed in?

All the times I had been encouraged not to wear this, all the times the flick in my wrist had been straightened, or the raise in my voice had been muffled. We are policing people before they even know the person they are. We are punished for when we fail.

Last week on a Tube a mother called me an abomination to mankind, and I said isn't that an oxymoron? Isn't man already an abomination?

Two weights hang in equilibrium, they force us to stand with one toe upon them, and if you unbalance them there is this fear that the scales will smash and so will everyone else's compliance and you will be punished accordingly. This is all about order. It's about structure. It's about regulation and to be unregulated is to be dangerous. There are billions of people in this world and somehow we will decide two boxes to fit all these people in. As if fitting billions of people in two boxes could ever be comfortable. We will decide who you are before we know you, decide which box to place you in, and then not let you change even if we can tell it was the wrong box.

Sorry, what was the instruction again?

MAN. Travis, before you can make the burger, it is important you decide the type of box the burger must go in.

TRAVIS *opens the box to reveal two identical burger boxes. They continue to search other boxes for boxes.* TRAVIS *speaks this next text through the boxes until they are hidden.*

TRAVIS. It seems silly to hide in the very things that try to contain you. Two thousand years ago there were gods that looked like me. And maybe you. Worshipped in their plurality. Existing. Not cast aside. Castrated. Cast away. But seen in their plurality as a strength, not a hindrance. Hijra – South Asian. Bakla – Philippines. Kathoey – Thailand. Two Spirit – Native American. Quariwarmi – Inca. Femminiello – Italian. Up until the nineteenth century, Italian 'lady boys' had their rituals seen as a gift, they were seen as elite. People believed they were connected to the ancient practices of Hermaphroditus. The Sister Boys and Brother Girls of the outback, indigenous tribes, once celebrated.

TRAVIS *climbs into the back of a large box.*

And I wonder how we ended up here? I wonder how I ended up as the person struggling to decide which burger goes in which box, having to even make this burger for this box, having to think this whole time about burgers and boxes – and you became the people in charge? Who will decide if this was good enough? Done the correct way?

We hear the sound of an electric turkey carver start. TRAVIS *cuts the cardboard box to get out.* TRAVIS *pops through, now holding a box (similar to the one they put away but way more* TRAVIS*).*

I've got the box. Can you tell me the next step?

MAN *reads page two of the instructions.*

MAN. Mince.

TRAVIS *struts across the stage, finds the big mincer, puts on latex gloves and gets out a chunk of meat. The meat is minced.* TRAVIS *then places the mincer away.*

TRAVIS. I'm ready for the next instruction.

The page is turned.

MAN. Spice.

TRAVIS *grabs the spice rack from the kitchen and places it on the table.*

TRAVIS *goes to add spice to the mince, then stops.*

TRAVIS. I *really* should not be adding my own spice to this mince.

Looks at MAN, *to gesture they need help.*

Will you stand behind me?

It's quite important that we get this right. Not enough spice and things can really feel quite bland. This burger can't be bland. Will you shake some in and I'll tell you when to stop.

MAN *shakes some spice in.*

Keep going. I know you are nervous, we are always nervous when adding spice into the mix. Stop. Stop. Not too much. We need enough to know it's there but not enough that we notice it fully. Keep going. Bit more. Go on. We need just enough that we can brag about this being a spicy burger afterwards, but don't name any of the spices on the ingredients list – it's better to leave it out. Keep going. A bit more. Is that too much for you. Does it feel too present. I would say pick up another spice but you know if there's two types of spices in one mix then shit really fucking hits the pan. Go on. Stop. Take a breather. I know all this work is hard on you. It must be so exhausting. To constantly have to respond to people's requests for more fucking spices. I can tell you're tired. So in a minute I'm going to say 'go on', and you will add the last bit of spice. Then you will take your seat. Later you will go home. And write a long Facebook status about how good you feel that you did this, and that when this burger is made you will make sure everyone knows it could not be made without your invaluable, groundbreaking, spice-related work. People will comment on that Facebook status and tell you that you are such a good person, and if you ever make a mistake in the future, people will say, 'This person could have never made that mistake because one time they added spice, to this fucking burger.'

Go on.

MAN *adds the spice and goes back to their seat on the stage.* TRAVIS *begins to mix the mince with their hands, intensely, eventually forming a patty.*

I can often feel a room become heavier as soon as race is brought up. A sticky, dense feeling where the room becomes... almost hotter. The temperature kind of rises and I feel we suddenly have less space. Steam always rises to the top. Of course, I do not feel this shift or the rise in heat... the steam; some of you do not either, because for us, it never left.

I was caught stealing once when I was fourteen, I should have just said I was trying to integrate myself in British tradition!

The third time I met someone online to have sex he left because he said, 'I thought you'd be more masculine because you're Black.'

I think often about what happens when we die. I wonder if hell is just a place where we watch white people in a club try and find rhythm, whilst they continuously dance to 'I'm Coming Out' by Diana Ross as they awkwardly-off-beat gyrate their hips in your face whilst impersonating the Black sassy women they met last week.

It's not just that, before colonisation, gender non-conformity existed in different forms, it's that colonisation and race continue to completely affect how gender continues to be formed. To think it is only trans people that are misgendered is the whitest way to think about bodies. Black bodies have known what it means to be de-gendered, hyper-gendered, misgendered since the beginning of your slavery. You know in these hate-crime adverts they always advise the poor trans person to call the police, and I always want to ask back, 'Why would we bring more trouble to our door?' And then I remember we aren't all in the same house… are we?

TRAVIS *has formed the patty and placed it down.*

(*To the* MAN.) Are you still okay with staying with me? Can I get you another drink?

They serve a drink if requested.

TRAVIS *goes to put the spice rack away and notices something else under the table: the burger buns. Feels them. Brings them above the table and begins to play with them until they place them on their chest.*

I never really wanted breasts. I don't think. I mean, I'm not sure. I probably had the same urge to have breasts as I occasionally get to shave my hair. Fleeting. It's not always present, and it comes and goes. But there comes a moment when I start to wonder, if I made more effort, stuffed more things into me, turned some things over me, chopped some parts up, would you start to believe me when I say that I am hurting?

If I got these breasts, and changed my face, and blended into the walls, would we start to hear me when I scream? Would I even need to scream? I wonder how many bodies have forced parts onto themselves in order to be seen as fixed, legitimate, so they no longer need to stop traffic.

Why when I say I'm trans does someone ask, 'What will you have done?' 'What is next?'

As if trans can never be a destination. As if trans is synonym for broken body.

As if I cannot say I'm trans and have someone say, 'You do not need to change. I will protect you the way you are.'

(*To the* MAN.) Can you get me the tape? It's in the top drawer.

They gesture to the MAN *to bind the burger buns on top of* TRAVIS *as they say the text.*

I imagine myself with breasts a lot more now.

Feeling them over my chest.

Stuffing my top to see how the weight would feel.

I cannot tell if this is something I really want, rather than something I need. I do not know if that matters.

TRAVIS *takes off their buns in an instant. Back to the task at hand. They place a new bun on the surface. Cut it. Get out the lettuce. Onion and tomato.* TRAVIS *takes the lettuce and the tomato, and slides the onion over to the* MAN. *Carefully gives them a knife.* TRAVIS *begins to chop. And the* MAN *starts cutting the onion too. The next three questions are asked in gaps whilst the* MAN *is cutting the onions with* TRAVIS. TRAVIS *allows space for natural conversation to form.*

When was the last time you cried?

What does it feel like to be a man?

Are you scared of being outside?

TRAVIS *will signify when they finish by stopping cutting and saying:*

Thank you.

When they have finished, they place the three chopped items in three clear bowls.

What's the next instruction?

MAN. Cook.

TRAVIS. Oh yes…

TRAVIS *starts as if to cook, but then brings back out the hand sanitiser.*

'For old times' sake!'

They sanitise their hands one more time.

TRAVIS *gets out the pan and places it on the hob.*

TRAVIS *starts the timer that is preset to three minutes.* TRAVIS *starts by placing the burger in the pan.*

TRAVIS *tries to focus on the cooking. As the cooking amplifies, you can hear the noises of the past and present.* TRAVIS *tries to remain focused on cooking.*

No one will sit next to me. My eyes go from floor, to their eyes, to door. Their eyes never leaving me. It was the Victoria line, Oxford Circus southbound to Brixton and someone had finally occupied the seat next to me.

Things felt closer. I had my headphones in, but I had no music on; a melody is a privilege for those that do not need to be aware.

'What the fuck are you?'

I wanted to reply: 'A person, another human, someone who deserves respect.' Or I wanted to hear the six other people that heard say something too.

We all stayed in silence. His hand was on my inner thigh for the rest of the journey.

Heat intensifies.

Dalston Overground Station, it was after a gig, a man followed behind me, breathing down my neck.

Heat intensifies.

Busy shopping mall. Group of girls laugh at me. Someone tries to trip me down the stairs. They say it's an accident.

TRAVIS *goes to add salt.*

(*To the* MAN.) Taxi driver pulled up to pick me up, saw what I was wearing, and said I was disgusting and drove off.

I'm on a bus back home and a group of schoolchildren get onto the top deck to join me. Instantly they notice my pink skirt, matching pink jumper and pink eyeshadow. A young girl smiles at me and I smile back. I forget for a moment about all the other stares that day.

Her friend sees the exchange and is scared by the possibility. 'Why is that man dressed like a girl?' The teacher sees: 'It's rude to point, lower your voice.'

The kids continued to point and laugh.

I became a spectacle, an object of other people's ambitions.

'When I grow up, I want to be just like you, but I'm too scared to say that so I'm just going to point and laugh.'

(*To the* MAN.) Have you ever been pointed and laughed at in public? Or had a whole room stop as you walk in?

The timer buzzes. The burger gets flipped.

(*To the* MAN.) Can you get me a glass of water, please?

November 11th. '*Children sacrificed to appease trans lobby*', an article written by Janice Turner in *The Times*. I was the subject of that article. I tried to go into a single-stall changing room in Topshop and was kicked out cuz I made the other customers feel uncomfortable. They lied in the press and said that I changed the rules of Topshop and I was the reason they were now 'gender-neutral' – ignoring the fact there'd been gender-non-specific changing rooms nine months before November 11th. There were photos of me in every major newspaper, misgendering me, pulling apart my appearance, telling me I was an imposter; people were tweeting at me saying they wanted me to die thousands of times a day; in the street people would come up to me and call me a freak; a group of mums told the theatre I was working in at the time that I should lose my job, and my mom saw photos of me on *Good Morning Britain* whilst doing the dishes. She sent me a text saying, 'I don't understand what's happening, but would you like to come home for dinner?'

The heat rises.

Everyone's busy debating whether or not I'm a snowflake whilst a group of lads throws snowballs at me and my friends. It didn't feel like a game.

Anti-trans billboards go up around Liverpool the same week that one of our sisters is murdered in the streets.

They're debating our existence on the television again, whilst a trans friend was held up at knifepoint the day before.

I think about the first time I was slapped round the face.

The bus, the Tube, the mall, the shop, outside my house, online, in my house, in my bed, at the doctor's, at the airport, in the newspaper, on the stage, in the bathroom.

Harassment isn't just one moment. It doesn't just start and stop.

I walk outside. The world will say I have privilege. That I have the choice to avoid it. And I want to yell: 'What choice. What choice gives me the honour to hide myself on the streets.'

It is not in split seconds, it is in every single pain in my body I am still yet to discover. It is the pain my doctor notes from my head never looking up, it's the UTI my friend has from never feeling safe to use the bathroom, it's the anxiety that has induced my head to look for eyes when they are not there, it is the continuous cloud surrounding me, it's me grabbing at my body and not knowing which parts need fixing. It's trying to breathe when the whole room feels like it is closing in, it's crying and not knowing for which moment, it's grabbing at your body wanting something to work. It's not knowing what changes I am making for myself, or for you. It's knowing I was not born in the wrong body, rather born in the wrong world, but still grasping at my chest, longing for something to change, for me to change, for me to do better, it's wanting to gi–

We reach a point of climax with both sounds, as the timer goes off again.

TRAVIS *starts to walk away from the kitchen.*

The timer remains beeping.

(*To the* MAN.) Can you turn it off?

The power in the kitchen and to the hot pan is killed off. TRAVIS leaves the kitchen to walk away.

If I walk out of this room right now, leave you, and leave like this, like how I want to be, in these clothes, in this gender – I will be beaten, I will be bashed, I will be shouted at, I will be hurt. And you will go home. We have gotten into this cycle. Where bad things happen and we have to go onstage and perform for them in order for us to be believed. We have to be polite, bring in lights, bring in costume, make you laugh, bring in a show, and hug the very people that have their hands around my neck. You have your hands wrapped around my neck. I asked you here. You've helped me. But I can still feel the hands.

I'm so confused.

I need you, but I can't tell what that looks like.

Am I doing this wrong? Have I done this wrong? What are we asking for that seems more than just breathing? What is the debate in breathing? What debate? What debate is left? Who is left? It feels like both of us can't do this alone.

I just want to figure out who I am outside of violence. I just want to make this fucking burger and be done with it. To finish it. To make this burger and be able to have you believe me, understand me, want to be there, without me having to ask.

They look in the pan.

It feels like we were always set up for failure?

Throughout the past speech TRAVIS *has been getting further and further away from the* MAN. *A shift in sound as* TRAVIS *reaches the top of a box.*

And sometimes I close my eyes. Sometimes, when I am being shouted at, thrown abuse, followed home, shaken up, or the world feels like too much to hold on my shoulders, or I am too tired for the weight of my lids – so I just hold them tight. And closed. And I think about the dream that I had last night. Where I was no longer here. Dead in this time. But not in an awful state, just peacefully somewhere else. Close my lids and imagine I am no longer feet-on-ground, but in air, floating. And I'm floating next to my ancestors in the Philippines. The Baklas. And we are both floating in a time before we were punished. Floating in and out of genders, the Bakla turns to me and speaks in their own tongue. 'We have been creating these words long before they were shouted at us.'

The Bakla holds me in their arms and lifts me above the weight of my shoulders, and places me on the finger of the Femminiello, just above the atmosphere. The Femminiello looks at me in my eyes.

'Why are you scared?'

'How can you hold all of me on just one finger?'

'Darling, we have held so much more for centuries. We were not always treated like dirt, we were once seen as blessed. Of course I can hold you on my finger, that power never leaves you.'

The Femminiello spun me around, one hand painted, the other dry, and threw me over sidewalks of jeers, and mirrors of back pain and late nights, into the bed of a Hijra named Jaan, and in no words Jaan tidied the blankets around me, placed my eyes next to the pillow and tucked me in.

'Goodnight.'

'Are you not afraid?'

'I once was. When they first came over here, said "male or female" and we said "no". They called us a criminal tribe. I was afraid. Then I was scared. But when you close your eyes at night, and remember that we have survived all of this, that we have been here, have existed, have lived beyond the jeer, then you can breathe easier.'

'But the pavements feel so lonely...'

'Isolation is the best tactic of oppression. But I need you to open your eyes, your ears, your heart, and remember that we have been there too. You are not new, you are not the only one, the streets will make you feel like there is no one else, but remind yourself of the lands before they were walked on.'

Jaan blew out the candle, as the Femminiello closed the curtains, and the group of Baklas gently pushed me back down to the ground.

I opened my eyes to hear you say faggot, and remembered that there was more than this moment.

The mood shifts back to reality. TRAVIS *is back down at the kitchen. Looks at the* MAN. TRAVIS *asks:*

What's next after cooking?

MAN. Assemble.

TRAVIS *and the* MAN *assemble the burger.*

TRAVIS. Burgers are really messy. The texture of them can be quite coarse, invasive, sticky – sometimes they cost nine pound

and other times they cost three-twenty-five with chips and a
drink. It depends where you get them from. I know burgers
aren't everyone's favourite food, I don't think they are mine
either, but I didn't think people hated burgers enough to waste
them. I don't mean waste as in not eat all of the last tiny bits and
put the scraps in the bin. I know people don't always eat the
very last bite, or maybe leave the onion, or maybe the lettuce. I
mean fully waste them. Like a whole burger. Like to buy a
whole burger and then to not use it is to waste it. To not eat the
rest of your burger but instead to throw it.

The burger is assembled. The MAN *sits back in their seat.*
TRAVIS *sits across from the* MAN.

I became obsessed with how a burger feels and smells because I
needed to recreate an intimacy with it that wasn't forced. I
needed to get to know it so I could pretend that we had a choice
to meet each other. If I become obsessed with how the burger
works, how it flies, how it smells and how it lands, then maybe I
will have some agency over it. Maybe I would feel like I was
once in control. But truth is – there isn't really a way to do that
with this. Whenever I get down to it, whenever I really say it out
loud, whenever I utter the words to someone else, or myself or
even as I do it now, they still don't feel like my words to tell. It
still feels exactly as violent and as horrible as when it happened.
I can't lie and say I have any control.

A moment passes.

When I realised the burger had hit me I realised it was too late
to dodge. I'm not good at dodging things. Especially unplanned
things.

A burger was thrown at me in broad daylight in April 2016 on
Waterloo Bridge whilst someone yelled the word tranny. I think
over one hundred people saw and I know no one did anything.
To be trans and Black and gender non-conforming is to both be
accustomed to the violence whilst also dissociating from the
reality. I am a human being who was kind of not shocked when
a burger was thrown at me by another human being. No one did
anything.

I am yearning for one time, for me to say this, and to hear
someone shout out in the room, 'I'm sorry.' For someone to

shout, 'No, for fuck's sake, that happened.' For us to find this violence so repulsive that our bodies launch forward involuntarily to hug someone. But I do not think we are shocked. No one did anything.

I gave everyone around one minute to come up to me. To shout at him. To touch me. To look at me. To see me. To remind me that I was human. But everyone was still walking. I had to touch the mayonnaise on my shoulder for me to make sure that it was real, because if you looked at everyone else, it would have you thinking nothing in the world had changed. I guess nothing had changed though, if we really want to think about it. The world was working exactly how it had been made to. No one did anything. Mothers with their children, men in their suits, students with their feminist tote bags. No one did anything. And I'm left scared, I know that burger could be a fist, a knife, a choked neck, but what I do not know is if you will be there? You have never proved us wrong. No one does anything. No one did anything.

The man who threw the burger at me did pause though. We both did. For a split second. I wondered if he was going to scream, '*I was afraid, I am hurting so I hurt you.*' Maybe he was waiting for someone to hold him back, to tell him off for the action I still do not know if he planned to have.

But, he saw the world had not noticed, and continued with his day.

TRAVIS *gestures for the* MAN *to sit, this time not onstage, but back in their seat in the auditorium. We allow this moment to happen.* TRAVIS *looks at the* MAN *as they leave.*

No one did anything.

But someone else did notice. I remember there were two people's eyes I saw after the burger had been thrown. The man, and a lady across the street. Her eye caught mine for two seconds. She saw me holding back tears. She saw what had happened. She saw the man, and then saw me, and then she looked down. And she carried on walking. With everyone else, who carried on walking. And I'm not going to say any more that no one did anything, because walking away is action, is action that you choose. Because doing nothing is not neutral.

I often think about that woman. I often wonder if she went home and cried too. If she saw the safety I was mourning, and cried for how much worse hers could be. Maybe she thought that if she touched me she would catch it too. As if we exist on a ladder, and in that moment she realised she was not at the bottom, but that my hand could grab her and pull her down if she offered to wipe the mayonnaise off my dress.

Maybe she caught my eye like you just caught mine.

TRAVIS *gestures to a* WOMAN *in the audience. Gestures for them to come up onstage. When they do, they stand opposite* TRAVIS.

TRAVIS *hands them the opened recipe book. The* WOMAN *reads:*

I vow to protect you, more than others have before. I vow to protect you, as in the plural, as in more than just you. I vow to realise that in my safety, in my comfort, in my silence, comes your danger, hurt, and entrapment. I vow to know that I cannot possibly be free, whilst you, the plural, are still hurt. I vow to know that I cannot remain silent when others are hurting, to recognise that silence is part of the hurting. I cannot, on my own, make them stop. Make them turn away. Make them look less. But I know that I can wake up. I know that I can do better. I vow to make sure that every day I go outside I realise that I am not alone, that I am together, with you, the plural, and me, the plural – that there cannot be singular any more. That we have tried singular, and we continue to fail. My freedom is not just tied to yours, but is not freedom without yours.

TRAVIS *hands them the real burger in the box.*

When I throw this burger I will throw it, not to hurt you again, but to acknowledge that I have hurt you before. That my hand may not have thrown the bun, the beef, the patty, but my silence still burns. I did not need to throw the burger with my own hand to still hear it hit. I throw this burger, to bring this vow of words into action. An action born out of violence with a hope to turn into some promise. A promise to do better. For each other. For others. I will say sorry. We will count to three, together. I will throw this burger at you. It will fall to the ground. And I will go back to my seat. And you will leave the stage. And I will go home. So will you. But outside, we are now together.

I'm sorry.

One… Two… Three…

The burger is thrown at TRAVIS.

End.

40 DAYS

Firdos Ali

Introduction

I like to write in short bursts, so in 2017 I gave myself 40 days to write a new play. The 40 days coincided with the election period, so I chose to use the same timeline for the play and zoom in on the home of a Black, British Muslim family with a sick son.

I had struggled with chronic pain and fatigue for years and wanted to write about what it was like to be a sick person, 'doctor' and spiritual guide all at once. I lent those three parts of my experience to the boy, the mother and the father in the play, respectively.

Black, British Muslims sit at a painful intersection. To predict the next outrageous political scandal against Black Brits, you'd only have to look back. It would likely have happened to Black, British Muslims already but few would have noticed. To live with the twin devils that are racism and Islamophobia, to feel the painful push of 'Muslim-but-Black' from Muslims and 'Black-but-Muslim' from the wider Black community, there is little rest for Black, British Muslims. Their bodies keep notes. The notes hurt. It is a miracle that some Black, British Muslims remain healthy.

40 Days took 41 days to write. I love how it rebelled against me – that one extra day it made me spend with it. A single draft, shared with a handful of people – until now. It has not been produced.

F.A.

Characters

ANGRY BLACK WOMAN, *Black woman, mid-thirties to mid-forties*
ANGRY BLACK MAN, *Black man, mid-thirties to mid-forties*
WHITE WOMAN, *white woman, forties, working class*

And
THE BOY, *unseen behind a curtain*

Note

A forward slash (/) in the text indicates the point at which the next speaker interrupts.

Scene One – And so it began on the 4th of May 2017

Dim light. ANGRY BLACK MAN (ABM) *is sitting on the floor, completing a prayer. A table, surrounded by a curtain, sits in the middle of the space.*

ABM (*as he turns to look at his right shoulder*). Asalamu aleykum wa Rahmatullah.

(*As he turns to look at his left shoulder.*) Asalamu aleykum wa Rahmatullah.

(*Looking down, hands up.*) My Lord, the Guide, show us the best way, the middle way. Ameen.

ABM *stands and picks up a bowl of water. He approaches the table and circles it without looking at it.*

I've been reminding myself of the stories of the greatest men that lived. I'm reminded of Moses who had to face the fearsome Pharoah and who turned to his Lord:

'My Lord, put my heart at peace for me and make my task easy for me and remove the knot from my tongue, that they may understand my speech.'

ABM *blows into the water three times.*

Speak!

ABM *resumes walking in a circle.*

I'm reminded of Job who cried to his Lord, 'Adversity had afflicted me,' and God ordered him, 'Strike with thy foot.'

ABM *blows into the water three times.*

Walk! And God returned his health and his family to him.

ABM *stops circling and sits away, still holding the bowl with both hands.*

Smoke.

ABM *recites verses under his breath and blows on the water every now and then.*

ANGRY BLACK WOMAN (ABW) *enters with a folder and urgency. She lays the papers out on the floor.*

ABW. I think I see a pattern. Clues. They've been right here in front of my eyes. I've made pie charts, and graphs from the spreadsheets – time on the Y axis, progress on the X, you'd love it. Undeveloping. Is that even a word? Shall we look it up? Never a bad time to learn new words, is it? Where's that dictionary? Ah, 'Undeveloped: Not having developed.' But that's not true, not completely, is it?

ABW *walks around the table backwards.*

Backwards. Backwards. But to where? Where's better than here? Where's safer than here? Oh my God. The womb. Oh my God. That's it. There's a book here somewhere. The one about what to expect when you're expecting? That one. I should stop collecting books, shouldn't I? They're taking over this house. Here, here, I found it.

ABW *returns to the floor and charts and compares them against the book.*

I've found a pattern, I've found a bloody pattern. I'm closer to understanding this. A breakthrough. Can I say Eureka?!

ABM *returns to the table and walks around it.* ABW *gets up and walks around the table in the opposite direction.*

All I have to do is find the patterns, follow the clues.

ABM. Prayer is the weapon of the believer.

ABW. I'll find the key that   ABM. I will use it to pry open
unlocks this box.   this box.

ABW. You wanna hear a joke? Donald Trump is even more orange now.

ABM. I was thinking, can you try praying?

ABW. You think he binge-eats carrots while he decides who deserves freedom of movement?

ABM. Imagine yourself in prayer, standing, bending, bowing, sitting. Just run it through your head. Walk.

ABW. That Hopkins woman-demon tweeted something the other day, 'Dear Black people. If your lives matter why do you stab and shoot each other so much.' She's vile but they keep giving her the platform to spew her hate. Because white people can do that, speak freely, their speech is never inciting hatred or violence, it's free, it's worthy.

ABM. Can you recite the opening chapter of the Quran? It may open the box. It's not called 'the Opener' for nothing. Speak.

ABW. And as we hurtle towards a sudden election, our unelected Prime Minister is not speaking to journalists except to say there are many complex reasons why nurses are using food banks. I mean really.

ABM. You are a traveller in this world. Never become attached to anything on it or in it.

ABW. And good old UKIP has pledged to ban the headscarf because that's just what this country needs to focus on right now. Oppressing women. And nothing will get better until we band together as Muslims, as Black people, as Black Muslims to stop this global far-right leaning. The world is tilting to the right, and it is our job to bring it back to neutral.

ABM. Everything is in God's   ABW. It's in your hands.
    hands.

    ABM *and* ABW *bump into each other.*

ABW. What are you doing here?

ABM. I want to come home.

    Doorbell.

ABW. Is that a philosophical home or the home you left /

ABM. / Things need to change. We need to do something different. I'll get that.

    ABM *leaves to get the door.*

ABW (*to no one in particular*). He left one eve with not so much as a by your leave, his fears in his bag and his tail out of wag.

    He doesn't look at me like he used to, doesn't look at me like *I'm* used to.

He doesn't talk to me like he used to, talk to me like *I'm* used to.

ABM *returns with* WHITE WOMAN (WW). ABW *rushes at* WW. ABM *grabs her.*

(*To* WW.) You can't come in here! (*To* ABM.) Lemme go. I want her out of my house. Lemme go.

ABM. Calm down.

WW. I was under the impression /

ABW. / You have no right. I told you I didn't want anyone /

ABM. / Calm down and I'll let you go.

ABW (*to no one*). Six weeks' absence, on an undeclared trip and he returns with his hard grip.

WW *begins to walk magnetically towards the table. She peeps through the curtain.*

ABM. Right. Now we can talk properly, like adults.

WW *moves in a circle around the table.* ABW *and* ABM *begin to move in a circle of their own.*

ABW. Don't you patronise me. You think, you actually think you can come back in here and run things? Just like that.

ABM. I only want what's best /

ABW. / Best for whom? You!! That's who /

ABM. For us. For him.

ABW (*to no one*). Another short cut, in and out of this marriage like a shoulder popping out of its socket.

ABM. We can make it work this time, if we get the proper help. If we let her help –

ABW *looks to find* WW *reaching out to the table.* ABM *holds* ABW *back.*

ABW. Get away from my /

ABM. / Professor, please.

ABW. Get out of my house.

ABM *holds* ABW *close and they both begin to circle around the table, following* WW. WW *walks backwards around the table.*

WW. I urge you to consider this properly.

ABM. Just hear her out.

ABW (*to no one*). They conspire behind my back, here to hijack.

ABM. You know we've tried everything else. We can't do this alone any more.

ABW. There is no 'W' in ME, I did all the work while you faffed about in a spiritual cloud. I did all the work.

ABM. That's not fair.

ABW. When are you going to learn life is not fair. Fair is for people like her.

WW. Look, I can get you help. Relationship counselling. You must be under /

ABW *throws something at the* WW. *It may be a bracelet.*

ABW. And now you bring her into my house to rub it in my face. Get out!

ABM. Stop this nonsense. Hear her out first. She can /

WW. / I think it's time for me to leave.

ABM. Please stay.

ABW (*to no one*). They negotiate my life like they have a say. They will hound and hound until I sway.

ABM. Ten minutes. That's all. Give her five minutes.

ABW (*to no one*). She thinks she brings me hope.

ABM. And if she hasn't got anything to offer in those ten minutes /

ABW (*to no one*). / I'll hand her a rope.

ABM. I'll ask her to leave.

ABW. Five minutes. And I never want to see her again after that. You. Go. Let's see what you've got.

ABM. Thank you.

WW. What's his name?

ABW. Ask him yourself.

> WW *moves closer to the table, draws the curtain back a little and looks down.*

WW. Hello. I'm Professor Jones. What's your name?

> *Silence.*

> May I?

ABW. No.

ABM. Let her do her job.

ABW. Four minutes.

WW. Not responsive to touch or speech. Normal reflexes.

ABW. You moved the tube! I knew we shouldn't have let you touch him.

ABM. Just put it back. Here, let me, you're shaking. Hand me the syringe.

WW. I'm sorry. I didn't mean to.

ABM. Do you think, does it look like?

ABW. Don't give her the answer, that's cheating.

WW. How long has he been feeding through the tube?

ABM. A year or so. Hand me the pH strips.

ABW (*to* ABM). 24th of June 2016.

WW. His health generally, before he got here?

ABM. Fine. Healthy, bright, active. But then things… he began to decline, and then finally this. Professor, do you think it's what we think?

ABW. What *you* think.

WW. Resignation Syndrome. If it is, it would be the first of its kind in the UK.

ABW. But it's not, so you're wasting your time.

ABM. Give her a chance. You were saying.

WW. It's as though, exhausted physically and emotionally, some children give up... fall into this state, like Snow White.

ABW. Except he's a little Black boy.

WW. Race is irrelevant to this.

ABW. Race is never irrelevant. (*To* ABM.) Did you think to get one that understands the ramification of race on physical and emotional wellbeing? No. You got Snow White herself. And the dwarves, are they in a seven-seater outside?

ABM. Just let her finish, will you? The professor has recently returned from a tenure at a university in Sweden. She's had first-hand experience of children like our son /

ABW. / And how many of them were Black?

WW. None. That is not to say /

ABW. And how many were Muslim?

WW. None as far as I am aware.

ABW. Our son is both those things. Both those things. (*To* ABM.) What is she saying we haven't heard before? (*To* WW.) I believe you have two minutes left.

ABM. It's the right colour; his stomach pH is fine. Now give me the feeding syringe. Thanks. You have the feed there? Pour it in. Gently.

WW. 24th June, that's when you were denied leave to remain in the UK.

ABW *claps her hands.*

ABM. We're British.

WW. Oh. This normally happens to refugee children whose families have faced deportation.

ABW. That wouldn't be us.

WW. He stopped speaking his mother tongue.

ABW *claps.*

ABM (*to* ABW). Will you stop that?! (*To* WW.) He stopped speaking English, not his mother tongue. He couldn't make sense of English any more.

ABW. The words became noise to him. White noise.

ABM. The school had to get him a teacher's assistant who could speak /

WW. / Your mother tongue.

ABM. Arabic.

ABW. Except Arabic is not our mother tongue.

ABM. Arabic was the only language he said he could comprehend. So we got him an Arabic-speaking TA. And we did what we could to improve our basic Arabic.

WW. Why would he choose Arabic?

ABW. He's Muslim. It chose him.

ABM. He learns it at the Islamic school, on Saturdays. I mean he used to.

WW. Why would a British boy want to withdraw?

ABW *claps in mock mirth.*

ABW. From British life? More reasons than you have dwarves, Snow White. Your time is up. Say hi to the boys.

ABM. Hang on, hang on.

ABW. She came in here sure of herself and her knowledge and now she is leaving more bewildered than us.

ABM. Professor, is there anything you can do for us?

WW. I would need time, to sit and talk to you two, take a history, understand /

ABW. / You will never understand us.

ABM. Wouldn't that be better than doing nothing?

ABW. I have given up everything to be by his side day in, day out, everything and you call it nothing. Get out and take her with you.

ABM. We can't leave him like this, to…

ABW. Die? Maybe it's better he does.

ABM. Don't you dare say /

WW. / I'm sorry. I was only trying to help. It's time for me to leave.

ABW. It's been time for a long time. See yourself out. Take this man with you. We have no use for him either.

ABM. I'm sorry, Professor. We best be going.

WW. Just one last question /

ABW. No, Columbo. Take your clues and leave.

WW. The significance of the date, the 24th of June? Did something happen to finally push him into this unmoving state?

ABM. No, nothing that we can think of.

ABW. That was the day after, you and a small majority of this country voted us out of the EU. He saw the result on the morning news, went upstairs, still in his uniform, lay down and never got up again. Now, for the tenth time, get out of my house!

WW *and* ABM *leave*. ABW *stands in front of the table*.

ABW (*to* BOY). Everything's going to be okay. Trust Mummy to bring you back. I know you can hear me. I know you love me. I know you'll find your way back. You don't have to rush just to make Mummy happy, okay? Take as long as you need to. Come back when you feel safe. Mummy will be here. I will wait forever but it won't be that long, will it? No. Forever is for fairytales, silly Mummy, and fairytales are not meant for little Black boys.

ABW *backs away from the table*.

He doesn't look at me like he used to, doesn't look at me like *I'm* used to.

He doesn't talk to me like he used to, talk to me like *I'm* used to.

My boy, my boy, my boy.

Scene Two – Papa and Mama drama

ABW *touches the* BOY.

ABW. You're wet, why are you wet? Have you been sweating?

Pause.

What have you been doing to him? I'm letting you visit him, can you not drown him, please!

ABM. Why do you talk like that? Like I'm harming him.

ABW. He'll catch a cold.

ABM. The water is warm and it's good for him.

ABW. How do you know?

ABM. I believe.

ABW. Yes, but how can you measure it?

Silence.

How can you track it?

ABM. Why does it matter? As long he gets better /

ABW. / Of course it matters! If you know which verses you're reciting are having an effect and which aren't, wouldn't you start doing more of /

ABM. / All of the Quran is healing.

ABW. Oh for goodness' sake. I'm not disputing that /

ABM. / Sometimes I wonder.

ABW (*to no one*). Back again to this button-pushing, this pushing and shoving.

(*To* ABM.) You wonder what?

ABM. Nothing works without belief.

ABW. Faith doesn't work without work.

ABM. I want to make things right.

ABW. Maybe stop bringing white women home?

ABM. Things need to change. We need to do something different. For him. Get him help.

ABW. You've given up on the prayers?

ABM. I will never give up on prayer. We've tried everything else. He's not got any physical illnesses.

ABW. So it must be psychological? I don't want those people in his head. Feeding him /

ABM. / Better than what you feed him.

ABW. Love, you mean. Dedication, you mean.

ABM. You feed him racism and Islamophobia.

ABW (*to no one*). When did the love turn to this? Guns blazing.

(*To* ABM.) That's the world he lives in. The one you hide away from in a haze of spirituality. When you should be teaching him how to be a boy, a Black boy. A Black Muslim boy.

ABM. I am a good father.

ABW. And I am a bad mother?

ABM. I didn't say that! It's just you talk to him about all this stuff, this political garbage.

ABW. Did I bring this 'political garbage' into his life or did his school? Did the TV? Did the kids at the playground? Tell me. Remember how this all started? Do you? The day the school made him take that questionnaire, 'to identify the initial seeds of radicalisation with children of primary-school age', they said. Remember that day?

ABM. Course I remember.

ABW. Do you really? 'Cause I don't remember you being there to comfort him, give him context when he came home upset that he had gotten the questions wrong. That he hadn't studied those questions in class? Was it Science? Was it English? What was it? He thought he had failed, the questions were so hard. He didn't like to fail.

ABM. I wanted him to stay a child. It was too early for /

ABW. / But it's too late to keep him childlike; they beat us to it; they profile our children without our consent, and turn them into suspicious adults so we are forced to talk to them like they are adults, before their time, before they are ready, before we are. You think I want to talk to him about this?

ABM. You get lost in it. It's like you enjoy it.

ABW. How dare you! You think I enjoyed contacting the school and demanding to see the questionnaire? Sitting in the headteacher's office while they made me wait 'cause there was an angry Black woman they wanted to calm down first? You think I enjoyed that! You think I enjoyed having to pore over the questions with him… did you actually read the questionnaire?

ABM. Hun /

ABW. / 'Religious books are to be understood word for word.' Did you? 'I believe my religion is the only correct one.' You read that shit, didn't you? Leading questions. I never stopped to ask, did you actually read them?

ABM. I did /

ABW. / 'God has a purpose for me.' You must have read it. You didn't sleep, stood in prayer most of the night. Primary-school children being asked to answer Yes or No to: 'I would do what a grown-up told me to do even if it seemed odd to me.'

ABM. I'd never read anything so vile. But what was the point of going over it with him? He was distraught by the end of it.

ABW. He was already distraught! He'd compared answers with his friends. His teacher had said there was no right or wrong answer. It didn't make sense to him.

ABM. You didn't have to tell him everything. He's free to practise his faith as he chooses.

ABW. Is he? You don't believe that, do you? That you are free?

ABM. I do.

ABW. And is that what you told him when you took him to the bookshop the next day? Brought him back home with a badge that said, 'I love Islam'. The one you pinned to his school bag. You think you can talk about love without talking about hate?

ABM. I don't want him /

ABW. / To reject his faith because it might get too hard?

ABM. He'll never leave Islam.

ABW. So much for freedom.

Silence.

You want him to stay a Muslim and not give him the tools.

ABM. His faith gives him the tools.

ABW. He also needs to know how to use them in the context of the world he is living in.

ABM. I want to come home.

ABW. You said.

ABM. He needs us both. He also needs what we can't give him… someone… a professional.

ABW. His faith gives him all the tools he needs.

ABM. Don't throw that back at me.

ABW. Easy really.

ABM. I want the professor /

ABW. / Over my very dead, very Black, very Muslim, very womanly body.

ABM. So fucking melodramatic.

ABW. Language, O Saint.

ABM. We shouldn't argue in front of him. We never did that before, before this.

ABW. We never argued full-stop. There was nothing to hide from him.

ABM. This whole thing; it's put a big strain on us. I want to, I want to do better by you. You deserve more from me. He deserves more from me.

Silence.

Look, I'm not perfect but between your persistence, your charts and scientific ways and my Islamic healing, we can bring him back.

Silence.

Okay, if not for me, for him. He needs us both. I want to come home.

ABW. No.

Scene Three – WW and ABM plot

WW *walks around the table.*

WW. There is no precedent for this, yet. The first of its kind. A reverse Resignation Syndrome. A child born and bred in the UK withdraws into wilful death. Unheard of. Typically seen in refugee children who are triggered into this state when their parents are denied asylum. The child eventually returns to life when the parents appeal, supported by the new detail of the child's illness, and are successful. No indication the children are deliberately placing themselves in this state or have control over it.

WW *stops and stands over the* BOY.

What is it that you are running away from, little one? If we took that away, would you come back like the others? They wanted to stay in their new countries but you, what do you want? The opposite?

Pause.

You want to leave! Is that it? You want to leave.

ABM *walks in nervously.*

ABM. We have an hour, at the most. I convinced her to go to some yoga thing.

WW. Yoga! I didn't expect that.

ABM. She says it originated in Africa. I found her a Black-focused women's yoga group. She won't hurry out of there quickly but we can't take the risk, we have to be quick. I hate that I have to resort to this.

WW. You want him well, don't you?

ABM. Yes, yes, of course, he's the priority. What are you thinking, Professor?

WW. He shows all the symptoms of other children with Resignation Syndrome.

ABM. At least we have a name for his condition. It's better than all the not knowing we've had to endure.

WW. Perhaps. The children are always refugee children, your son isn't. They go into this state when their parents are refused asylum, but you two are citizens. We have to identify the trigger in this case.

ABM. I don't know. His mum thinks, doesn't matter, I can help /

WW. / His mum thinks what?

ABM. I think it's just a coincidence.

WW. Brexit.

ABM. And other things. She thinks she sees relationships between his decline and what was happening at his school and politically. She's quite obsessed, she keeps meticulous notes of his progress: dates, global events, school incidents, all /

WW. / Do you have them?

ABM. Yeah, they're over here. You think she has a point?

WW. I need the history, in order to find out the final trigger. Let me see. The children, we think they go into this state following a period of prolonged stress and depression.

ABM. Depression? No, no he wasn't depressed; he is just a child, for God's sake.

WW. Look, I understand this is difficult to hear as his parent but it's important not to get bogged down, I'm not looking to blame, I'm here to help you bring him back.

Pause.

You and your wife, what were things like between you in the months, year leading up to this.

ABM. I know what you're thinking, I know what you saw but she, we were fine until this. It's put an enormous pressure on us both and we take it out on each other.

WW. What else was happening in his life? At school? What's this here? It seems to begin here. 'Questionnaire.' What's that?

ABM. The school made the children take a quiz – to root out radicalism.

WW. Disgraceful! How did he take it?

ABM. Pretty badly, we all did to be honest. His mum, she marched into the school accusing them of targeting Muslim children.

WW. She wouldn't be wrong. How did he respond?

ABM. Confused, he felt like a failure. His mum, she, she then gave him a run-down of world politics, Islamophobia, Trump. To give him context she said, but I felt she'd gone too far. He withdrew from his teachers from then on. Almost as though he stopped being able to comprehend them and it was unlike him, he was a smart boy, so he would come home and we would have to go over lessons with him. She started talking about home-schooling him.

WW. You think she added to his plate?

Silence.

This here, what's this, the next point he declines significantly. It says Secret Census.

ABM. The Department of Education had a secret agreement with the Home Office to share the data of up to fifteen hundred children a month for immigration-enforcement purposes. It was kept secret from parents, the press and the public until a Freedom of Information Act request was made.

WW. Diabolical. They were using children /

ABM. / As a proxy for immigration services. His teacher singled out the brown and Black children in the class, in the guise of a game. She asked everyone to write and draw where they were born and what their citizenship was. She then collected only the brown and Black children's work, said she was going to put them up on the board, they were the best.

WW. What?! But that's, that's heinous.

ABM. He was already sensitive and when he saw who was being singled out, albeit for 'good work', he came home saying he could no longer understand his teachers. He'd lost the ability to comprehend English.

WW. I'm so sorry. He's been through a lot, poor guy.

ABM. You think she has a point. That it's definitely related?

WW. This sort of thing occurs in the meeting between certain cultures. She may have a very valid point, yes. Your little boy feels rejected and has withdrawn.

ABM. And all this time, I didn't want to believe she was right.

WW. She's not fully right.

ABM. Oh?

WW. He could do with hearing less of the 'context', or be provided with a softer version of matters. We can't change the world around him but we can /

ABM. / change how much we expose him to. So I was right.

WW. You both are. So.

ABM. How can I stop her sharing so much with him? She's now talking to him about the coming election.

WW. Maybe you don't have to. Maybe all you have to do is keep her busier. Keep her away so he has time to de-stress.

ABM. Professor, are you saying for my son to come back to us, I will have to keep his own mother away from him?

Silence.

Scene Four – Together

ABW *is practising the Hudu Air Movement.* Drums beat.*

ABW. It's hard to pull answers into existence. To pull together dates and facts and emotions and work out how to push the pain away. Once I know, once I have the answer, I will be able to push it away and it will be easier than all this pulling. Pulling, pulling. I want you to imagine, son, that you are at the end of this rope and I am pulling you to me, each day I bring you closer back to me. I sense your willingness, you want to come back to me. Mummy will pull you back from… where are you, son? Do you want me to come to you? Is that it? I would if I knew how.

Am I supposed to be thinking about this laterally? That out-of-the-box thinking they talk about. I wish I were more creative. Maybe that's what this needs, blue-sky thinking, not numbers and graphs.

Where are you, son? I hate that this world has pushed you away instead of pulling you into its arms. Are you like those refugee children? They love their new countries, in fact the more they love their country of refuge, the more they feel they belong, the more likely they are to withdraw into this state. Hah. That's the opposite of you though, born here, African roots, you've been nagging me to take you to Africa ever since…

You want to leave! They want to stay and you want to leave! Is that it? Oh my God. Those other children wake up when their parents are finally allowed to stay. Would you wake up if you were allowed to leave? How would I move you? There must be a way. It might not be easy. To take you to Africa. Yes, that's what I'm going to do. I'm going to take you away before this damned election throws this country into further chaos. Can't tell your dad though. Hmmm. Mummy needs a plan. I'll work it out, son, but can you hear me? I'm taking you away from here, to Africa.

ABW *assumes a position.†*

ABM *walks in.*

ABM. How is he?

ABW. Same.

---

* See youtu.be/4FlB_Byb6CY

† https://s-media-cache-ak0.pinimg.com/originals/ee/77/ab/
ee77abf0ac5557af91032599b047b43c.jpg

ABM. What's that?

ABW. Yoga. African Yoga.

ABM. You look like /

ABW. A queen on the walls of an Egyptian pyramid.

ABM. Kind of sexy, actually.

ABW. Don't be getting any ideas. You could do with this though.
You're shaped like the couch.

ABM. And whose fault is that? I do my own yoga five times a day.
And at night. I miss praying with you.

> ABM *sits on the floor to the left of* ABW *and mimics* ABW*'s
> yoga position.* ABW *is faced away from him.* ABM *faces* ABW.

ABW. What's got into you?

ABM. Have you forgotten how it used to be?

ABW. Pressed delete when you left.

ABM. I needed a restart. We had lost our way.

> ABM *touches his right hand to her left hand.* ABW *tries to pull
> away.*

> Stay. I was overwhelmed. You seemed to have a plan, all that
> doing, doing, doing, it was overwhelming. Just wanted to sit
> still with you sometimes and just be. Still. Stop resisting. Look
> at me. I'm sorry. Give me your heart again. A sliver of it. I'm
> lost without you.

> ABW *turns to look at him.*

> I want to make it up to you. I have an idea. There's a woman's
> spa in Turkey.

ABW. A spa?

ABM. A retreat surrounded by forest, with wholesome food,
massage therapists, saunas, swings hanging over pools, thermal
waters to ease tired bodies and healing.

ABW. For our baby!

ABM. For my baby. I've bought you a package. I want you to go
alone. Recharge.

ABW. That's insane. I can't go /

ABM. / Shhh. Close your eyes. Come on. Close your eyes and
listen with your heart. I want you to go. Alone. Recharge. Close
those eyes. You're safe.

ABW *closes her eyes*. ABM *follows suit*.

Imagine taking a walk in nature, blue sky peeping through.
Imagine lowering yourself into a hot spring full of minerals.
Imagine swinging above a cool pool. Imagine healing hands
rubbing hot stones on your back. Imagine sleep, uninterrupted
sleep, waking up to birdsong, refreshed in the morning. Three
days.

ABW. That sounds so dreamy.

ABM. It's real. I've bought you a three-day spa package. The
Queen's Package, they call it. Close your eyes.

ABW. How did you know I'd opened them?

ABM. I know you deeply. Close them. I've taken a couple of days
off. I'll be with him twenty-four hours. Trust me with him. Trust
yourself to rest. Remember how we used to sit in remembrance
of our Lord, how we contemplated nature, this world and its
wonder? (*Chanting*.) Allah. Allah. Allah.

ABW *and* ABM. Allahu Akbar. Allahu Akbar.

ABM. It's settled then.

ABW. Three whole days?

ABM. It's not like you're going to Africa. Up you get. Let's pray,
baby.

ABW *and* ABM *stand*. ABM *raises his arms, palms facing
forward*.

Allahu Akbar.

ABW. Allahu Akbar.

ABM *and* ABW *fold their hands over their bellies*.

Scene Five – Promises, promises, promises

Friday evening, 19th May 2017.

BOY (*voice-over*). Africa.

WW. Hello? Hello? Yes, yes, this is she. I can talk now.

ABW. Mummy's going to be back in three days. Seventy-seven
hours to be exact. Dad's taken Monday off; you know how rare
that is. He's going to be with you twenty-four hours, praying
probably, eh? He's either working or praying, your daddy.
Mummy fell off the to-do list at some point. Gosh, that sounds
wrong. He's making up for it now though. Daddy's done well.
SPF that'll make me look like a ghost – check, passport – check,
Lonely Planet Guide to Africa – check, burkini – check, a copy
of the Quran, UKIP should see this suitcase, haha. Mummy's
looking forward to this.

ABM. You mother will pray for you while she's gone. The prayer
of the traveller is accepted. It's also raining – another time when
prayers are accepted; that's double the prayer power. And I'll
keep praying too, son. Our Lord tells us not to give up on His
Mercy. He will bring you back to us. Just a little break from
Mummy and her politics, son.

ABW. And when I come back, Mummy's gonna find a way to get
us to Africa, before these stupid elections make things even
worse for us. Twenty days left. You'll like that, won't you? An
adventure? We can decide where to go, east, north, west or
south. Daddy doesn't need to know. He worries too much.

WW. I'm going to monitor him over the next couple of days and
see how he responds to his mother's absence.

ABM. You deserve to stay a little boy as long as possible.

ABW. Mummy's got to go now, honey. I'll carry you in my heart.
Mummy's never far from you. You are half of me. Daddy will
take care of you.

ABW *and* ABM *leave.*

WW. I should be available for interview at the end of next week.

WW *leaves.*

BOY (*voice-over*). Stranger danger.

Scene Six – Surprise

Late Monday evening, 22nd May 2017. ABM is washing the BOY with a wash-cloth and a bowl of warm water.

ABM. He's ready now, Professor. Nice and clean for you.

Silence.

ABM *begins circling the* BOY *slowly.*

What are you doing there?

WW. I'm rubbing his sternum. No reaction. None when I apply some pressure to his fingertips either. Does he move at all?

ABM. His big toe, when I wash the sole of his foot.

WW. That's a good sign, means there isn't any structural damage.

ABM *starts circling the* BOY *quickly.*

ABM. Any change, Professor?

WW. It's only the second day. We should be cautious about our expectations.

ABM. What do you have there?

WW. An ice-pack. Checking if his pulse and blood pressure change. Nothing. It's like I haven't placed an ice-pack on his belly at all.

WW *walks out.*

ABM *begins to pace around the* BOY *quickly.*

ABM. Day three. My Lord, I have prayed and prayed for our son. My heart has shattered and my mind risks following suit. I am almost at breaking point. Today, I need you more than he does. I'm floundering, floundering, please do not forsake me. Don't the heavens shake when I call your name in pain, don't the angels follow the light that beams from our home every night when I stand in prayer. Don't I remember you when I eat, when I walk and talk, when I make love to my wife and foresake all others, when I forgive the racist and the bigot, when I go hungry for you twice a week, when I give to the needy? Does the dark circle on my forehead not mark me as your subject, do my grey knees not humble me as your servant? Do I not put all those I love before me? Am I not your slave? A nothing. An everything.

I know you hear my cries. You love to hear my voice, so you make me call you by all your names, by day, by night and even in my dreams. My Lord! Truly, I am in need of whatever good that you bestow on me! Ameen.

ABM *opens his eyes.*

Son! Your tube, here let me. Professor! Professor!

WW *enters.*

WW. What's wrong? Is he okay?

ABM. I found his feeding tube out of place.

WW. Well, did you move it when you washed him earlier?

ABM. No, no. This was after. I didn't touch him again, not a finger, not after his wash. I was praying over him, the prayer, glory be to Allah, the prayer worked.

WW. Let's not forget /

ABM. / Son, son, can you hear me? Are you returning to us? Say you are. Say you are.

WW. His mother *has* been gone for three days.

Silence.

ABM. But the prayer /

WW. You've been praying and praying all along. Why now? What's different?

ABM. Persistence. Prayer favours the consistent person.

WW. I understand, I really do, why you would prefer to believe that than /

ABM. / The important thing is that he's shown progress. That's never happened before. He must have moved his head.

Pause.

You didn't move him, did you?

WW. I can assure you I did no such thing. Whatever this is, whatever progress he could have made, we must continue to ensure /

ABM. / She'll be here soon.

WW. It might interrupt his progress.

ABM. What's the alternative?

WW. Tell her!

ABM. That her presence makes him sick? Look, Professor, I appreciate everything you have done for us. Maybe we don't have to do this any more. Maybe this is enough – to jump-start his healing, bring him back.

WW. Find a way! For his sake.

ABM. She'll be back soon. Please gather your things and leave before she returns. I'll be in touch. Give me a few days. Son, son, well done, well done. Do it again, son. Can you move? The camera, my phone… I need to record this in case he…

ABM *leaves the room.* WW *takes a photo of the* BOY *discreetly.* ABW *walks in.*

ABW. Get away from him! What were you doing? If you've hurt him, I swear to God /

WW. / I haven't! He's fine.

ABW. Who let you in?

WW. Your husband.

ABW. That bastard.

ABW. Are you okay, honey? Did she hurt you? Let me see, let me see /

WW. / I haven't harmed him. I wouldn't. I'm here to help him back. I have an idea.

ABW. I don't need your help. All people like you do is reinforce sick children's symptoms. You can't bring him back.

WW. And you think you can?

ABW. I'm his mother, his mother. I know more about him than you do. I want you out of my house!

WW. What are you afraid of?

ABW. Don't you try and psychoanalyse me!

WW. What are you afraid of for him?

ABW. Me? You mean what this society is afraid of? Black boys. Muslim boys. They're afraid of him so they hurt him. Doesn't matter that he is a little boy. No, no. Annihilate his self-esteem and sense of belonging early so he doesn't grow up to be a Black man. A Muslim man. They want him dead and he has obliged.

ABM *walks back in.*

So this is how it's going to be from now on?

ABM. Babe, let me explain. I wanted to give her a chance; see if it would make a difference.

ABW. So you wait until, no, you set this whole thing up. Silly me.

(*To no one.*) He sends me away to another land so he may force my hand.

(*To* ABM.) You betrayed me. Again. Is this who you've become. A traitor!

ABM. It's for his good. Our good ultimately. We want the same thing – to bring him back.

ABW (*to no one*). By any means necessary, how contrary to his belief.

(*To* ABM.) The system that has made him withdraw, become sick, cannot bring him back, make him better. Don't you see that?

ABM. That's not true. Let's stay calm.

ABW (*to no one*). Calm in the face of betrayal, while he stares at his navel.

WW. Are you going to tell her?

ABM. Please, Professor. Leave us to talk about this alone.

ABW. Tell me what?

WW. Your son /

ABM. / Professor, please, not like this /

ABW. / Someone better start talking.

WW. Your son has /

ABM. / Professor, do you mind!! I'll take care of this.

WW. Your son moved. While under *my* care.

ABW. What? What's she talking about?

ABM. It's true. Honey. He moved.

ABW. How? Where?

WW. His head.

ABM. I found his feeding tube out of place.

ABW. And you believe her?

WW. Your husband found the tube himself.

ABW. You moved it. (*To* ABM.) You're really falling for this bitch's moves, aren't you?

WW. How dare you /

ABM. / Why would she do such a thing?

ABW (*to no one*). A man is blind if he can't see through his heart, his first eye.

ABM. It's the prayer, hun. I prayed for three days in a row, finally I made a prayer for my own self, you know the one the prophet Musa made when he had nothing, that's when it /

ABW. / Oh, shut up. You're both as bad as each other.

ABM. You're being disrespectful now and I won't have it.

WW. So if it wasn't the prayer, what was it?

ABW. Why are you still in my house, Snow White? Don't the dwarves need seeing to?

WW. He moved because you were gone, because he had a break from your endless talk of politics and pain. He could rest in a peaceful environment, away from your constant chatter of Brexit, racism and the elections.

ABW. So this is my fault? I'm to blame for the state of the world and the Black man's place in it? How convenient! Blame the victims for their oppression. Snow White, you're showing your true colour of privilege.

ABM. Professor, I think you should leave now.

WW. I'm just getting started. (*To* ABW.) You don't have to bring that into your home. It should be his refuge /

ABW. / There is no paradise on earth for people like us. You can look down your nose at my lived experience with your theories all you like, all you like, but you will never get it. Now you heard my husband, out of my house.

WW. You're not going to pretend you didn't invite me here!

ABM. Of course not, and I appreciate all that you have done for him but can you leave it to us as a family now?

WW. I'm not going anywhere until you tell her /

ABM. / There's nothing more to tell. Now, if you don't mind.

ABW (*to no one*). There is no bottom to betrayal. It falls deep and dark.

WW. You're not going to pretend you didn't want her gone because you thought it would do him good. There she is. Tell her. What are you afraid of?

ABM. Nothing.   ABW. Everything.

ABW. You think I make our son sick?

ABM. No. I wanted him to have a break from it all. Just for a few days.

ABW. You conspired with her behind my back because you think I make our son ill.

ABM. Not make him exactly, just make it harder, baby, I love you.

WW. This is pitiful.

ABM. Get out!

WW. Gladly. Between the two of you, it's no wonder your little boy doesn't want to return. The Coward and the Rebel Without A Cause.

WW *leaves*.

ABM. Hun.

ABW. Don't touch me. You came back into my life so you could betray me. Deprive a little boy of his own mother to satisfy your theories. You're pathetic and weak.

Pause.

I'm taking him to Africa. The answer's been staring us in the face all along.

ABM. What are you talking about?

ABW. Those other kids, the refugee kids, they wake up, they return when their parents are allowed to stay in their new country.

ABM. What's that got to /

ABW. / Use your head! For once. He will come back when we take him to Africa, back to his roots. I'm taking him /

ABM. / No.

ABW. Before this election.

ABM. You can't move him /

ABW. / I'll find a way. I don't need your help.

ABM. He's my child too.

ABW. Get out!

ABM. You can't keep kicking me out of my own home.

ABW. Funny thing, betrayal. It destroys everything.

ABM. Hun /

ABW. / Just go.

ABM *leaves.*

You ready, young man? For Africa? Mummy has seventeen days to find a way to get you there.

Scene Seven – Boom

Very early hours, 23rd May 2017.

ABW *is on her tablet.*

ABW. I'm researching airlines that go to Africa. Makes sense to go to the closest African country, doesn't it, so we don't have to be travelling for a long period of time. Where do you think that might be, baby? Take a guess.

Pause.

Morocco! Some town, peaceful, close to the sea. You like the sea, don't you? Shit, oh my God. Manchester. Suicide bomber? Oh my God. Those poor babies. Why? Why? At a concert! We have to get out of here, fast. They'll be coming for us. They'll want us Muslims to apologise and feel bad and they'll harass us on the streets like always happens after one of these incidents. I'm booking tickets right now. I'm not having us exposed to one more of these things!

Silence.

Just when we're getting close to the elections. Typical. Typical. Well, I see through it. Work the people up into a frenzied, frightened state, and Pied Piper them into an election win. I'll be damned if I'm going to let you go through another one of these fiascos.

Silence.

Mummy's looking for a wheelchair for you. Something robust, that won't jerk you around. How about one of those electric ones? You charge them up and off you go. You won't need it for long once we're in Africa, will you?

Silence.

That evil Katie Hopkins. She just tweeted something again, we have to get you out of this country. You're not safe here. Imagine tweeting something that vile. Mummy's in the next room, getting a paracetamol. She has the worst headache, she barely slept after her return from Turkey last night. BRB. We need a final solution, she said, we need a final solution. Evil! She wants us exterminated.

ABW *leaves.*

BOY (*voice-over*). Mark Duggan – August 2011.

Eric Garner – July 2012.

Michael Brown – August 2014.

Sheku Bayoh – May 2015.

Anton Sterling – 5th July 2016.

Philando Castille – 6th July 2016.

Mzee Mohammed – 13th July 2016.

Me – 8th June 2017.

Black boys

Black boys die

Black boys die in the summer.

ABW *returns*.

ABW. Feels more like a migraine to be honest. Must be all that healthy food I had at the spa. This detox business is not all it's cracked… your tube, dear God, you moved, did you move? Talk to me! Did you move, hun?

Silence.

I can't believe… I'm so happy. You moved. That's two days in a row now. You're coming back to us! Oh dear God, all praise is due to you. Thank you, thank you. I'm so proud of you, baby. Your dad was right.

Silence.

You did move. While I was gone. You moved. While I was gone. Mummy was gone when you moved. You moved when Mummy was gone.

ABW *holds her stomach*.

Mummy feels a little sick. All that green food's making Mummy green! Get it? Joke. Mummy will be right back.

ABW *leaves. We hear her retching*. ABW *returns*.

That's better. Better out than in, eh? Better away than here. Is that… is that what you need, hun? For Mummy to go away?

Will you come back if Mummy goes away? I will, you know. I
will do anything to have you back even if it means leaving you.
Don't feel bad if that's what you need. Mummy can take it.
Mummy's sorry if she made you worse.

Silence.

Mummy's going to go lie down next door. She won't sleep next
to you tonight. Mummy wants to give you the space you need.

ABW *leaves.*

BOY (*voice-over*). I want Africa.

Scene Eight – Alone

Saturday evening, 27th May 2017. Day One of Ramadan.

ABW *has got her notebooks out. She circles the* BOY *as she
scribbles.*

ABW. That's five days Mum's been leaving you by yourself.
You're doing really well. I hope you're proud of yourself.
You're on Mummy's mind every second she's gone. Mummy
has to be vigilant when she's out there, you know, some angry
people want to take out what happened in Manchester on
Mummy. They're starting to get bolder. Yesterday, this bad man
shouted at two young girls telling them they were nothing and
should kill themselves. That's how much he hates Muslims and
Black people. He then killed the people who tried to help the
girls. Mummy needs to get you out of here. It's a circle of terror,
everything in life is circular. Our planet is circular, its path is
circular, what happens in the East, happens in the West, the
water cycle is circular, our body's systems are circular, our cells
are circular. We are atoms, circular.

(*To no one.*) You can't destroy evil, it finds new bodies to inhabit,
new ideologies to hijack, new bombs to ride the back of, new
rhetoric to decorate, new leaders to shake hands with. It lives
inside its own cycle and you can't destroy it. You can only stay
outside of it as much as possible. It is cunning and manipulative.
It appears as self-preservation and masquerades as success.

(*To* BOY.) Shall we try those tests again? Shall we? Can you squeeze Mummy's hand? No? Not to worry. Can you move your head? Let's try something simpler. How about you... blink? Focus really hard on your eyelids and see if you can. Let's try that one more time, say Bismilaah, go. Oh my God, you blinked, you blinked, baby, you blinked. Mummy's so proud of you. I knew you could hear me all this time. You're coming back.

ABW *scribbles in her notebook.*

(*To no one.*) They would have a field day with this. The Black Muslim mother who made her own child sick. They must never know of this.

(*To* BOY.) It'll be our little secret, won't it?

Doorbell. ABW *leaves and returns with* ABM.

(*To no one.*) It's Daddy! Here with his prayers beads and spiritual deeds.

ABM. Ramadan Mubarak, son. How are you doing?

ABW. He's fine. Ramadan Ka... kaka /

ABM. / Kareem. You ok?

ABW. Fab-dab-doozy.

(*To no one.*) Very clever of him coming round when I'm fasting knowing I can't give him a blasting.

(*To* ABM.) Could have sworn I kicked you out.

ABM. Surprised you let me in.

ABW. Can't swear while I'm fasting. What can I do you for?

(*To no one.*) The boomerang's back looking for a bang. /

ABM. / Any progress?

ABW. They fired her. I laughed out loud. LOL. No, it was more of a LMAO.

ABM. What are you talking about?

ABW. Katie Hopkins. They fired her from the radio show.

ABM. What's that got to do with... I hope you're not sharing that stuff with him still.

ABW (*to no one*). Course I am. Can't seem to stop.

(*To* ABM.) Course I'm not. You don't want to fear the facts.

ABM. Fear what?

ABW. Hear it. I said you don't want to hear it.

ABM. No, you didn't. Are you okay? You know you don't have to do this alone?

ABW (*to no one*). Nothing worse than spiritual heroes and their twinkly toes, ready to spring to help.

ABM. It's Ramadan /

ABW. / Hence the headache and gibberish. I'll be fine. He's fine. No progress.

ABM. That's a shame. I was sure we'd made a breakthrough. We should remain hopeful, it's his first Ramadan since /

ABW. / I have to go.

(*To no one*.) Betrayal makes me sick, every word of his a stick.

ABM. Go? Go where? You're not going to leave him by himself, are you?

ABW. Don't be ridiculous. I mean, I have a headache, I need to lie down. Here, your polling card.

ABM. I don't need it to vote.

ABW. Just a reminder.

ABM. You and I need to sort this mess out.

ABW (*to no one*). He hasn't said sorry yet, but he expects me to forget.

(*To* ABM.) Not now, okay? Maybe later in the month, when we've both had some time to get used to the fasting and have a clearer head.

ABM. If you need me /

ABW. / I won't. Now will you please leave before we have an argument and lose our fast?

ABM. Son, I'll be praying for you at night prayers tonight. Asalamu aleykum.

ABM *leaves.*

ABW. Mummy's gonna break her fast soon. Aren't you proud?
Eighteen-point-five hours. I've made a couple of Moroccan
dishes.

ABW *busies herself with going back and forth to the kitchen,
laying the floor with a cloth with African print, and placing
dishes on the floor. She sits and waits.*

It's time to break my fast, hun. O Allah, for you have I fasted
and by your provision I have broken my fast. Please bring my
son back to me fully and wholly and make our journey to Africa
easy. Ameen.

ABW *eats dates and drinks milk.*

You've done so well so far, haven't you, when Mummy's left
you by yourself? Mummy's going to try something new, I'm sure
you'll agree, we have to keep experimenting until we find the
optimum condition which will make it easiest for you to return.
Mummy's always near even when she's away. Remember that.
She wants you back so badly, she's willing to leave you alone
during the night – that's what's new. We're going to see how you
respond when I leave you at night. It won't be for long – three
hours at the most. And Mummy will be keeping herself busy in
those hours so she can keep strong. She'll be at the mosque
praying night prayers. Isn't that wonderful? Win-win. Mummy
loves you. I'll be back as soon as I can.

ABW *leaves walking backwards, slowly.* ABW *returns. 28th
May 2017.*

I'm back. Let's have a look at you. See. All is well.

ABW *leaves.* ABW *returns.*

Well done, that's a second night now.

ABW *leaves at a quicker pace this time.* ABW *returns in a
quicker pace still. 29th May.*

Oh, there you are. Jeremy Paxman, I thought he'd died. There
was an interview on tonight, hun. He snapped at Corbyn like he
was a guard dog. I watched the highlights on the bus back. And
the Prime Minister will not debate Corbyn. What a farce. Oh,
my joints hurt so badly. I feel light after all the prayers but my
bones feel like they're going to snap. Don't worry, hun, soon

we'll have vitamin-D. Let's try that test again, shall we? There. Can you squeeze my hand? Focus, say Bismilaah. Oh, oh, was that a squish? Do that again. Yes, yes, that's my boy. Hurry, son. Ten days left before election day. You can do it.

ABW *leaves at an even faster pace. She returns in a jog. 30th May.*

There you are. Safe and sound. A bomb went off outside an ice-cream parlour in Baghdad. Mummy's tired. So tired. The fasting is harder this year. Mummy feels like her legs are made of rubber and her skin feels flushed with heat. But Mummy must keep going.

ABW *leaves faster.* ABW *returns faster still. 31st May.*

Baby. Good. Here. Huge car bomb in Kabul. Hundreds injured. Mummy's still standing though. Every night we pray at the mosque for everyone, everyone, everyone in this circular world. What hurts one person hurts us all.

ABW *leaves running.* ABW *returns running. 2nd June.*

BBC *Question Time.* They faced the audience separately. Are we living in the Twilight Zone? You won't believe the number of people in this country who want to press the nuke button. We'll be gone before all that happens, eh? One week left. Come on, to Africa. Baby. Baby. Baby. Are you moving? My eyes are so blurry. You're moving. You're moving. God is great. It's working, it's working.

ABW *leaves running, she stumbles.* ABM *walks in. He looks around, checks on the* BOY. *Waits. 3rd June 2017.*

ABW *runs back in, bent over.*

London Bridge, they're killing people on London Bridge. Get up, baby, get up, they're coming for us. You can do it.

ABM. Stop it! Stop it! What are you doing?

ABW. What are you doing here?

ABM. Son, are you okay? Where have you been?

ABW. We have to leave. For Africa. They're saying already it's Muslims that have done it. The backlash this time, I can't, I can't /

ABM. Calm down. Look at the state of you. No one's coming for us.

ABW. They are. They are. It's all a big ruse /

ABM. You left our son alone /

ABW. / Days before a big election. Wake up! You think it's accidental that it's Muslims killing.

ABM. So-called Muslims… killing people in Ramadan of all months. They want to cause fear. This is no time for conspiracy theories.

ABW. You're asleep. They're evil. All of them. One big circle of evil. How convenient for Theresa May when the Labour Party has been catching up with the Conservatives, how convenient.

ABM. Stop this nonsense!

ABW. Two bombs in, what? Ten days? Have you not been paying attention to what has been happening globally?

ABM. I'm not listening to this. You have lost all sense of reason. You've become reckless. Where were you? I said where were you?

ABW. Mosque.

ABM. Mosque?

ABW. Yeah, you know the place you practically live in.

ABM. I don't know what's got into you but you've become a liability to our son. I've let you have your way for too long. I'm not leaving you alone with him again. In fact, I think it's your turn to leave.

ABW. I haven't got anywhere to go.

ABM. I found somewhere. You can do the same. Leave.

ABW. But, but.

ABW *sinks to the floor, breathing hard.*

ABM. Dear God, what's the matter, what's the matter?

ABW. Can't breathe.

ABM. In through the nose, out through the mouth. Stay calm, stay calm. My Lord, relieve my wife of her burden. What's happening to us? What's happening to us, Lord?

ABW. He moves.

ABM. What?

ABW. You were right, he gets better when I leave him. I didn't want to admit it to you but he's been getting better.

ABM. God is great. I knew it. I knew it. Our Ramadan miracle.

ABW. I can't move. It hurts everywhere.

ABM. You can stay. In the spare room.

Pause.

I'm moving him into the main bedroom with me. I want you as far away from him as possible. Do you understand?

ABW. Anything. For. Him.

Scene Nine – Breakdown

Sunday 4th and Monday 5th June 2017.

ABW. It's all my fault. I should have shielded him from the circle of evil, instead I pulled him further into it. I didn't mean to. I was trying to do my best. There's no manual for motherhood, is there? Wish there was. But it's art and art is subjective. I don't do subjective well. I do analysis, give me numbers and graphs. Katie Hopkins and Donald Trump have both been tweeting about London Bridge. I can't stomach any more of this. I've become one of them. They pulled me in and I fell for it and worse I dragged my son into it. Can't go back though. Must keep moving forward.

ABM *comes in.*

How is he?

ABM. Keep your voice down. I don't want him to hear you.

ABW. Sorry.

ABM. You're right, he's moving now. It's a miracle.

ABW. All praise is due to Allah.

ABM. I'm still mad at you but I wanted to say, I'm grateful – for your sacrifice. How are you feeling today?

ABW. Worse. If that's possible. My brain jiggles. I'll make us some brain for Iftar.

ABM. Brain? What are you talking about? Are you fasting? Tell me you're not fasting.

ABW. I want to feel close to Him. I feel so disconnected from everything.

ABM. You're being silly now. You need to eat and rest. Don't worry about the meal, I'll take care of it.

ABW. I'll make some… those circular things, triangular things, forget what they're called, he likes them.

ABM. Samosas?

ABW. Maybe the smell will help, and those red jewels sprinkled over a papaya and mango salad nestled in a pillow of watercress.

ABM. Jewels? Pillows? You don't sound right. Why don't you go lie down.

ABW. Can't. We have a guest coming.

ABM. Who?

ABW. It's the month of forgiveness.

ABM. It's not Uncle Mahmood, is it? I don't think I can deal with him, why would you invite him when you know /

Doorbell.

ABW. I'll get the window.

ABW *leaves. She returns with* WW.

ABM. Professor!

ABW. I apologised. The professor was gracious enough to accept it. She will be joining us for our brain food tonight.

WW. Sorry, but I… I don't mean to offend but I don't, I can't eat brain.

ABM. We don't eat brain! What are you talking about? Just what is going on?

WW. Your wife wanted to talk. I hear he's been making progress.

ABM. Yes, yes. It's a blessing. You're welcome to join us tonight but we really don't need your help, Professor. It's all under control.

ABW. I have a light bulb.

WW. Okay?

ABM. What are you on about?

WW. An idea?

ABW. An idea! A double-whammy, two heads are better than one, two for the price of one, BGOF!

ABM. I'm sorry, Professor. My wife hasn't been feeling herself lately.

WW. Understandable, she's been /

ABW. I want to talk to the TV.

ABM. This is insane. You're breaking your fast right now.

ABW. We're going to the media. About him. I think it's time we shared our story.

ABM. More madness. What's gotten into you? You need to eat and sleep. I'm making you an appointment with the GP first thing in the morning. Here, sit down. I'll bring you some dates.

ABW. I want you to be there, talk to them also, give them your professional opinion. We have to let people know, parents know that they can't bring the evil into their homes. We have to let people know what racism and Islamophobia can do to children, British children.

ABM. Honey, you don't need to do anything. Don't punish yourself, he's getting better. There's no need.

WW. Why now?

ABM. This is madness. I won't be a part of this.

ABW. The election is in three years.

WW. Days. Three days.

AWB. After the bomb and the murders, there is a chance people who were undecided or wanting to vote for Labour will panic and vote Conservative.

ABM. I can't believe I'm hearing this.

ABW. Sharing my son's story, it will make people think, realise we're pawns in a circle of evil and we can choose to step outside of it.

ABM. Our son! The one you left alone, remember?

WW. You left him?

ABW. For his own good. He's moving now, isn't he? It's working – keeping me away from him.

ABM. And that's all we've wanted. But now you want to, what, interfere with politics? Change votes with our son's story? You've lost your mind.

WW. It could work.

ABM. You're both out of your minds! And what's in it for you?

ABW. The professor who brought the boy back.

WW. It's more than that. How did you know?

ABW. I YouTubed you. Googled you. You're a mental-health worker in the NHS. I saw a photo of you at a demonstration highlighting the cuts to the NHS. Easy, really.

ABM. Professor, you're not actually considering this, are you? I won't be a part of this, you hear me? I won't.

ABW. We don't need you. We have the power to do something about the state of this nation. People need to know what Brexit has done to our children.

ABM. Professor, you need to leave. My wife is not feeling well. Her judgement is clouded. Please, leave.

WW. That's all I seem to do. Get invited and then get thrown out.

ABM. I'm sorry, please, leave.

WW. Call me.

ABW. No. I mean, yes. Yes.

WW *leaves*.

ABM. You don't have my consent. Are you listening to me?

ABW. I'm going to make fried triangles and wash red jewels. Only three days, right.

Scene Ten – Cycle

Very early morning, 9th June 2017. ABW is sitting, slumped in a chair, staring into her tablet, following elections results as they come in. ABM rushes into the room.

ABM. He's opened his eyes.

ABW. I'm so happy. Thank you, God.

ABM. He recognises me.

ABW. Can I see him? Please?

ABM. I don't want to interrupt his progress.

ABW. I miss him so much. He's doing so well, without me. Without me.

ABM. He has me.

ABW. I miss you too.

ABM. You have God.

   ABM *leaves*.

ABW (*to no one*). When we first saw me, he said I blew his mind

   He followed the trace of gold I left behind

   Gathered the gold in his palm and panted

   I think you dripped this, I mean you dropped this

   Gold.

   Pause.

   Now it's empty this gold mine

He's dug and dug and it's in decline

So I resort to this: adornments, incense and rancour

To bring him back to where he used to

Back to when we used to

Love.

When he first saw me, there weren't these frown lines,

When he first saw me, not so many of these belly lines,

Not so many down-times.

Pause.

He doesn't look at me like he used to, doesn't look at me like *I'm* used to.

He doesn't talk to me like he used to, talk to me like *I'm* used to.

ABM *rushes in.*

ABM. He's talking, he's talking!

ABW. Oh, oh, my boy, I'm so happy. What did he say? My boy is coming back. What did he say?

ABM. He said, 'Daddy'.

ABW. Has he asked for me, for his mum?

ABM. No.

ABW. He did! I'm so glad.

ABM. No, babe. I said no.

ABM *leaves.*

ABW. Oh.

ABW *lies down on the table.* ABM *returns.*

The Conservatives have the majority.

ABM. Don't worry yourself over that. What are you doing on the table?

ABW. Tired.

ABM *leaves*.

Long pause.

18th June 2017. ABM *returns*. ABW *is looking at her tablet*.

ABM. It's been a week now, hun. You need to sleep in the spare room. He'll be walking soon.

ABW. Fire! Fire!

ABM. What? What's wrong?

ABW. London's burning. People are jumping out of their windows, throwing their children out.

ABM. Give me that. Oh my Lord.

ABW. I can't see, I can't see. The fire's burned my eyes.

ABM. Honey. Calm down. Calm down. You're safe. Oh those poor people. Those poor people.

ABM *holds* ABW.

I'm sorry, my love. Please forgive me. I'll get you help. I'll get you help. Honey, honey? Talk to me, baby. Talk to me. Can you hear me, darling?

Long pause.

19th June 2017. ABM *is still holding* ABW.

A man ran over people coming out of our mosque. What is happening to the world? Talk to me, babe. Help me make sense of this. You were right. I was such a fool to bury my head in the sand. He stood up a little today. We have to get him out of here. I have to get you out of here. My love. My everything. Wake up. Don't do this. Don't leave me. Come back. Come back to me.

The End.

a profoundly affectionate, passionate devotion
to someone (*—noun*)

debbie tucker green

a profoundly affectionate, passionate devotion to someone
(*—noun*) was first performed at the Royal Court Jerwood Theatre
Upstairs, London, on 28 February 2017. The cast and creative team
was as follows.

MAN	Gary Beadle
B	Gershwyn Eustache Jnr
A	Lashana Lynch
YOUNG WOMAN	Shvorne Marks
WOMAN	Meera Syal

Director	debbie tucker green
Designer	Merle Hensel
Lighting Designer	Lee Curran
Sound Designer	Christopher Shutt
Movement Director	Vicki Manderson
Assistant Director	Jade Lewis
Casting Director	Amy Ball

Characters

PART ONE
A, *female, Black*
B, *male, Black*

PART TWO
WOMAN, *Black or Asian*
MAN, *Black*

PART THREE
MAN, *same character from Part Two. Some years later.*
YOUNG WOMAN, *the daughter of A+B. Some years later.*

He is significantly older than her. The Young Woman is of legal age.

A forward slash / marks an overlapping point in the dialogue.

Words in brackets are intention only.

Names appearing without dialogue directly above/below each other indicate active silences between those characters listed.

A name appearing without dialogue indicates an active silence.

PART ONE

Scene One

A   So is it –

B   no.

A   Is it that / you're –

B   No it is / not.

A   so it's

B   there is no 'it's' it's nothing there's nothing

A   you're not –

B   no. Nothing. There isn't.

         Beat.

A   My bad.

B   Yeh.

A
B

B   'My bad' – piss off.

A   I've always –

B   no you haven't.

A

B

B   It's not always all about you.

A   Well. It usually is.
         Isn't it.

         Beat.

         …So there is –

B	no there / isn't.
A	you're –
B	no
A	you have a –
B	(*quietly*) fuck / me.
A	something's not right
B	you're jumping / to –
A	something about you's not / right.
B	(*dry*) really? Right. Me. Right.
A	I'm just –
B	is it? Me. Right. (*dry*) My bad.

Beat.

You jump to conclusions. You always jump to – jumped to conclusions and wrong conclusions in leaps and fuckin bounds

A	I know / you.
B	come to conclusions where there aint none
A	I do know / you.
B	makin me make conclusions where there ent / one.
A	I do still know you.
B	Makin me *want* to make conclusions where there ent none to make, me makin them to make you feel better bout concluding there are conclusions, when there aint no conclusions to be had. Shit.
A	You ent never said something just to make me feel better.
B	I ent lied to make you feel better / no.
A	When have you ever said something to me to make me feel / better?
B	I'm not gonna lie to you to make / you –

A   Something considerate to – something mindful –
           and I'm not talking bout your / lies.

B   you wanting me to say somethin to say anythin just
           so you can feel somethin – somethin good about
           y'self – no – and I don't lie –

A   thass one right there

B   and I won't say somethin just to say anything and
           lies ent got nuthin to do with what I do and don't
           say what I will and won't say what I won't and
           don't say – want to say and don't – to you.

A   I think –

B   *jump* to conclusions –

A   I think that –

B   jump to your conclusions.

A   I think that this is still about / me.

B   (You) get me nervous to say anything me not
           knowin how you'd 'conclude' about it wrongly

A   you're nervous of nothing.

B   Nervous of you

A   couldn't make you nervous of nuthin that you didn't
           wanna be nervous of even if I wanted to.

B   You wanted to.

A   …I did not

B   you tried to

A   I do not

B   you wanted to try to.

A   I did (not). I –. I… No.

           Beat.

           You've never been nervous of me.

B   Y'sound disappointed.

           Beat.

A	You've never been nervous of anything about me.
	And there are no conclusions jumped to. Nothin in fuckin 'leaps and bounds' thank you – nuthin needed to be jumped to regarding you as you're / quite –
B	Here we / go.
A	quite straightforward.
B	Here. We. / Go.
A	In a straightforward sort of way.
B	That the best you can do?
A	No.
A	
B	
B	...You didn't understand my complexity.
A	I think I / did.
B	You never did understand how complex I could / be.
A	I think I did. I think, there weren't much *to* understand – I understood what was understandable.
B	
A	What was coherent.
B	You didn't try to understand.
A	I understood what was there to-sometimes – and this is with respect – sometimes you mistook – I felt you mistook, complexity, for... confusions.
B	
A	
A	You were confusing – could be confusing.
B	For you.
A	(*dry*) Hmm no – you were, a bag of confusion. Bags a contradiction, inconsistent –
B	if you weren't able / to –

A	confusing generally and sometimes-sometimes – you mistook 'confusion' for actual… crap (*gestures*) was a bit crap about you. Not complex. Shit crap. About you. Bags of it.
B	…You weren't able to support my / complex –
A	Bit of a fuck up bit of a crap fuck / up.
B	You didn't have it in / you to –
A	(A) bit self-indulgent.
B	Patience wasn't one of / your –
A	Well, very self- / indulgent.
B	compassion wasn't something you ever –
A	I was compassionate
B	you were condescending
A	I was more than compassionate
B	and I / knew –
A	you drained my compassion well dry
B	knew you didn't understand me
A	I was desert-like you got me – you drained me to a desert-like / state.
B	knowin you didn't understand want to understand never did understand me was quite an underwhelming experience. Generally.
A	I went from bein an oasis of understanding to an – and I understood your lack of complexity which pissed you off I was more than patient with you which pissed you off more and you knew I could read you better'n you knew yourself – and underwhelming?
B	(*dry*) With all due respect and all that.
A	'Underwhelming'?
B	Or am I not bein straightforward enough for / you?
A	After seein y'mouth never sayin what y'mind was thinkin for years –

B	thass depth
A	now you got the-the no iss not – thass not depth thass *boring*. Was your eyes sayin one thing and your mouth not havin the bottle to follow / through.
B	Thass knowin you won't get what I got to say you won't have the patience compassion or complexity –
A	you were / boring.
B	so I didn't bother sayin it.
A	You were borin.
B	Don't bother sayin it.
A	In all aspects.
B	'All aspects' – borin'?
A	All aspects.
B	Fuck off.
	Beat.
A	Do you miss me?
B	
A	Do you even –
B	you leapt and fuckin bounded…?
A	Do you miss –.
B	
A	
A	You miss me…?
	…Did you miss being… 'Underwhelmed'?
	About me. At all. Then?
B	…

Scene Two

A *is busy*.

B   I want you. Yeah.
I want you to me. Want you with me want me us.
I want you beyond what I can say
beyond what I got words for
beyond my vocabulary
beyond any vocabulary
beyond language
beyond imagination,
beyond what words can do beyond what my words
can do. Beyond what words have been known to do,
have yet to do, beyond what they will ever do.
I wanted you beyond sentence in between syllables
above vowels under consonants and after
punctuation.

A *is busy*.

And.
Getting up aint gettin up when you ent got up with
me.

A *is busy*.

No. And
gettin up is like I never got up once when I wake up
and get up with you, or-or if you-you aint yet got up
and still lying by my side –

A   *what?*

B   But.

A   What?!

B   Not gettin up and layin by you with you on you too
hot next to you, too cold far from you, lookin at my
favourite bit.
Of you.
Breathing on my favourite bit.
Of you.
Touchin it. A bit. That bit. Of you. Just. Soft like –

A   I feel / it –

B	so soft you don't even know it
A	I know / it.
B	too soft for you to even feel / it.
A	I know it. Knew it. Felt it.
B	And-and you taste better'n my food ever did. And
A	seriously?
B	But.
A	God.
B	But my days-our days seemed shorter with you in em, you shortened the hours, made minutes not matter and seconds seem shit, racing to build our old age together. Days couldn't be long enough with you in em and nights was like blinkin before daylight dawned quick –
A	this is –
B	you was my –
A	(this) is a real revelation –
B	yeh you / was.
A	(you) never said you wanted me that much –
B	I –
A	never said none of this-this poetical... *shit* –
B	shit?
A	Then.
B	'Shit'?
A	That you seem to find so easy to say now.
B	'...Shit'?
A	(*dry*) Hmm. Yeh. *Shit*.
B	You liked it.
A	I never said I liked / it.

B	You never said you never liked / it.
A	I tolerated it and then just blocked it. Blocked it off blocked it out. Turned up the TV faked a phone call or somethin... Y'know.
A	
B	
B	...I didn't have to say...
A	
B	how much I... Shouldn't have to say, how much I...

(I) showed it instead.

Didn't stop showin you.
Did I?
Couldn't stop showin you.
Could I.
Wouldn't stop. Would I.

Thass how you did know – do know.
You did know. You did know you did know, you
knew how much...? How much I...
Don't you?

Didn't you?

Scene Three

A   …When you do that thing…

B

A   …When you do that-did that (thing), that you do –
           did. With your thing. To me –

B   with you.

A   That you did a lot to me.

B   With you.

A   Thinking I liked / it.

B   You liked it you did like me doin / it.

A   When you did that – kept doin / that

B   That thing that you liked

A   I didn't.

B

A   Like it.

B

A   I didn't like it.

B   …You didn't say you didn't like / it.

A   I never liked it.

B   You never said you never did like it.

A   I –

B   ever. Never. Not once. You never said that.

           Beat.

           You looked like you liked it.

           Beat.

           You sounded like you liked / it.

A   What does that look look like then?

B	You made that sound that you made – that sound you make when you like – when you like it. While I was doin / it.
A	How did I sound then?
B	You know how you sounded. The sounds you-you – givin the looks you looked never sayin nothin bout not likin (nothin) – *I* didn't particularly like doin it but done it cos I knew you liked it and wanted to-wanted you to, y'know... Something you liked that I could do you-give you – do with you doin it right. That you liked. Even though I didn't like doin it. Selfless. Generous.

Beat.
Beat.

A	...That look that looks like I'm enjoying that thing that something you do – did – done back then... that look weren't that look that I liked it. It weren't that. And what you was doin you were doin cos you-you liked, *really* looked like you were enjoying doin more'n me –
B	that look weren't / that.
A	as you were doin it really *sounded* like you was enjoying doin it more'n / me –
B	That sound weren't / that.
A	while you was doin it
B	I dunno how you're-how you're looking at me now – how do I take (that) – how do I take this – what's this look / now?
A	I'm not looking at / you.
B	What is that what is that then what is / that?
A	You're lookin at me.
B	I don't even know now where to even (look) or to let you look, let you even look at me or I should look at the floor or summink, is it that? Look at the floor or su'un in silence. I know you –

A   stop lookin at me.

B   What doin that thing –

A   stop lookin at / me.

B   me doin that thing *with* you, meant to you and know
           I know that you liked it – what you look like when
           you liked it what you liking that thing looks like. I
           know.

           Beat.

           I do know.

           You did.
           …You did.

           Fuck.

Scene Four

A	When she looks at me (and) she looks at me, I see you I see you I – it's the weirdest thing / that –
B	It's great.
A	It is great – in the great way she looks at / me.
B	She looks at you a lot
A	(I) love lookin at her
B	I love lookin at her, it's great, love lookin at you
A	she's lovely to look at
B	still love lookin at / you.
A	she's got your eyes –
B	thass great
A	you see that? Got that depth –
B	great
A	that you got, she got that same complexity behind her eyes that you got she got the same colour as well although they say eye colour don't settle for the first few / months.
B	She looks at you a lot. She looks at you loads.
A	They say it's smell as much as anything –
B	(she) don't stop lookin at you
A	their eyes can't focus yet that young, they / say.
B	won't stop lookin at / you.
A	She's lookin but not lookin I don't think, don't think iss lookin how we think about lookin –
B	I think she's looking.
A	I think it's scent
B	looking at you.
A	She looks at you.

B	She looks at me and sees it's not you and looks for / you.
A	She looks at you
B	she looks *for* you.
A	I… think it's the milk she's sensing – scenting, the breast milk, instinct – built in, amazin – senses and that, thass why she looks for me – I'm sayin 'looks' y'know what I mean lookin but not lookin how we would / look.
B	She looks over my shoulder. For you. She turns her head when I have her. For you. Tries to lift her head when I hold her, looking for / you.
A	That don't really mean –
B	I look at you.
A	…Right.
B	But you're busy lookin at her.
A	
B	'Instinct' and all that, aye?
A	
B	
B	Amazin. I instinctively look at you. …You instinctively look at her.

Beat.

A	It's amazin lookin in her eyes.
B	She got your / eyes.
A	Lookin deep into her eyes deep in them eyes and seein… you – thass what's amazin. Thass what I'm seein. All you. Only you. Really.

…None a me in there at all.

Really.

Scene Five

B	Just-it's-that it aint – it's that it starts to feel a bit… Y'know.
A	…No.
B	A bit by-the-numbers – a bit goin through the motions – y'know?
A	…No.
B	A bit – 'Cos we should do' not that 'we want to do'
A	I want to / do.
B	which gets a bit can get a bit
A	I want to / do.
B	a bit y'know
A	no
B	I get a bit –
A	no
B	bored.
A	
A	…I –
B	it is borin. That was borin.
A	I –
B	weren't it.
	Beat.
A	I –. I… I'm not bored though.
B	Kinda routine borin even the – is actually borin. It actually is. Y'know you do what you do –
A	I thought it wasn't me
B	no no no iss not / you.
A	you said it wasn't me

B yeh no iss not. But it is. You.

A

B Anyhow. Y'know…

A

Beat.

Right.
…Are you tired?

B Yeh.
No.

Well… no.

Beat.

A Are you tired of me?

Beat.

B …Yeh. No.

Well…

Scene Six

A	…After Mum. After my mum… And I thought there was no after. When. After that. After then. I thought you'd… I thought you would… I did.
B	
A	But you didn't.
B	
A	
A	Did yer. You wasn't.
B	
A	Was yer? You couldn't.
B	
A	Could yer. Weren't yer?
B	
A	And I shouldn't have to say. Have had to say –
B	you never said anything about –
A	I shouldn't have to say anything.
B	…Don't say. Then. Nuthin don't say nuthin. Again.
	Beat.
A	I can't –
B	don't say anything cos after that, after then, after your mum, you saying nothin was your new sayin somethin / except –
A	I wasn't able to say anything.
B	I can't know –
A	was I? Wasn't able / to –
B	except I can't know what I don't know. I really can't –

A	you knew what was / happening
B	you didn't speak.
A	You saw what was happening.
B	You didn't speak
A	I didn't speak
B	you didn't speak to me, wouldn't speak to / me.
A	in all your poetical bollocks with how well you think you know me you coulda picked up on what I was goin through – I *couldn't* / speak.
B	After that, after then –
A	I couldn't speak –
B	after your mum you –
A	which was obvious. To someone with a bit of sense.
A	
B	
B	Nuthin about you –.
A	
B	Nuthin about you's obvious. And I didn't know what this new you of not sayin nuthin / was.
A	A blind man could see what I was goin through.
B	A clue a hint a sign an indication about your non-verbals to help me / out.
A	I wasn't there to help you out
B	woulda helped me to help you out and you weren't there –
A	I wasn't able to be (*taps head*) –
B	you weren't there
A	and you were no help
B	you didn't give me / the –

A	you helped nothing –
B	you didn't give me the chance / to –
A	I wasn't there to give you chances. I wasn't able 'to help you out'. I wasn't able. That was the point and you were no help are no help. Can't help. Couldn't help. Didn't help. Didju?
B	
A	
B	…When I tried to help / you –
A	You didn't try.
B	When I tried to help you –
A	you didn't try hard enough.
B	You said I couldn't help.
	Y'said that much.
	Before you stopped speakin. You told me I couldn't – told me I had no idea told me I couldn't imagine, *insisted* that I wouldn't-wouldn't get close couldn't get close couldn't get-get nowhere near close enough to know what you was…
A	
B	I know what you was going through –.
A	You've never been through it.
B	I could see you were –. I was waiting to help –
A	'waiting'
B	you wouldn't let me help.
A	'Waiting'.
B	You stopped speaking.
A	I stopped speaking, to you.
B	
A	

Beat.

B   ...I stayed.

A   No / help.

B   You, mute or otherwise I stayed.

A

B

B   Creepin round the house in your / silence I stayed

A   I weren't mute I was silent

B   you weren't speaking to me

A   I couldn't speak to / you.

B   just mute with me, quiet with me, silent with me.
           (*dry*) Nice.

A

B   And I talked to you.

A   You talked at me.

B   I talked to you – you not talkin back was your
           choice, talked to you through – talked you through –
           never stopped talkin never stopped tryin. (I) stepped
           up stepped in stepped to, even when you wouldn't
           let / me.

A   What you was sayin was wrong.

B   You dint let me / know.

A   What you was sayin weren't workin.

B   You could have let me know cos ten months of your
           bein mute –

A   I weren't / mute.

B   you bein morose

A   I was / in –

B   you bein fuckin miserable your fuckin silent way,
           got a bit grinding. You could have let me know
           sooner what I was sayin weren't workin coulda

dropped a hint so I coulda saved my time saved my
effort saved my tryin and saved my breath.

Ten months. Ten months of it: forty weeks three
hundred and seven days and nights of it. Of silent
you – and those nights…

He shakes his head. Says nothing else.

(*quietly*) Fuck me.

Beat.

I more than know you.

Beat.

Ten months of you sayin nuthin to me when I dried
your tears and your tears.
And your tears.
When I fed you healthy
when I watched you not sleep.
When I rubbed your aches and set your baths
when I dried your body and lay you down
then watched you not sleep more.
When I dressed you-undressed you, combed out
your hair, oiled your hair creamed your skin and (I)
didn't touch you when I wanted to and I wanted to –
when I wanted you
and I wanted you.
When I sat with you
when I excused you
when I drove you – walked you, walked with you
stood by you and when I tried to fill the gaps your
gaps with sayin somethin with sayin anything tryin
to fill you up with what little I had to offer with
what I had left to give and now you're tellin me that
was all wrong? That that was all no good that
weren't what you wanted weren't what you needed
and weren't a piece of it right or done right anyway
– and that I was the 'let down'? Really?

Really?

Beat.

Fuck.

Beat.

Y'know…

He watches her.

Is this straightforward enough for you am I bein
straightforward enough for you – after your mum.
After that. After *then*.
Or am I bein confusing?

Cos, no.
No.

I don't miss that. About you.

At all.

Scene Seven

A	When I'm watching something…
B	
A	You listening?
B	Yeah.

He is not listening.

A	When I'm watching something, I am watching something. I am watching it. It's not just 'on'.
B	
A	You / listening?
B	Yeah.

He is not.

A   I don't just put it on. I'm not you, not you like that. I don't just put it on and leave it and leave it on and not watch it. If I put it on I'm watching it. I'm relaxing – trying to relax. You walk into the room – you walk in and it stops bein – I get – you walk in and I'm already distracted wondering how long I've got, how long till you start talkin or frapsin or looking for the remote or asking for the remote, or askin the kids for the remote or askin the kids to look for the remote – askin the kids to ask me for the remote cos I aint answered you, when I am still watchin – still trying to watch, halfway through – partway through my programme.

Beat.

Y'know?

Beat.

Are you / listening – ?

B	Yeh.

He's not listening.

A   And iss not right that I should have to – not that
           I do – but it's not normal to hide the remote – want
           to hide the remote, in your own house. Just so you
           can get through a programme.
           See you lookin, noisy lookin knowin you won't find
           it but the vibe is already – you've already mashed
           up the – talkin loud so I can't hear – well not the
           kids cos they know, but you, really talkin loud askin
           loud where it's at so I get distracted – thinkin iss
           funny I get distracted, when all I'm doin wanna do
           is watch my one programme without no
           interruptions. Y'know?

B

A   You lissenin?

B   Yeah.

           He is not.
           Beat.

A   Y'know?

B   …Yeah.

A   …Yeah.

           Cos that's not relaxing.

           Thass not relaxin.

           Beat.

           At all.

Scene Eight

>   *They watch each other.*

A   …That bit you can't see that bit you can't see of
            yourself… thass mine of you that bit-a-you-there
            that last nook of your neck that no one normally –
            that / bit.

B   The back of your right thigh –

A   that back-of-the-neck-bit there for me to-to remind
            you of / me –

B   no disrespect to the back of your left thigh but the
            back of your right thigh is mine.

A   When your head's down and they think they've
            bowed you tested you but not able to bruk you that
            piece of you is mine that part of you is all (mine)

B   sometimes I look down – head down deliberate not
            nuthin that they've done, not nuthin they could do
            but just enough just waiting for you, to have your
            feel just to have your touch just to have you on your
            favourite part a me there.

A
B

B   Sometimes I do that. Did that.

A   Miss that.

B   Do that. Still.

Scene Nine

B	He's perfect
A	he is perfect
B	ten fingers ten toes
A	juss like his dad
B	thank you
A	don't thank me it's us
B	it's you
A	took us to make / him
B	twenty-two hours of labour is all you
A	well, twenty-seven if we're counting.
B	You did / it.
A	He's perfect
B	he is perfect.
A	He's worth it. She'll love him
B	she'll love bein a big sis
A	even though she didn't want a brother.
B	She's got a brother she'll love him.
A	Even though she said clearly she didn't want no brother being brought home.
B	She will love / him.
A	She'll look at him / and –
B	She'll take one look and fall into these eyes of his.
A	She'll make a great, big sis
B	you're a great mum
A	(*dry*) you're an okay dad

342   a profoundly affectionate…

B   and he's a beautiful boy already.

Thank you yeah.

Thank you.

Scene Ten

A	Lock it then –
B	what I'm sayin / is –
A	lock the door then
B	there isn't a lock on the door.
A	Put the lock on the door – you been sayin you was gonna do that for ages been sayin that for / years.
B	All I'm sayin is that / sometimes –
A	If you want one put one on
B	sometimes it would be –
A	if you want to put one on then I'll know –
B	sometimes I'd just like / to –
A	then we'll all know not to – when not to disturb you.
B	Sometimes, I'd just like to tek time to take a shit on my own is all / I'm –
A	So the kids know not to disturb Daddy
B	it's not even nice it's not even –
A	you come in when I'm on / the –
B	I leave if you're havin a shit.
A	Thass cos you're funny like that. If I have to come in –
B	no one has to come in then
A	if the kids need to come / in –
B	there's nothing the kids need enough bad enough to have to come in for the two minutes it takes / me –
A	it's not two minutes
B	takes me to have a –
A	it's never two / minutes

B   takes me to have a solitary shit. How is that –

A   if you –

B   how is that too much to ask?

A   If you wanna fit something fit an extractor fan. Stop
         you stinkin out the / place.

B   How is asking to have a – too much to fuckin…? I
         don't even know why I'm askin. Don't come in.

A   You're tellin me?

B   Don't come in when I'm takin a dump.

A   (*dry*) Very commanding.

B   How is this even / a – ?

A   You tellin me where I can and can't go in our own
         house / now?

B   It's a bathroom. I'm on the bog. Don't come / in.

A   I'll go where I like

B   I want some privacy.

A   I'll go where I / like.

B   I want some privacy when I –

A   I'd like some privacy when I'm getting undressed.

B   What?

A   In the bedroom when I'm – I've always hated
         getting undressed in front of / you.

B   *What?*

A   At night –

B   where did –

A   in the bedroom –

B   where did this –

A   at the end of the day –

B   where did this come from and thass different.

A	Feels like I'm bein judged.
B	I don't judge / you.
A	Feels like –
B	I've never judged (you) and you've always got undressed in front a me
A	always felt judged.
B	It's a bedroom.
A	Don't come in.
B	It's our bedroom.
A	It's our bathroom
B	you're not taking a shit
A	it's uncomfortable. I'm uncomfortable.
B	No you're not
A	always been uncomfortable
B	no you haven't
A	it's always uncomfortable getting undressed in front of you. Put a lock on the bathroom door I'll get changed in there.
A B	
B	…I don't make you feel uncomfortable…
A	
B	I make you feel (uncomfortable)…? You're not – you're not. You're…
A	
B	Are you?

Scene Eleven

A   Iss nuthin about you wouldn't be nuthin about you. You're still as – as you ever were, as you always are. Y'know y'that.

Beat.

B

A   It's just, that it's... that it aint... It's that it's... starts to feel a bit. Y'know?

B

A   A bit... ...By the numbers y'know?

B

A   A bit goin through the motions a bit routine... if you get what I / mean?

B   No

A   y'know?

B   ...No.

A   And iss me iss not you, it is all me.

B

A   And I don't want you to feel that –

B   yeh. No.

           I don't feel that it's like that.

A

B   With you.

A

B   With you with / me.

A   It's feelin like we, that we sorta 'we should do' in a routine sorta-sorta – tedious sorta – y'know –

B   no

A   not that 'we want to do'

B	I want to / do.
A	which gets a bit –
B	I want to / do.
A	can get a bit y'know –
B	I / want –
A	I get a bit y'know
B	
A	…Bored.
B	
A	But. It is boring.
B	I –. I'm not / bored –
A	Kind routine kinda borin even the doin it differently… is actually borin.
B	
A	It actually is. Ennit?
B	
A	Isn't it?
B	
B	(*quietly*) No. I –
A	y'know, you do what you / do –
B	you said it wasn't me.
A	Yeh iss not-no iss not it's not you – I do what I do as well it's as much me I – y'know you're –. It is you, it is you it is that.
	Anyhow…
B	Are you…
A	
B	…Are you tired of me?

A   You? No.
           …Yeh.
           No.

           Beat.

           Well…

Scene Twelve

B	How is it –
A	piss off.
	Beat.
B	How is it that it's only / your –
A	Piss off *really*
B	only your decision when I'm the
A	do I really need to / explain?
B	I'm the – and I do have a say –
A	you have a / say.
B	I should have a say –
A	you do have a say I'm lissenin to your say – again – you've said your say – again and you're still sayin it.
B	You're not listenin
A	I've heard it
B	but you're not / *lissenin.*
A	I've only got one way to listen –
B	which is the / problem.
A	two ears and whatever shit you're sayin reachin them.
B	You lissen closed you are closed. I lissen to you
A	nuthin about me's / closed.
B	have always lissened to you and you've always been closed
A	been too open to your / bullshit.
B	I listen to you
A	you talk over / me.
B	I lissen open to you and have to talk over you to be heard.

A	I've heard you. And I disagree. But, generously, I'm still listening to what you're sayin but you're always sayin it so I can't act surprised every time I hear / it.
B	You're not changing your mind.
A	I *hear* you, but, you're still talkin shit. You sayin what you're constantly sayin, again, don't mean I'ma change my mind bout this but-so as I've said, I've heard your say, heard you say so much I'm bored a fuckin hearin it and I do 'know who you are' and I hear that this shit seems 'unfair' but I'm not changing my (mind) you're not changing my (mind) you haven't never yet bout nuthin and y'won't about this, and if you actually heard what I been sayin –
B	what you're 'actually' sayin don't make no / sense.
A	*lissened* to why I'm sayin what I'm sayin –
B	what you're sayin is wicked.
A	Hear-wot. This ent no fifty-fifty I've heard your twenty per cent and my eighty per cent is still sayin the same consistent 'no' – and 'wicked'?
B	Spiteful and wicked
A	piss / off
B	I'm a good dad
A	'spiteful' – piss / off
B	I'm a great dad
A	'you're a great dad' I'm a great mum – or a 'spiteful and wicked' mum accordin to / you.
B	A spiteful and wicked wife – a good mum
A	but not a great one? Only you thass got the greatness is it? (I'm) not as great a parent as you is it?
B	
A	
A	(You) fuckin wish.

B	…One more.
A	No.
B	Just one / more.
A	We've got the set, boy and girl.
B	Two boys one girl –
A	no
B	two girls and a brother in between
A	no
B	I've always wanted three –
A	can't always get what we want
B	always said to you / three.
A	can't always get what we ask for. Can we.
B	…You're a / fuckin –
A	Hard horrible pregnancies
B	control freak / fuckin –
A	horrendous for months
B	bein a fuckin bitch –
A	distressing awful labour for days
B	fuckin bitch of a wife with how you're carryin on.
A	
B	
A	Nice. Nice.
B	Fuck you.
A	Well, no actually, seein as we're not tryin for another one –
B	cunt.

Beat.

A
B
A
B

A   …Nice.

             Thank you.

             Thank you.

             For that.

Scene Thirteen

A   You know she needs talkin to.

B

A   You know she needs you to talk (to) – she needs you
           talkin to – she needs to be able to talk to / you.

B   She can talk to me.

A   She wants to talk to / you.

B   She can talk to me I'm easy to talk to.

           Beat.

A   She's not talkin.

B   Got somethin of her mum about her then.

           Beat.

A   …That was different.

B   After your mother –

A   that was different

B   and so after her mother… she's not speaking.
           Sound familiar?

A   Thass not fair

B   not a lot fuckin is.

A   …She cries most nights you know that?

B   Then she's crying over you.

A   She is crying over me but you're still / here.

B   If she wants to cry over / you –

A   And it is most nights

B   that's up to her.

A   It's most every night

B   if she wants to cry over you and doesn't want to
           come to me / then –

A   she wants to come to you. But you don't hear that,
            you don't hear her over your TV the crap TV you
            have on loud too loud so loud or the crap radio
            thatchu you have on so loud too loud and then turn
            up, you don't hear her over that do yer?

B   I miss turning over your crap programmes.

A   She needs you.

B   I miss makin noise lookin for the remote halfway
            through what you was watchin –

A   she needs you to talk to her.

B   Don't hear her crying over my tears.

A   You're the adult.

B
A

B   She hasn't cried since your service.

A   She hasn't shown you her cryin since my service.
            But, she does cry most nights most of the / night.

B   When she's ready –

A   she's ready

B   when she wants to talk to / me –

A   she's ready but she doesn't know / it.

B   I'm here. I'm always here – which is more than you
            are. I don't go nowhere. Don't got no one to go
            nowhere with. Now. Have I? I don't go out. She don't
            go out. He don't go nowhere. We're all here. All the
            time. Great. It's just, great. Here. Without you.

A

B   And after getting it so wrong wid you, apparently *so*
            wrong with you, after your mum after all that, after
            all that tryin and after all that talkin that you said
            was shit and useless and wrong, after all *that* I'm
            now tryin to get it right. Give her space, give her
            time, give her the shit you wanted –

A	she's not me
B	I know-she's-not-you-I-know-she's-not-you I still want… I know she's not you.
A	
B	…I cry most nights.
A	
B	(I) cry every / night.
A	You're the adult.
B	I got things to say but no one to say them / to.
A	You're the adult. She's our / daughter.
B	I got things to share but no one to show them to.
A	You're grown.
B	This is / so –
A	She's our daughter
B	this is so fuckin –
A	he's our son
B	so-and-because there's nowhere I wanna go without you nuthin I wanna do without you bein / here.
A	they need / you.
B	Nights are fuckin endless and days are a disaster. That soft neck-back piece a me yearnin for that touch by you has given up waitin and gone hard so if she wants to-to – to speak to me –
A	she's a child
B	I'm here but I'm / not –
A	she's the / child
B	not chasin her with words
A	she's our child

B	and-but – 'ours' has just become 'mine'. All mine only mine. Because of *you* – they've got each other thass somethin, I've not got –
A	they need their dad.
B	They got each other
A	they need their / dad.
B	I need my wife. I want my wife.

Beat.

I'd swap my place for your place –

A	don't.
B	…I'd swap her place for you
A	*don't*
B	to have you back and her gone.

A *slaps him hard.*

Both of them for one a you –

A *slaps him harder.*
Beat.

Ask me again what I miss.

A	
B	Ask me.
A	
B	Ask me. *Go on go on.* I'll do a you. I'll do a sullen. I'll do a morose I'll do a silence I'll do seven – no ten months of silence I'll do that.
B	
B	
A	…They need their / dad.
B	I need my wife. I want my wife. I want my-you, back.

A

B   You shouldn't have left me.

A   I didn't leave / you.

B   You shouldn't have left us

A   I didn't leave / you.

B   you left / us.

A   I died.

B   …You left me.

A   I died.

A

B

A   …Don't let them –

B   what?

A   …Don't just let them –

B   what? 'Just let them'… what?

A

A   You're bein –

B   what? I'm bein exactly, *what*?

A

           He gestures.

B   Name it *name* it, or would that be somethin that's
           too fuckin complex for me to understand an' all?

A
A
A
B

Scene Fourteen

They watch each other.

Beat.

Gently she touches the back of his neck, he leans his head forward to accommodate. They are tender with each other.

He touches the back of her right thigh.

PART TWO

> *They are busy.*

> WOMAN *watches the MAN. He is busy. He feels her looking.*

> *Beat.*

> *He continues to be busy.*

WOMAN ...You don't lissen. You look – like you're lookin now – you'll look like you're listening but you're not. Got no intention. But lookin like you've heard – wanting it to look like you're hearin, lookin like you're hearing me.

MAN What?

WOMAN But you're not.
Is what you're doin.

> *He says nothing. He is busy.*

> Can tell can see can see it, andju know it sends me which is why y'do it – which is what *pisses* me off – if you was doin it in ignorance not outta ignorance, but in ignorance thass one thing but doin it and knowin you're doin it –.

> *She becomes busy.*

> And I lost count got tired of sayin got tired of repeatin myself bein made to repeat myself sayin how irritatin it is when you got two good ears – last time I looked – two good hearin ears thatchu choose not to use when it comes to hearin me.

> *He is busy.*

> And you do it on – doin it on purpose to make me look bad when it aint me at all it's all you, you and your passively, pathologically, aggressively

fuckingly not-right-in-the-head bullshit version of
'listening' thatchu do. Are doin. Are doin badly.

They are busy.

MAN   …I / don't.

WOMAN   (*dry*) But iss alright.
            It's alright.

            Beat.

MAN   I don't.

WOMAN   (I) see you thinkin of doin it before you've done it
            that look that you do thass lookin at me but not
            lookin to see me –

MAN   I / don't.

WOMAN   that shit look you do where it never gets to me never
            gets that far, that far over – falters just beyond your
            eyeballs. *That.* And thinkin I don't notice – I notice,
            you don't notice I notice but I see it cos I look, look
            properly – and you're doin it now / your –

MAN   I'm / not.

WOMAN   your eyes are doin the equivalent of your ears.
            Vacant. Vacating the place vacating the space that's
            in between makin you look (stupid) – it makes you
            look stupid nuthin goin on behind the eyes – and I
            know you do this to get a reaction – get a reaction
            from me – iss not getting a reaction from me, it's
            not workin you need to know it's not workin,
            thought you woulda realised that by now an'
            changed your tactic – your one tactic you got. It
            don't work. Not at all. No. …And if it was really an
            apology –

MAN   it / was –

WOMAN   if it was a really proper heartfelt – properly from
            somewhere in there –

MAN   it / was –

WOMAN   from somewhere in there *meant* –

MAN   it was / you –

WOMAN   from somewhere deep down that *matters* –

MAN   it was you who should apologise to me.

             They are busy.
             Beat.

             It's you who should be apologising to / me.

WOMAN   I woulda thought about thinking of accepting it,
             that's all I'm sayin. If it was somethin from
             somewhere heartfelt from you

MAN   you sayin so much I –

WOMAN   but there was nothin to accept –

MAN   you always sayin so much that / I –

WOMAN   was there? Nuthin to (accept) – and me should be
             'apologising to you'?

MAN   You always sayin so much but not sayin nuthin –

WOMAN   I should apologise to *you*?! An' if I was *gonna* say /
             something –

MAN   I do / lissen.

WOMAN   gonna say anythin / it –

MAN   I do lissen but it's like tryin to separate the shit from
             the shovel tryin to lissen to you and I got nuthin to
             apologise for.

WOMAN   Cos you've never got nuthin to apologise for have
             you? Cos y'live life Saintly. You don't know how to
             apologise thass you, that's / your –

MAN   I don't know / how?

WOMAN   that's your problem part a your / problem.

MAN   I don't know how to apologise?

WOMAN   I thought it was-there was somethin wrong with –
             an illness or summink I / thought –

MAN   What are / you – ?

WOMAN	thought you had a somethin psychological – a blockage or summink – some mentally constipated something that's stopped it comin / out.
MAN	What are you talkin –?
WOMAN	But now I know it aint that
MAN	you thought I was / mental?
WOMAN	givin you too much credit –
MAN	you think I'm mental?
WOMAN	Know now there's nuthin wrong with you, know now you're just ignorant – although that is an affliction in itself –
MAN	there aint nothing wrong with / me.
WOMAN	a self-inflicted affliction like the-the lung cancer of a smoker or the diabetes of a fat fucker thass your ignorance affliction – you're a drain – drain on me like they drain on the NHS –
MAN	if I'm constipated up here (*taps head*) you're a shower of shit from there (*gestures mouth*)
WOMAN	so I don't feel sorry for you.
MAN	'Dia-fuckin-/betes'?!
WOMAN	Learned a long time ago to not bother to feel sorry for / you.
MAN	'Lung-the-fuck-/cancer'?!
WOMAN	Don't feel that, don't feel anything – just / feel –
MAN	You aint right wishing that on / me.
WOMAN	just feel pissed off mostly
MAN	you wishin that on / me?
WOMAN	just feel that now. Most of the time, pissed off.
MAN	That's fuckin –
WOMAN	andju don't *lissen* cos I didn't *wish* it on yer – did you hear me wish it on you? You did not. I'm not

	like that, not that kinda – it was an example y'thick fuck.
MAN	And I'm not mental
WOMAN	I was bein meta-fuckin-phorical.
MAN	
WOMAN	My metaphors are lost on you.
MAN	You wouldn't know what one is
WOMAN	you clearly gotta lacka understandin – y'shoulda listened harder at school.
MAN	Woulda done if you'da shut up in class
WOMAN	O-level English –
MAN	grade C
WOMAN	takin criticism from the CSE drop-out? Don't think / so.
MAN	'Transferred use of a phrase'. Metaphor. Use it properly or not at all.

WOMAN
MAN

They are busy.

WOMAN	…(An) apology would stick in your friggin throat.
MAN	You're like the MRSA then –
WOMAN	oh we've moved / on
MAN	'metaphorically' speakin, eatin people alive –
WOMAN	moved on we've moved on and y'dunno what that is you don't even know what / that *is*.
MAN	Know that it fucks people up – affects where it shouldn't – outlives antibiotics and anything man-made – thass you – and it can't / be –
WOMAN	What does it stand for –
MAN	it can't be –

WOMAN	what does it even stand for?
MAN	
MAN	It's like…
WOMAN	What does the M even stand for?
MAN	

She gestures 'go on'.
He is busy.

WOMAN   You don't know.

He is busy.

So whatever that dig was meant to be didn't work
don't work – and when have I ever had an apology
from you?

MAN   If you shut your / mouth –

WOMAN   This the / apology?

MAN   shut your mouth and give your ears a chance –

WOMAN   that an apology? Nice.

MAN   (I) never said –

WOMAN   never faltered never failed never wronged nobody
never wronged me never made no mistakes –

MAN   I never / said –

WOMAN   have you? Thass you. Lived the life of a fuckin
Saint – forgot who I was talkin to there for a minute
forgot I was talkin to Christ in the corner cos for a
moment I thought you was just you, just you and
your ignorant self who still aint apologised to / me.

MAN   I've got nuthin / to –

WOMAN   Amazing.

MAN   I never / said –

WOMAN   *Stunning. Unique* – you're unique you are –
wish I could live like you – no conscience.
Wish I could be like that, live life like that,

self-centered. Selfish. Psychopathic. And 'shut my
mouth for two minutes' – ?

MAN   Psychopathic?!

WOMAN   That's nice –

MAN   psychopathic??

WOMAN   *That's nice* that is, a nice way to talk to me. Very
Christian, 'Christ'.

MAN   Only one psycho from where I'm / standing.

WOMAN   Thass another apology stacking up.

MAN   Must be hard bein you –

WOMAN   it's great.

MAN   Must be horrible.

WOMAN   Only horrible thing that spoils it about bein me is
you.

MAN

WOMAN   And how you speak to me needs an apology all of
its own.

MAN

WOMAN   And –

MAN   must be hard work keepin yourself in the state
you're in – effort. Workin yourself up for no good
reason – exhaustin.

WOMAN   Harder to think of others than yourself – I think of
you – yes, that is consistently hard for me but
I do it. Easy bein you

MAN   you don't think of me

WOMAN   you don't think of *anyone* –

MAN   consider you

WOMAN   you don't consider no one.

MAN   Consider you to stop talkin.

WOMAN   You don't consider me y'never have you ent got it in / you.

MAN   It's exhausting bein with you.

WOMAN   Piece a piss bein you in comparison to bein me.

MAN   Shit bein you.

WOMAN   Shit listening to your shit.

MAN   Shit bein with you

WOMAN   shit bein with *you*

MAN   shit havin to be with you.

WOMAN   You don't 'have to be with me' nuthin.

He pretends to be busy. She sees it.
Beat.
She is busy.

MAN   (*quietly*) …(I'm) not gonna say something I don't believe in sayin just cos –

WOMAN   what?

MAN   …I'm not gonna say something just cos you want.

WOMAN   You don't say anything I want.

MAN   I'm not / a –

WOMAN   You don't do anything I want –

MAN   don't 'do anything you / want'?

WOMAN   it's not 'anything' I'm talkin about it's '*something*'. Specifics.

MAN   I 'don't do / anything you – '

WOMAN   There's so much I could want that I trained myself to not. To stop. To not bother to want at all. Because of you.

MAN   The things I wanna do but don't cos I know you and know you won't, so I don't even bother say. All the things I'd love to do but let slide cos you –

WOMAN   all that I'd love in life, love in my / life –

MAN	let slide because of you.
WOMAN	The things I'd *love* to do in life –
MAN	you do whatchu want.
WOMAN	I do what I can.
MAN	You do exactly what you / want.
WOMAN	Do what I can, despite you.
MAN	Y'do what you do to spite me.
WOMAN	…And I don't want you to just 'say it', an apology needs to mean something. I need you to feel it and understand it and understand what it means to me and why you need to say it. Just sayin somethin don't mean nuthin. And I wouldn't spite you. Do somethin do anythin I do to 'spite you'. Thass a sign of you – *thass* a sign of how you're takin it if you're takin it / like that.
MAN	I take it how it's given –
WOMAN	now you're just talkin shit.
MAN	(*dry*) Nice.
WOMAN	I am. Y'need to apologise
MAN	if it don't need to be said –
WOMAN	I feel it needs to be said.
MAN	You feel everything needs to be / said.
WOMAN	What I feel matters –
MAN	you feel every fuckin thing matters thass the problem –
WOMAN	just apologise.
MAN	You over-talk y'know that?
WOMAN	Apologise
MAN	y'never stop and the fact is you *feel* I need to apologise. I *feel* I don't.

WOMAN	…You aint got no feelings.
MAN	Oh. Right. Mature.
WOMAN	You don't feel.
MAN	Not like you.
WOMAN	Couldn't feel like / me.
MAN	Don't wanna feel like you
WOMAN	(you) don't feel me, no
MAN	cos you feel hard.
WOMAN	Long time since you were.
MAN	Wonder why that is?
WOMAN	I stopped wondering with you a long time / ago.
MAN	You don't want a man, you want / a –
WOMAN	Still lookin for the man in / you.
MAN	you want a version of you with a dick.
WOMAN	That'd be nice.
MAN	You want a self-help book-of-shit tellin you what you wanna hear – you want a robot with a dick that don't answer back –
WOMAN	something with a dick would be nice –
MAN	my dick would like something nice
WOMAN	y'dick must be dusty haven't seen it for so / long.
MAN	lacka excitement it's bored you bore it and it aint been hard cos you're hard to get hard for.
WOMAN	
MAN	What?
WOMAN	

She is not busy enough.

MAN	…What?

Beat.

WOMAN   …Y'don't hurt y'know, you don't hurt me – that /
            kinda –

MAN   (I'm) not tryin to hurt / you.

WOMAN   that kinda… sayin that kinda… it don't hurt me /
            y'know.

MAN   Not trying to hurt you just stating a fact. Fact. Thass
            how I feel.

            He tries to stay busy.

            Seein as we talkin bout how we 'feelin'.

            She watches him.
            He stops being busy.

MAN
WOMAN

            She starts being busy again. Not busy enough.
            Beat.

WOMAN   (*quietly*) …The reason I wouldn't recognise an
            apology from you is cos I aint never heard one. Aint
            never had one. Never. Not once. Not a half word,
            not a whisper in the wind, nuthin.

            And if you wanna start with one, there's a *really*
            good reason to start now.

MAN

            Beat.

WOMAN

            Beat.

            (*quietly*) …Right.

MAN

WOMAN   …Be a shock getting an apology from you. Cause
            me a condition.

MAN   Comin from you.

WOMAN   Bring me out in sweats or summink

MAN   if you're gonna have a turn have one quietly, lemme
            know when you're done and I'll scrape up what's
            left of yer.

WOMAN   …Oh. Nice. Nice. You'd just stand and watch.

MAN   I'm busy.

WOMAN   Would let me suffer.

MAN   I'm / busy.

WOMAN   Like you did before –

MAN   you weren't suffering.

WOMAN   I have to get to suffering before I get a reaction from
            / you?

MAN   You weren't (suffering) even how you talk,
            even how you – 'suffering'? You were under-
            the-weather.

WOMAN   I was ill.

MAN   Y'felt a bit rough

WOMAN   that what you call / it?

MAN   thass what *you* called it. You 'felt rough' you said –

WOMAN   what I said don't matter when you could see that I
            was – you could see I weren't right. Normal people
            would see and say something.

MAN   I said to you that you didn't look right –

WOMAN   you said it once.

MAN   You said to me 'you felt a bit under-the-fuckin-
            weather is / all'.

WOMAN   You said it / once.

MAN   I said it once cos I *lissen* – I heard you. And
            respecting what you say –'said', I took you at your
            word.

WOMAN

MAN   And I was there and I stayed / there –

WOMAN   Must've been ill for you to / do that

MAN   stayed there and never left your side –

WOMAN   to 'respect what I / said'.

MAN   couldn't leave your side never left your side cos
             I could *see* something weren't right with you.

             Beat.

WOMAN   ...You was there in body not mind and sat there
             resentful.

MAN   (*quietly*) For fuck's / sake.

WOMAN   Could feel it. Vacant and resentful

MAN   I was / there.

WOMAN   be better you not bein there.

MAN   I stayed / there.

WOMAN   Felt bad about feelin bad havin you sittin there with
             your awful aura in the room. Bad airs, bad air, bad
             aura.

MAN

WOMAN   You didn't even ask how I was feeling.

MAN   I *knew* how you was 'feelin'. Fuck. I could *see* it.

             ...And a thank you for changing your sheets woulda
             been nice
             and a thank you for spoonfeeding you
             and a thank you for lifting fresh water to your lips
             and a thank you for cooling your fever
             and a thank you for easing your shakes,
             a thank you for takin out the sick bucket – for takin
             out the shit bucket, a thank you was it for cleaning
             you gently and thank you again for redressing your
             dressings gentler than they did and a thank you for –
             I could go on.

WOMAN
MAN

MAN   ...And a final thank you, for not sayin how fuckin
             frightened I was.

I should wait for that 'thank you' from back then should I? Or I should wait for an apology from you now…?

WOMAN

MAN   …You tell me how long I should wait.

Beat.

WOMAN   (*quietly*) …If I took a turn again. I'd turn to you.

Beat.
Pause.

I would.

They both become busy. She can't sustain her business.

WOMAN

Beat.

MAN   What?

WOMAN

MAN   What?

WOMAN   Nothing.

Beat.

(*quietly*) …I know how frightened you were.

Beat.

MAN   (*quietly*) …Knew how frightened you were.

WOMAN
MAN

He nods, just.

WOMAN   (*quietly*) I was –.

WOMAN
MAN

WOMAN   I do…

MAN   what?

WOMAN

MAN   What?

            She becomes busy again.

WOMAN   (I) do want to say…

            She doesn't continue.

MAN   …Whatever.

WOMAN

WOMAN   If you would just say –

MAN   a thank you shouldn't come with no conditions.

WOMAN   It's not no condition –

MAN   from there's a 'just' and a 'you' in there, there's
            a condition.

WOMAN

MAN   'A thing that must exist if something else is to exist
            or occur'. Condition. By definition.

WOMAN   A figure of speech.

MAN   (*dry*) A metaphor?

            Beat.

            I wannit unconditional.

WOMAN   That's a condition of your own.

            …You do still owe me an / apology.

MAN   You're doin terms and conditions now

WOMAN   I'm-we're not-I'm not…

MAN
WOMAN

            Beat.

WOMAN   …If you say what you need to say to me first

MAN   first?

WOMAN   I didn't mean –

MAN   '*first*'? Terms, conditions and a timetable. / Shit.

WOMAN   I meant, 'as well'. I meant…

MAN

WOMAN   I meant –.

MAN

WOMAN   …I didn't mean that.
           Like that.

           Beat.

WOMAN

           Beat.

MAN   …Howdju want me? All ears?

           She is uncomfortable.

           Seated?
           Stood?
           Eyes on yer, eyes away, what? Nuthin vacant.
           Looking, all the way over?

WOMAN   Don't take the piss.

MAN
WOMAN

MAN   (*quietly*) I'm not.

           Pause.

WOMAN   And I'm… we've got a –. (*she gestures*)

           If I do, you do.

           He gestures back, a little ambiguously.
           Silence.

           …

           …I just wanna say…

           then…

           She exhales quietly.

MAN

WOMAN   …Thank…

               Thank you.

MAN
WOMAN

WOMAN   And…

               Sorry.

               Beat.
               He nods, just.
               Beat.
               She nods back, just.

MAN
WOMAN

               She gestures to him.

MAN
WOMAN

               She gestures for him to say something.

MAN

MAN

               Silence, for as long as it can be held.

PART THREE

MAN   Nothin.

The YOUNG WOMAN *isn't particularly listening to him.*

Y. WOMAN

MAN   Nothing about you.

Y. WOMAN

MAN   Nothing about you to change. You know that?
I wouldn't change nothing about – nuthin about you
could be better.

Beat.

You know that?

Y. WOMAN   What?

MAN   Wouldn't change a thing.

Y. WOMAN

MAN   Wouldn't wanna change anything.

He smiles.
Beat.

About you.

Beat.

…Me?

Y. WOMAN   What?

He gestures.

What.

MAN   …Would you change anything about…

The YOUNG WOMAN *isn't paying attention.*
Beat.

Wouldn't change even a little thing about you…
but…

He watches her. She feels it.

Y. WOMAN   What?

He gestures 'me'?
Beat.
She isn't particularly paying attention.

MAN   Don't matter.

Beat.

…You should talk to him.

Y. WOMAN

MAN   You should, I think, that's all I'm…

Y. WOMAN

MAN   You should talk to / him.

Y. WOMAN   I talk.

MAN   You should talk to him properly it's obvious it's –

Y. WOMAN   (*dry*) I 'should talk to him'

MAN   obvious it's on your mind –

Y. WOMAN   it's not.

MAN   Playin on your / mind.

Y. WOMAN   He's not.

MAN   Y'look like you wanna talk to him.

Y. WOMAN   I don't.

MAN   …You do.

Y. WOMAN   I do know what I look like and I don't look like
             I want to talk to –

MAN   you're not lookin at you I am – and iss lovely – and
             you do look like –

Y. WOMAN   I don't and –

MAN	you've looked like that for weeks
Y. WOMAN	I've talked to / him.
MAN	you've looked like this for months.
Y. WOMAN	I've talked at him for years tried with him for / years.
MAN	Do you good to say somethin.
Y. WOMAN	You do me good.
MAN	Not good enough by the look of / it.
Y. WOMAN	You do great you do me great. It's great – what.

Beat.

MAN   …Talk to him –

She goes to say something, before she can he continues.

not for him to nuthin-about-him but for you to feel better for you / then.

Y. WOMAN	'Feel better for me'?
MAN	Make it about –
Y. WOMAN	I need to 'feel better' for / me?
MAN	make it about you is what I –
Y. WOMAN	is that what I look like an' / all?
MAN	is what I mean. / It –
Y. WOMAN	I 'look like' I need to feel better about it is it? That I 'look like' I need to feel better about him?
MAN	It wasn't –
Y. WOMAN	I've tried talkin to / him.
MAN	it sounds selfish but –
Y. WOMAN	I've tried talkin / to –
MAN	talk how you talk, / talk –
Y. WOMAN	talking to him / doesn't –

MAN   talk how you talk to me to him, you don't stop
               talkin to me – in a good way, y'never shut up.
               In a good way –

Y. WOMAN   which you –

MAN   which is what I like. Love. Bit of what I like
               amongst the lot of what I love. About you. Y'know
               that. But be selfish – if you have to, talk to him to
               get what you need to feel better about –

Y. WOMAN   I don't need to talk to him to 'feel better about'
               anything, I got nuthin to feel better about – I feel
               fine and talkin to him wouldn't be how to make me
               feel better if I didn't.

Y. WOMAN

MAN   Love you talkin. Y'know that.

Y. WOMAN   I know / that.

MAN   Love how you talk –

Y. WOMAN   I / know.

MAN   love that it's non-stop. Love your lovely noise in my
               ears. All the time.

               She smiles, says nothing. He sees.

               Hmmm.

               He kisses her lightly.

               …And me?

               She is distracted.

Y. WOMAN

MAN   …Anything about me…? That you (love)…

Y. WOMAN

MAN   (I) like how you wake up with words – your words.
               Bathe with a dialogue and breakfast with a chat.
               Like how you go to work missing me, call me up on
               your way. Like how you talk quiet when you're
               outside in public on the phone to / me –

Y. WOMAN   You said –

MAN   like how you text me when you can't talk and –

Y. WOMAN   you said / it –

MAN   and-and FaceTime me in your first break.

Y. WOMAN   You said it got on your nerves.

MAN   Like how on your lunch break you'd –

Y. WOMAN   (you) said I got on your / nerves.

MAN   find the time to phone and say the right – not 'on my nerves' –

Y. WOMAN   'on your last nerve'

MAN   I was havin a – only said that when – I was bein- havin a-a-… no. Not on my nerves. You don't –

Y. WOMAN   did sometimes.

MAN   Y'didn't.

Y. WOMAN   Do sometimes

MAN   I –

Y. WOMAN   sometimes you say to me –

MAN   on occasion I might have said –

Y. WOMAN   say to me

MAN   on an occasion I might have said somethin when sometimes I weren't in the right – sometimes I get in my – y'know –

Y. WOMAN   moods

MAN   sometimes y'know –

Y. WOMAN   moods

MAN   that I get up in my – a bit and

Y. WOMAN   moody

MAN   and stay there. Too long. Till you talk me out of it. Like you do like only you do, can do.

Y. WOMAN	
MAN	…But, 'moody' I dunno if I would – don't think I would quite… y'know, (put it) like that.
Y. WOMAN	I'd change that –
MAN	'moods' is a / bit –
Y. WOMAN	change that about yer
MAN	'moody' is a bit strong –
Y. WOMAN	change that about you in a minute.

Beat.

MAN	…Talk to him. He's your dad.
Y. WOMAN	He won't talk to me about you.
MAN	Talk about somethin else / then.
Y. WOMAN	I wanna talk about you talk about me and you
MAN	talk about what he wants to talk about.
Y. WOMAN	Thass not a conversation
MAN	that's not a conversation about what you want, but iss something.
Y. WOMAN	Thass him controlling the subject
MAN	that's you engaging with him.
Y. WOMAN	He talks about nothing
MAN	let him talk about anything.
Y. WOMAN	He talks about anything but me
MAN	listen to what he wants to talk / about then.
Y. WOMAN	he doesn't talk. I end up listenin to he's sighs and shit efforts and his silence again, I want him to talk like he used to talk like he talked before Mum… and then there was after Mum. When I thought there was no after. And he's had years to get over that, years to get back to talkin how he did before, years to stop turning up his TV too loud, so loud or the

crap radio that was on so loud too loud then turned up thinkin I couldn't hear – tryinta mask he's tears over that and-when-and-and he's never listened to me. Ever listened to me.

MAN   (It) won't hurt to try again

Y. WOMAN   he thinks you're too old for me.

MAN   I am too old for you.

Y. WOMAN   (He) said old men are temperamental

MAN   'old' I wouldn't / say –

Y. WOMAN   said they don't know what they want, unless it's something new and shiny.

MAN   Knew I wanted you, was / sure.

Y. WOMAN   That is somethin he does say – one of the only things he does / say.

MAN   Given him somethin to talk about then –

Y. WOMAN   thinks there's somethin wrong with you going out with someone as young as me.

MAN   Seems to say a lot for someone who don't say much. He's, obviously still got opinions

Y. WOMAN   still got somethin to say about / that

MAN   well –

Y. WOMAN   will only talk about that will only talk about you in that way, has always talked about you in that way so we end up – we always end up, y'know…

MAN

Y. WOMAN   …And 'tryin' – me tryin, does. '…Hurt.'

Y. WOMAN

             MAN *kisses her gently.*

MAN   He's older than me.

Y. WOMAN   What?

MAN   He's older'n me.

Y. WOMAN   Not much.

MAN   He's – there are a few years in between –

Y. WOMAN   not enough. He says

MAN   well

Y. WOMAN   not by much at all. He says. And then he's silent
               again. It's not even a argument, I have my say he
               shuts up – I'm arguing with silence his silence,
               again, then that shuts me up.

MAN   …Talk to your brother about talking to him.

Y. WOMAN   He thinks I'm too young for you.

MAN   …You are.

               He kisses her again.

Y. WOMAN   He don't know what's wrong with me going out
               with someone as old as you.

MAN   Right.

Y. WOMAN   Goin out with someone as old as you for as long as I
               have.

MAN   Right

Y. WOMAN   he thinks I lost my mind (he) thinks I'm goin
               through a phase – thought I was going through
               a phase – thinks it's linked to Dad in some way
               (and) tries to psycho something about me says
               I got psychologicals –

MAN   right

Y. WOMAN   says you're gettin more out of this than I am –

MAN   okay / that's –

Y. WOMAN   he thinks there's some trophy su'un going on
               somewhere with you and thinks we've got nothing
               to say that can cross the age gap to say it in.

MAN   …Right.

Y. WOMAN   Thinks I'm missing out on life not seeing someone
my own age.
Yeh.
Me and my brother talk.

MAN   …Your brother talks a lot.

Y. WOMAN   And after Mum…

MAN   I know

Y. WOMAN   you don't

MAN   I know that must –

Y. WOMAN   no you don't. After Mum was…

MAN   …Talk to your brother about that.

Y. WOMAN

MAN   I know.

Y. WOMAN   You don't.

He kisses her.

Scattered to the four fuckin winds which is what she
wanted, Dad said.
Feel a breeze think of Mum. Dad said.
Feel a breeze… and I don't feel nothin. But cold.

MAN   …Talk to your brother –

Y. WOMAN   I think she would have wanted a grave. I want
a grave-would want a grave when – whenever –

MAN   I'd come and tend it –

Y. WOMAN   you're older than me you'd go before me I'd be
tending yours.

MAN   …Talk to your brother about your –

Y. WOMAN   my brother only wants to talk about you.

MAN

Y. WOMAN   And the wrong decisions I'm makin – he thinks I'm
makin.

MAN   …Right.

Y. WOMAN	And the fuckin up of my life he thinks I'm –
MAN	maybe your brother –
Y. WOMAN	thinks I still am doin
MAN	maybe your brother / isn't –
Y. WOMAN	pointin out what I'll regret what he thinks I'll regret by bein with / you
MAN	your brother isn't the best / person to –
Y. WOMAN	and you said I talk to my brother too much you said you wanted me to talk to you, you wanted me to talk to you more – you wanted me to talk to you as much as I talked to my brother. And my brother won't talk to me as much as he did cos he only wants to talk about me and you which I ent talking about no more. To him. But he's got plenty still to say about what he thinks, of me. Got even more to say bout what he thinks of you. So I talk to you, talk to you as much as I talked to him and then you tell me you can't take it. You tell me that I should learn to listen learn to be quiet which I learnt for most of my years with Dad after Mum and that. After all that. My talkin has started to get on your nerves 'got on your last nerve'. You said. Have said. Moody or not moody.

Beat.

MAN	…I might have said that once…
Y. WOMAN	more than once.
MAN	On the way back from seeing her or something
Y. WOMAN	more than once and you –
MAN	she puts me in a – she punishes me with her moods.
Y. WOMAN	You've said it when you haven't been and don't go. Don't go, if it's that –
MAN	I don't wanna go
Y. WOMAN	don't go if / it's –
MAN	I don't wanna go but I go, should go cos –

Y. WOMAN   you don't owe her anything.

MAN   I go cos it's decent.
             I go cos she's not well.

Y. WOMAN   Again.

MAN   She's not been well

Y. WOMAN   again.

MAN   She's / not –

Y. WOMAN   She's not your responsibility.

MAN   She's not my responsibility.

Y. WOMAN   No.

MAN   I go and when I go I talk about you, that pisses her
             off

Y. WOMAN   shouldn't go at / all.

MAN   I go to be decent, go to see she's alright, see she's
             alright talk about you, piss her off and leave.

Y. WOMAN   She's not as sick as she says she / is.

MAN   I go. I check on her. We sit down. She makes a bitter
             brew (of tea), I don't stop talkin about you, she
             bangs down the kettle and doesn't offer me
             a drink. I tell her how great you are. She clatters
             open the cupboard and avoids eye contact, (I) tell
             her how great bein with you is – she throws hot
             water into her mug – still not offering me mine in
             mine, and I count off the good years of bein with
             you. She sugars her hot drink – too many to count,
             while I think of you. She slices her latest bake effort
             not offering me none, while I look at her and wish it
             was you. She sits down heavy – face like thunder
             sips on her hot drink halfway eats her cake watching
             my mind wander on to you, when she says what she
             says –

Y. WOMAN   your own / mug?

MAN   says what she always says –

Y. WOMAN   you have your / own –

MAN	says about herself goes on about herself –
Y. WOMAN	how have / you –
MAN	sayin it tight through her teeth clenched tight –
Y. WOMAN	you have your own mug round there?
MAN	What?
Y. WOMAN	Your own mug.
MAN	She –
Y. WOMAN	you.
MAN	What?

MAN
Y. WOMAN

She half-laughs a little.

(*dry*) Whatever.

MAN	…When she talks she doesn't talk like you. When we laugh she don't laugh like you, when we –
Y. WOMAN	(*dry*) she bakes for –
MAN	when we watch what we watch she don't watch what you / would.
Y. WOMAN	she bakes for you.
MAN	She bakes.
Y. WOMAN	(*dry*) You gotta special plate?
MAN	Are you – ?
Y. WOMAN	Are *you*?
MAN	…She says you're 'lucky to have me'.
Y. WOMAN	Are you / that –
MAN	Says 'you don't know how lucky you are'
Y. WOMAN	you that / gullible?
MAN	says I'm unique – well, actually says I'm 'fuckin unique'

Y. WOMAN   or just that / stupid?

MAN   then goes into all her metaphorical shit that was
always borin and how she's happy to be not
disappointed no more, so I make a brew myself and
sort myself / out.

Y. WOMAN   She's not sick.

MAN   She is.

Y. WOMAN   Not as sick as she –

MAN   she / is.

Y. WOMAN   and I'd change that. Change that about you. Change
that about you bein so gullible.

MAN   She's old.

Y. WOMAN   You're old.

MAN   …You jealous?

Y. WOMAN   Nuthin to be jealous of knowin you don't date old
(people) – people your own age.

MAN
Y. WOMAN

Beat.

Y. WOMAN   (*dry*) Make a brew in your own mug do yer?

MAN   …So you catch me in a mood and maybe you catch
me in a mood comin back from that, comin back
from her and I might say somethin sharp
I don't mean.

Y. WOMAN   You've said it more than –

MAN   and I'm not counting – you counting you doin that?

Y. WOMAN   I'm just –

MAN   thass kinda –

Y. WOMAN   was / just

MAN   kinda a little bit juvenile. If you're doing that.
Counting up the times –

Y. WOMAN	countin up your moods?
MAN	Really. A bit childish.
Y. WOMAN	
MAN	Are you doing that?
Y. WOMAN	
MAN	Stackin your grudges against me?
Y. WOMAN	
MAN	Are yer?
Y. WOMAN	This isn't –
MAN	are yer? Cos if we're countin –
Y. WOMAN	this isn't / that.
MAN	I could count up your silences –
Y. WOMAN	this isn't –
MAN	could count up your silences with your mind wandering on to y'mum or y'dysfunctional –
Y. WOMAN	don't talk about / my –
MAN	well I couldn't count would lose count and wouldn't count up anyway cos that is a bit... isn't it. I don't do that.
Y. WOMAN	
MAN	Y'know I don't do that. Don't hold grudges, don't count grudges don't stack em up. Like you are –.
Y. WOMAN	...I don't –
MAN	like you're doin
Y. WOMAN	this isn't that.
MAN	You are you are –
Y. WOMAN	I'm –
MAN	you're holding grudges
Y. WOMAN	I'm not

MAN	yes you –
Y. WOMAN	I'm / not.
MAN	say if you are, I mean, y'know –
Y. WOMAN	I / would.
MAN	y'know –
Y. WOMAN	I would say
MAN	say it if you mean it –
Y. WOMAN	I wouldn't not / say.
MAN	and if I've y'know – it's that upsetting to you –
Y. WOMAN	I'm not upset
MAN	if it affects you that much to the point where you're –
Y. WOMAN	your gullibility doesn't upset me
MAN	if I'm upsetting you to the point you're holding grudges against me – and it's not – I'm *not* / gullible.
Y. WOMAN	you dunno whatchu / are.
MAN	if me seein my sick friend makes you / so –
Y. WOMAN	and I'm not 'upset'
MAN	seein my sick / friend –
Y. WOMAN	y'think this is an 'upset' look is it? Gullibility –
MAN	I'm / *not* –
Y. WOMAN	doesn't upset me and she wasn't just your 'friend' and you doin whatever 'tea and biscuits' y'doin round there doesn't make me anythin
MAN	it makes you somethin you holdin it against me it obviously makes you feel / something.
Y. WOMAN	nuthin obvious about me.
MAN	And it's cake.
Y. WOMAN	What?
MAN	She don't do biscuits.

Y. WOMAN   (*quietly*) Fuck / off.

MAN   You're obviously pissed off

Y. WOMAN   no.

MAN   Yeah you are –

Y. WOMAN   no.

MAN   I know what your 'pissed off' looks like. I do know
             that. Had plenty of…

             She shakes her head.

Y. WOMAN

MAN   …(*dry*) Another silence.

Y. WOMAN
MAN

             Beat.
             He kisses her gently.

MAN   Want me to apologise?

Y. WOMAN

MAN   Want me to –

Y. WOMAN   y'don't apologise.

MAN   Want me to say –

Y. WOMAN   you never / apologise.

MAN   if you want that, if that would make you feel –

Y. WOMAN   have never apologised. Never apologised to / me.

MAN   if that would get you outta your 'mood' if that's
             what you need to hear to make you feel…

Y. WOMAN
MAN

Y. WOMAN   …Y'know…
             I say so much, have to say so much – to you – cos
             I'm not sure it's gone in. I'm not sure that you get it
             that you got it.
             I can't tell if you've heard it, if you've wanted to
             hear it. If you've listened. To me at all.

MAN   I love hearing / your –

Y. WOMAN   It's not easy to tell with you with that look thatchu
               do, that one where y' look like y'listenin, like
               you've heard, but your glazed look that you're doin
               now never actually gets over far enough for me to-
               to… it is hard to tell.

MAN   …If you want me to –

Y. WOMAN   it's not about apologising – if I get on your nerves –

MAN   I can –

Y. WOMAN   if my talkin gets on your nerves

MAN   it was only

Y. WOMAN   no it wasn't, but thass alright.

Y. WOMAN

MAN

MAN   I wouldn't have you no other way you know / that.

Y. WOMAN   Thass what I told my brother.

MAN   Nuthin I would change about you.

Y. WOMAN   Thass what I told my dad.

MAN   I'm not askin you to change

Y. WOMAN   I know I know.

MAN   I love you.

Y. WOMAN   I know.

MAN   Love everything about you.

Y. WOMAN   (I) know that too.

MAN   Even though you do talk a lot but that's just a –

Y. WOMAN   you not lissenin I would change / that.

MAN   thass just a minor thing

Y. WOMAN   I would change that about you

MAN   but I wouldn't change nuthin of / you.

Y. WOMAN   Change your gaze of a look thatchu do, would get
             rid of that.

             Beat.

             Change your hard-edged sighs when I haven't even
             finished a sentence. Would change that.
             Change you kissin me to not solve nuthin – would
             change that.
             Change you bringin back cake from hers would
             change that.
             Change how you snap at me –

MAN   (I) don't snap at / you.

Y. WOMAN   yeh y'do would change that quick-time. Change you
             askin about you to / me --

MAN   Maybe juss a tweak –

Y. WOMAN   shit thass annoyin would change that would change
             your raised eyes of when you're bored of what / I'm
             sayin.

MAN   a tweak to the amount of talkin thatchu / do –

Y. WOMAN   Change how you talk about my dad – would /
             change –

MAN   a slight amend on the endlessness of / that.

Y. WOMAN   change your attitude and your tone / generally.

MAN   Maybe more than an amend

Y. WOMAN   change your moods in a minute –

MAN   cos that bit about you talkin –

Y. WOMAN   change all a them an' there's plenty a them / to
             change.

MAN   – and I'm not moody but that bit about you talkin
             does need that. A change to that – a change about
             that. That does get irritatin. Is more than irritatin –
             does my head in you doin that. Sittin wistful about
             your dad and lookin miserable about y'brother –

would change (that) – and yeah y'do look like that which is all the time half the time. Would change that. Ignorin me – which y'do –

Y. WOMAN

MAN   see!

Y. WOMAN

MAN   (You) do on purpose would change that about you

She ignores him.

the endless phone calls of insecurity and texts of drama – all of that would change – FaceTime – what is the point? You lookin exactly how you're feelin not maskin nuthin not able to mask nuthin – get them looks for free when I'm with you don't need to see it on no phone, that could change cos you could make the effort. If you could be arsed. Your endless reportin of what your fucked-up family don't never say – would love to change that about you – you talkin *at* me, you talkin at me –. All the time like that.
All the time.
That does need changin.
Would properly change that.
About you.
If you could change that.
About you.
For me.
Change that. Do that, some a that – all a that. Some a them – all a them.
That would... that would –.
Would be...
That would be...

Beat.

They kiss.

Thass all.

End.

Author Biographies

Travis Alabanza

Travis Alabanza is an award-winning writer, performer and theatre-maker. Their writing has appeared on the BBC, in the *Guardian*, *Vice* and *gal-dem*; they had a fortnightly column in *Metro*, and have been featured in numerous anthologies, including *Black and Gay in the UK*. After being the youngest recipient of the artist-in-residency programme at Tate Galleries, Alabanza's debut show *Burgerz* toured internationally to sold-out performances, including at the Southbank Centre, to São Paulo, Brazil, HAU Berlin, and it won the Edinburgh Fringe Total Theatre Award in 2019. In 2020 their theatre show *Overflow* debuted at the Bush Theatre to widespread acclaim and later streamed online in over twenty-two countries. Other works for theatre and live performance include for the Royal Court *Living Newspaper*, Paines Plough, Free Word Centre, Glasgow Transmission Gallery and more.

Their work surrounding gender, trans identity and race has been noted internationally, and they have given talks at universities including Oxford, Harvard and Bristol, among others. Noted for their distinct voice, in 2019 the *Evening Standard* listed them as one of the twenty-five most influential under twenty-five-year-olds – as well as being listed in the *Dazed 100*, the *Guardian* asking if 'they are the future of theatre', and recently being listed on the Forbes 30 Under 30 List.

Firdos Ali

Firdos Ali is a playwright whose full-length plays include *Struggle* (Talawa Firsts, 2015), *The Wrong Way* (Talawa Theatre, 2016) and *40 Days* (2017). Her short plays are *Stripped Black* (*Black Lives, Black Words* at the Bush Theatre, 2015) and *How I Feel* (Royal Exchange Theatre, 2016).

Firdos's short story *Emerald Waters* was chosen for the Bare Lit Festival, 2016. Her musical *New Life*, for which she wrote the book and lyrics, was showcased at BEAM, 2018. Firdos was named on the BBC New Talent Hotlist.

Arinzé Kene

Arinzé Kene is a writer and performer whose most recent one-man play, *Misty*, ran at the Bush Theatre and Trafalgar Studios to widespread critical acclaim, including receiving two Olivier nominations for Best Actor and Best New Play. Arinzé is currently working on a TV adaptation of *Misty*.

Further stage work includes *good dog*, produced by tiata fahodzi and toured nationally in 2017, and *God's Property*, which ran at Soho Theatre, co-produced with Talawa Theatre Company. Prior to that, Arinzé was on attachment at the Lyric Hammersmith as a recipient of the Pearson Playwrights' Bursary. *Little Baby Jesus* and *Estate Walls* both enjoyed runs at Ovalhouse, the latter of which earned him Most Promising Playwright at the Off West End Theatre Awards and a nomination for Best New Play. His play *Wild Child* was performed in 2011 as part of the Rough Cuts season at the Royal Court.

Arinzé was a member of the Young Writers' Programme and Writers' Super Group at the Royal Court Theatre. He was part of Soho Theatre's Young Writers' Group and was chosen as one of their Hub Writers. He was shortlisted for Off West End's 2010 Adopt a Playwright Award and the 2009 Alfred Fagon Award.

In addition to his stage work, Arinzé writes for the screen and is developing a number of original features. His first feature script, *Seekers*, was on the Brit List 2015. He is currently working on feature project *Indigo Bloom* with Element Pictures. For television, Arinzé was commissioned by BBC in-house to write an original drama for the BBC Drama Writers' Programme. He was involved in the storylining and development of the second series of *Youngers* for E4, in which he played Ashley and wrote for spin-off series *E20* for BBC Three. Arinzé was named as a Screen International UK Star of Tomorrow in 2013 and was invited to take part in the Channel 4 Screenwriting Course in 2012.

Natasha Gordon

Natasha Gordon is a playwright and actress of Jamaican descent. Her debut play, *Nine Night*, enjoyed a sold-out run at the National Theatre in 2018 before transferring to Trafalgar Studios, making her the first Black British female playwright to be produced in the West End. Natasha won the Charles Wintour Award for Most Promising Playwright at the 2018 Evening Standard Theatre Awards.

As a performer, her stage credits include *Nine Night* at Trafalgar Studios, *Red Velvet* at the Tricycle Theatre, *The Low Road* and *Clubland* at the Royal Court Theatre, *Mules* at the Young Vic and *As You Like It* at the RSC. Film and TV includes *Dough*, *Line of Duty*, *Class* and *Danny and the Human Zoo*.

Natalie Ibu

Natalie Ibu is a director, producer, curator and facilitator of ideas and change. In 2020, she became the Artistic Director and Joint Chief Executive of Northern Stage in Newcastle. Previously, she was the artistic director and CEO of tiata fahodzi – the only Black-led theatre company in the UK with a sole focus on new work. As director, credits include readings and productions by Arinzé Kene, Nathan Bryon, Charlene James, Nick Payne, Luke Barnes, Rachel De-lahay, Kenny Emson, Steve Hevey, Hywel John, Stewart Melton, Jesse Briton, Marcelo Dos Santos, Jon Brittain, Penelope Skinner, Sabrina Mahfouz, Ella Hickson, Frances Ya-Chu Cowhig, Laura Lomas and Tom Wells at a variety of venues including Paines Plough's Roundabout, Watford Palace Theatre, Riverside Studios, Young Vic, Lyric, Southwark Playhouse, Southbank Centre, The Old Vic Tunnels, Theatre503, The Gate, Latitude, HighTide, BAC, Òran Mór, Traverse, Royal Court, OVNV at The Old Vic, Waterloo East, Vineyard Theatre in New York, Royal Lyceum Theatre, Citizens', The Arches, Contact and Nottingham Playhouse, as well as national tours of regional theatres.

Chinonyerem Odimba

Chinonyerem Odimba is a Nigerian British playwright, screenwriter and poet. Her recent work ranges from *Medea* at Bristol Old Vic, *We Too, Are Giants* for Kiln Theatre, *Unknown Rivers* at Hampstead Theatre, *Prince and the Pauper* at Watermill Theatre, *The Seven Ages of Patience* at Kiln Theatre, and *Princess & The Hustler*, which toured across the UK for Eclipse Theatre, Bristol Old Vic and Hull Truck. She is also Writer-in-Residence at Royal Welsh College of Music and Drama. Her other work for theatre includes *The Bird Woman of Lewisham* at the Arcola, *Rainy Season* and *His Name is Ishmael* for Bristol Old Vic, *Joanne* for Clean Break, and *Amongst the Reeds* for Clean Break/The Yard Theatre. Her work for young people includes a modern retelling of *Twist* for Theatre Centre and *Sweetness of a Sting* for NT Connections.

She has been shortlisted for several prizes including the Adrienne Benham and Alfred Fagon Awards. In 2015 her unproduced play

Wild is De Wind was shortlisted to the final ten for the Bruntwood Playwriting Award. She is the winner for the 2018 Sonia Friedman Award (Channel 4 Playwright Bursary) for a new play *How to Walk on the Moon*, and was a finalist for the inaugural Women's Prize for Playwriting 2020 for her play *Paradise Street*.

Chinonyerem's TV credits include *Scotch Bonnet* for BBC Three and *A Blues for Nia* for BBC/Eclipse Theatre, *Adulting* for Channel 4, and *My Best Friend Married a Warrior* for CBBC. For radio, credits include *The Last Flag*, and *Eve* as part of *This Is Your Country, Now* series on BBC Radio 4.

As a director, Chinonyerem has worked for Bristol Old Vic, Theatre503 and Bristol Old Vic Theatre School. She co-directed her new play *Black Love* for Paines Plough, as well an audio drama for Live Theatre/BBC Radio 4 in 2021. In April 2021, Chinonyerem became the new Artistic Director and Chief Executive of tiata fahodzi.

debbie tucker green

Theatre includes: *ear for eye, a profoundly affectionate, passionate devotion to someone (–noun), hang, truth and reconciliation, random, stoning mary* (Royal Court), *nut* (National Theatre), *generations* (Young Vic), *trade* (RSC/RSC at Soho), *born bad* (Hampstead Theatre), *dirty butterfly* (Soho Theatre).

Film and television: *ear for eye* (feature film), *swirl* (short film), *second coming* (feature film), *random* (film).

Radio includes: *Assata Shakur – the FBI's Most Wanted Woman* (adaptation), *lament, gone, random, handprint, freefall*.

Directing includes: *ear for eye* (feature film), *ear for eye* (play), *a profoundly affectionate…* (play), *hang* (play), *truth and reconciliation* (play), *nut* (play), *swirl* (short film), *second coming* (feature film), *random* (film), *Assata Shakur – the FBI's Most Wanted Woman, lament, gone, random* (radio).

Awards: Gold ARIAS Award for *lament*, International Film Festival Rotterdam Screen Award for *second coming*, BAFTA nomination for *second coming* (Best Debut Feature Film), BAFTA for Best Single Drama for *random* film, MVSA for Best UK Film for *random*, OBIE for *born bad* (New York Soho Rep production), Olivier Award for *born bad*.

www.nickhernbooks.co.uk

facebook.com/nickhernbooks

twitter.com/nickhernbooks